CRIME AND IMPUNITY

Sexual Torture of Women
in Islamic Republic Prisons

Part 1: 1980s

Justice
For Iran عدالت برای ایران

Crime and Impunity

Sexual Torture of Women in Islamic Republic Prisons
Part 1: 1980s

Second Edition 2016
First Edition
Copyright © Justice For Iran 2012

Published by:
Justice For Iran

info@justiceforiran.org
www.justiceforiran.org

Page layout:
Aida Book - Germany

By Shadi Sadr and Shadi Amin
Justice For Iran

ISBN 978-3-944191-97-3

About Justice For Iran (JFI)

'Justice For Iran' was established in July 2010 with the aim of addressing the crime and impunity prevalent among Iranian state officials and their use of systematic sexual abuse of women as a method of torture in order to extract confession.

JFI uses methods such as documentation of human rights violations, collecting information, and research about authority figures who play a role in serious and widespread violation of human rights in Iran; as well as use of judicial, political and international mechanisms in place, to execute justice, remove impunity and bring about accountability to the actors and agents of human rights violations in the Islamic Republic of Iran.

About the Authors

Shadi Sadr is the director of Justice For Iran. She is an Iranian lawyer, human rights defender and journalist. She received her law degree and later her LLM in international law form Tehran University. She has performed research on women's right in Iran, particularly in the areas of family law, *hijab* and women's rights movements. Shadi Sadr is the founder and director of Raahi, a legal centre for women. Iranian authorities closed down Raahi in 2007 during a wave of repression against civil society. She was arrested and imprisoned in Iran in 2007 and 2009. Shadi Sadr has touched the lives of many women through her work and her support for campaigns such as the Stop Stoning Forever Campaign. She has received several awards such as Ida B. Wells award for bravery in journalism, the Alexander Prize of the Law School of Santa Clara University and the Human Rights Defenders Tulip.

Shadi Amin is an Iranian feminist and lesbian activist who was forced to leave Iran in the 1980s because of her political activities and is now living in exile in Germany. She has researched gender discrimination, systematic oppression against women and the state of homosexuals in the Islamic Republic of Iran. Her selection and translation of Adrian Rich and Audrie Laurd's articles were published in a book entitled Ghodrat va Lazzat (Power and Joy) which is one of the few Farsi resources on compulsory heterosexuality and lesbian existence. She is a founder of the Iranian Women's Network Association (Shabakeh) and is currently one of the coordinators of the Iranian lesbians Platform (6RANG). She joined Justice For Iran as the 'Crime without Punishment' research project manager.

Table of Contents

Acknowledgments

We are grateful to the many political prisoners of 1980s who agreed to be interviewed and who shared their painful experiences with us. Without doubt, they were the ones who taught us how to view this part of the history of Iranian women; the history of resistance, failure and victory. Many people were involved in this project- ranging from workshop participants, to colleagues, volunteers, relatives of the women political prisoners who are no longer alive. We are unable to name everyone, but we are incredibly grateful for all their input and support for this work. Our deepest gratitude goes to Homa Shadi who, without her passionate advice and her tireless assistance, the English version of this work would not have been ready. We would also like to acknowledge the important contributions of some of the former political prisoners who without any hesitation shared their vast network and valuable information with us, especially Monireh Baradaran, Mehri Elghaspour, Mojdeh Arasi, Soudabeh Ardavan, Mona Roshan, Golrokh Jahangiri, Shokat Mohammadi and Iraj Mesdaghi. We would like to express our appreciation to Dr. Nouriman Ghahari for providing her indispensible advice to us throughout this project. We are also indebted to Professor Yakin Erturk and Professor Payam Akhavan, the Justice For Iran advisory board members as well as Gissou Nia, who read the whole report and made valuable legal and theoretical suggestions. We would like to appreciate the courage of our colleagues inside Iran who we are not able to mention by name because of the security reasons. We would like also to acknowledge our colleagues, Leila Moeini, Raha Bahreini, Leila Nabavi and Goli Far. We are especially thankful to Rima Attar, Amanda Matijevic and Tahirih Danesh who spent a lot of time editing the English version of this work which was originally produced in Farsi. We also appreciate the Human Rights Defenders Tulip and Hivos for the financial support they provided for Justice For Iran to work on the 'Crime without Punishment' project. This acknowledgment cannot be completed without thanking Women Living Under Muslim Laws (WLUML), which supported us by hosting the project.

Executive Summary

Throughout the 1980s in Iran, thousands of individuals were arrested and detained for supposedly supporting or participating in oppositional political organizations that were critical of the Islamic Republic regime's undemocratic practices. So far, many reputable reports have been published detailing the various torture methods inflicted upon the political prisoners in that decade.[1] However, despite anecdotal evidence on sexual abuses in the prisons of Iran, the topic has not yet been subject to systematic study. This report based on the first phase of the research project, 'Crimes without Punishment', aims to document the cases of rape and other forms of sexual torture used against female political prisoners in the 1980s. The second report will cover the subsequent period between 1990s-2009, and the third will cover events following the 2009 elections.

Our goal in conducting this research and preparing these reports is to launch a public discourse on this subject, which has haunted many women's lives and has discouraged thousands of others from entering public politics for fear of being raped in the infamous prisons of Iran. Indeed the issue of rape in prisons has been known throughout Iran, but never discussed seriously in public due to extreme cultural taboos on the topic. This taboo and prevalent perceptions of shame and (dis)honor in Iran has meant that open discussion of rape or torture is perceived to negatively impact not just the victims, but also their wider family and associates. As such, the state escapes responsibility and accountability for not only letting these atrocities happen, but for its role in actively promoting sexual torture as a tool for political

---

[1] For instance, see the report: "Iran, Election Contested, Repression Compounded", Amnesty International, December 2009:
http://www.amnesty.org/en/library/asset/MDE13/123/2009/en/1e69a8fb-dcf1-4165-a7fc-a94369e364bf/mde131232009en.pdf,
and "Violent Aftermath - The 2009 Election and Suppression of Dissent in Iran", IHRDC, February 2010:
http://www.iranhrdc.org/english/publications/reports/3161-violent-aftermath-the-2009-election-and-suppression-of-dissent-in-iran.html.

control. We feel that unless these systematic occurrences of rape atrocities against female political prisoners are documented and presented to the public, nationally and internationally, the culture of sexual violence against women by the state will continue, and worse, encourage others to commit the same crimes without fear of punishment.

This report aims to uncover the degree to which sexual torture of political prisoners in the 1980s was widespread and systematic. The report is the result of an analysis of publically published records, as well as interviews with 77 political prisoners detained during the 1980s and 18 informed individuals whom either because of the position they held or family connection held detailed information relevant to the research. Furthermore, the report delves into how sexual torture against female prisoners was carried out, in what manner it was justified, and the goal the officials hoped to accomplish through inflicting the torture.

Based on our findings, some of the various forms of sexual torture, such as the rape of virgin girls prior to their execution, were conducted in a systematic way and were based on the interpretation of an order by Ayatollah Khomeini (1979-1989), the Islamic Republic Supreme Leader at the time (quoted by Ayatollah Montazeri, his deputy of the time). In addition, various verses from the *Koran* and *shari'a* based *fatwas* were used to claim that women who were captured in battle with the *kuffar* (infidels) were akin to property and slaves of the army of Islam (a practice of the Middle Ages which had subsequently been accepted, at least theologically, as a part of Islamic war practices). That is to say the prison and judicial authorities were treated as the victorious army and female political prisoners as their slaves, not as citizens with different political perspectives. These theological sources provided religious 'justification' for raping imprisoned women.

This report further indicates that female political prisoners experienced systematic and extensive instances of sexual torture and harassment. While all prisoners are subject to abuse, case studies in this report highlight how particular forms of torture were (and continue to be) systematically inflicted upon women.

The data in this report confirms that sexual torture against female political prisoners constitutes an undeniable systematic component of the dark history of human rights violations in Iran during the 1980s- by a state that claims monopoly of morality, no less, particularly in the area of sexuality. This report further indicates that the crimes discussed in detail in the body of this report have continued to go unpunished, after more than three decades. Worse yet, due to cultural taboos around sexuality and rape, despite the fact that these crimes have been committed by the Islamic state, the state has remained unaccountable. These crimes have destroyed not just the lives of victims, but also the lives of their families and affiliates. Until recently, few public discussions were launched to condemn these abuses. This report is only the initial step on the road to breaking this silence, casting light on the darker corners of truth and demanding accountability from the actors and agents of such atrocities. The ultimate goal of this report and the project at large is to contribute to the public discourse this hitherto silenced human rights abuse, whose perpetuators have felt immune to punishment because such heinous crimes are often beyond public belief. Or, there is a lack of public willingness to accept or debate such abuses by the regime, making it easier to ignore or deny the need for action to end such abuse. With this project we hope to carve out possibilities for demanding justice for these crimes that have distorted the lives of so many women forever, and to contribute to the prevention of such crimes against women and men in the future.

Introduction

When the results of the 2009 presidential election were announced, hundreds of thousands of Iranians stormed the streets of Tehran and other large cities to protest what they believed to be an incredible act of election rigging. Although the protestors' initial demand was that the election results be annulled and the votes recounted, in the following days and months slogans had evolved to express lack of trust in the state to the point that the initial vague slogan of "Death to Dictator" was replaced with "Death to Khamenei" (Iran's Supreme Leader) and in some cases even "Death to the Islamic Republic." Oppositional protest rallies and meetings continued into the months following the election, while the violent crushing of those protests started after the election results were announced. According to the Judiciary Spokesman, during the first month following the election, four thousand (4,000) people were arrested in Tehran alone.[1] Widespread arrests of civil activists and regular people who were protesting the election results continued well into the following months.[2] Those released told harrowing tales of the treatment of detained individuals, including the rape of males and females by prison officials. Mehdi Karroubi, one of the two contesting presidential candidates (a religious leader in his own right, who was also among Ayatollah Khomieni's trustees), established a committee to follow up on the conditions of the detainees arrested in the post-election unrest. The testimonies received by the committee revealed that one of the methods of torture used on post-election detainees was rape and sexual harassment. On 29 July 2009, in a letter to Ayatollah Hashemi Rafsanjani, then the Head of the Expediency Discernment Council, one of the highest centres of state authority, Karroubi wrote, "A group of those detained have expressed that some of the detained girls

---

[1] See http://www.aftabnews.ir/vdcewp8o.jh8wpi9bbj.html.
[2] See "Iran Election Contested Repression Compounded", Amnesty International, 2009, http://www.amnesty.org.uk/uploads/documents/doc_19994.pdf

were raped so violently that it caused tearing and injury in their sexual organ. A group of people have raped the detained men in a violent manner, and caused them serious psychological and physical ailments so that they are hiding in the corners of their homes." He publically demanded investigation to this matter.[1]

This was the first time that the topic of rape in prisons was discussed openly and widely by an individual member of the governing body of the Islamic Republic of Iran. Although, years prior to this event, Ayatollah Montazeri, who was the deputy leader of Iran during 1985-1989, had included a letter that he had written in a letter to Ayatollah Khomeini in his memoir which was published in 2000. In this letter he writes:

> Do you know that a large number of people have died under torture by interrogators? Do you know that in Mashhad prison, due to a lack of medical care and attention for young girls, they were forced to excise the ovaries and uterus of around 25 of those young girls and in that manner, deformed (*naaqes*) their bodies and reproductive organs?!... Do you know that they [sexually] took young girls by force in some of the prisons of the Islamic Republic? Do you know that when young women are interrogated, usage of vulgar and sexual (*namoosi*) related terminology is commonplace?[2]

The letter was published in Ayatollah Montazeri's memoir in 2000, after he was removed from power and placed under house arrest[3]. As a result, it had limited reach within wider society.

Yet after Karroubi's letter to Rafsanjani was published, and brave victims went public with their testimonies of rape and sexual abuse during the post-election arrests, the topic of rape in prisons pervaded the public discourse in Iranian society more widely. Some protestors in subsequent oppositional protest rallies in Tehran chanted slogans such as: "Canons, tanks and rape

---

[1] See "Karroubi's Letter to Hashemi Rafsanjani Was Published after Ten Days: Young Boys and Girls Were Raped in Prisons; Please Follow Up!", Saham News, August 10, 2009: http://news.gooya.eu/politics/archives/2009/08/091965.php.
[2] Memoir of Ayatollah Montazeri, Volume 2, P 1164, available at: http://amontazeri.com/farsi/khaterat/html/1097.htm.
[3] Ayatollah Montazeri was removed due to several objections by Ayatollah Khomeini and the officials' acts specially the massacre of the political prisoners in 1988.

are no longer effective" or "Rape in prison, is this in the *Koran* too?" Such slogans were also chanted in the religious city of Qom, and during the burial procession of Ayatollah Montazeri, who died in 2009.

The belief that rape was administered as an organized crime against political prisoners in Iran, particularly since the rise of Islamists to power, was strengthened by an increasing number of victims' public testimonies. Especially with the recognition, in public discourse, of rape as a form of torture in prisons, many more victims who had been raped while in custody during the 1980s and 90s began to speak out. Videos of their testimonies were widely disseminated on the internet. Available published prison memoirs and testimonies also gained greater attention and were reprinted and distributed on a wider scale. As a result, these important topics that had been silenced, or only discussed amongst victims themselves, were revived in the public sphere and attracted a wider audience. One of the most significant topics was the systematic rape of virgin girls before execution as an organized form of sexual torture, particularly during the 1980s. The Islamic Republic officials' reaction to such claims, testimonies, and news has been complete and unilateral denial and rejection[1]. Indeed since the 1980s, in a few occasions when such reports or testimonies would surface, the Islamic regime would rush to deny the existence of sexual torture in prisons as baseless accusations that were part of attempts by its enemies, particularly western powers, to delegitimize the regime[2].

Hence while the victims could bear witness to what happened to them while in custody, they had no documentation to respond to questions such as the scale of usage of rape and sexual harassment as an organized or widespread means of torture against political prisoners. Nor did the victims have documentation of the methods and forms of implementation, or the identity of actors and perpetrators of such torture. It was in this context that we saw the need for in-depth research that would shed

---

[1] See the reactions of the then Head of Judiciary, as well as then Head of the Majlis in Response of Hashemi Shahroudi to Karroubi's letter, Tabnak, August 14, 2009, available at: http://www.tabnak.ir/fa/pages/?cid=59567.
[2] Press Conference of Hojjatolislam Mir Emadi, General and Revolutionary Prosecutor of Shiraz: Rumors of the Unsanitary Prison Conditions and Situation of Prisoners, Execution of 300 Prisoners and Marrying of Girls to Boys Prior to their Execution is an Absolute Farce, Khabar Jonoub, No. 889, August 10, 1983, P. 1.

light on some of these questions and by examining how and where these sexual abuses occurred and the extent to which they were a systematic. Many of the political analysts have assumed that sexual abuse and usually harsh treatment of women political prisoners had been, a deliberate and systematic action by the Iranian regime aimed at discouraging women from public participation in politics. However, lack of a systemic study had prevented a systematic discussion of the topics. It was in this context that we decided to launch the project 'Crimes without Punishment' in order to shed light on these matters. We hope that the findings of this project contribute to the public discourse to this hitherto silenced human rights abuse, whose perpetrators have felt immune from punishment because of the public lack of willingness to accept or debate such abuses by the regime. Finally, we hope to not only carve out possibilities for demanding justice for these heinous crimes that have shattered the lives of so many women forever. Another important goal of the research is to help to launch an informed public discussion of the sexual abuses as particular forms of torture and cruel treatment and to demand an end to such crimes against women, and men, in the future by encoding unacceptability of such acceptation into public and political culture of the country

Conceptual Framework

In defining torture, we used the definition adopted from Article 1 of the Convention against Torture and Other Cruel, Inhuman or Degrading Treatment or Punishment.[1] Based on this definition, torture is:

> Any act by which severe pain or suffering, whether physical or mental, is intentionally inflicted on a person for such purposes as obtaining from him or a third person, information or a confession, punishing him for an act he or a third person has committed or is suspected of having committed, or intimidating or coercing him or a third person, or for any reason based on discrimination of any kind, when such pain or suffering is inflicted by or at the instigation of or with the consent or acquiescence of a

[1] Memoir of Ayatollah Montazeri, Volume 2, P 1164, available at:
http://amontazeri.com/farsi/khaterat/html/1097.htm.

public official or other person acting in an official capacity.[1]

In deciding the framework of this research vis-a-vis the definition of sexual torture, we decided to base our work on the definition of 'invasion'- a term extracted by Amnesty International from amongst the decisions of the International Criminal Court processing charges of 'crimes against humanity'. Based on this definition, "the invasion was committed by force, or by threat of force or coercion, such as that caused by fear of violence, duress, detention, psychological oppression or abuse of power, against such person or another person, or by taking advantage of a coercive environment, or the invasion was committed against a person incapable of giving genuine consent. [A footnote here reads: "It is understood that a person may be incapable of giving genuine consent if affected by natural, induced or age-related incapacity.]"[2]

Aside from the aforementioned definition, one of the fundamental questions posed by the research was the degree to which sexual torture against female political prisoners was widespread or systematic. Our definition for widespread or systematic torture and harassment was primarily adopted from the International Criminal Court's statutes and the Court's subsequent interpretations of those statutes.[3]

Article 7 of the Rome Statute considers any form of torture, rape, sexual slavery, enforced prostitution, forced pregnancy, enforced sterilization, or any other form of sexual torture of comparable gravity, to be crimes against humanity if subjected as part of an attack against a civilian population and in a widespread and systematic manner.[4]

Definitions and interpretations related to the meaning of crimes against humanity proved to be a useful tool for us particularly in two sections of our research: Raping of Virgin Girls

[1] Ibid.
[2] Rare and Sexual Violence: Human Rights and Standards in the International Criminal Court, Amnesty International, 1 March 2011, available at:
http://www.amnesty.org/en/library/info/IOR53/001/2011/en.
[3] See Rome Statute of the International Criminal Court at:
http://untreaty.un.org/cod/icc/statute/romefra.htm
[4] Complete text of the Rome Statute of the International Criminal Courts, available at:
http://untreaty.un.org/cod/icc/statute/romefra.htm.

before Execution, and Widespread Sexual Torture. For these two sections, decisions had to be made on whether or not sexual torture in the 1980s could be considered systematic, as well as which forms of sexual torture could have been widespread.

Following the *Prosecutor* of the International Criminal Court *v. Germain Katanga* and *Mathieu Ngudjolo Chui*[1]; The term 'systematic' has been understood as either an organised plan in furtherance of a common policy, which follows a regular pattern and results in a continuous commission of acts or as 'patterns of crimes' such that the crimes constitute a "non-accidental repetition of similar criminal conduct on a regular basis."[2] That is to say systematic refers to policies and practices adopted as a means of torture and intimidation of prisoners, with those who committed such acts feeling legally immune from repercussions of such violent abuses.

A review of Iranian law was also important because, in a few cases, the victims of sexual torture and harassment complained to the officials in charge but the complaints did not result in any effective action. In some cases, the actors were simply assigned to another penitentiary or were given different tasks inside prison. This did not stop them from interacting with political prisoners though, nor did it stop abuse from being carried out by others.[3]

The Islamic Republic of Iran is not a signatory to the Convention against Torture (CAT), but according to Article 7 of the International Convention for Civil and Political Rights (ICCPR) - to which Iran is a signatory and obliged to uphold- "No one shall be subjected to torture or to cruel, inhuman or degrading treatment or punishment. In particular, no one shall be subjected without his free consent to medical or scientific experimentation."[4]

---

[1] For further details about the case, see: ICC-01/04-01/07Case The Prosecutor v. Germain Katanga and Mathieu Ngudjolo Chui, available at:
http://www.icccpi.int/menus/icc/situations%20and%20cases/situations/situation%20icc%200104/related%20cases/icc%200104%200107/court%20records/chambers/appeals%20chamber/
[2] Prosecutor v. Germain Katanga and Mathieu Ngudjolo Chui, "Decision on the Confirmation of Charges", 30 September 2008, International Criminal Court, Decision No. ICC-01/04-01/07, para 397. Decision available at: http://www.legal-tools.org/doc/67a9ec/
[3] There are repeated mentions of an unconfirmed case regarding the execution of a Tabriz Prison Official due to his repeated raping of female prisoners. As mentioned, we were not able to corroborate the narratives with first hand testimony.
[4] See International Covenant on Civil and Political Rights (ICCPR) at:
http://www2.ohchr.org/english/law/ccpr.htm

Article 38 of the Constitution of the Islamic Republic of Iran establishes that: "All forms of torture for the purpose of extracting confession or acquiring information are forbidden. Compulsion of individuals to testify, confess, or take an oath is not permissible; and any testimony, confession, or oath obtained under duress is devoid of value and credence." Violation of this article is liable to punishment in accordance with the law.

However there is no specified office, except the judiciary system for such a complaint when it takes place by representatives of the state.

In the Iranian body of law no specific section has been devoted to sexual torture and the punishments that befall its actors. Punishment for the act of rape, described as *zina bih anf* (forced adultery) is execution, regardless of whether the act took place inside or outside prison (Section D, Article 82 of the Islamic Penal Code). However, to prove rape, one needs to have at least four impartial male witnesses, or three impartial male and two impartial female witnesses, who attest to having seen the rape with their own eyes. The rapist's confession must be repeated four times. Another way of proving rape is what is known in Iranian Islamic judiciary as 'the knowledge of the judge', which does not rely on any kind of evidence but rather on opinion of the judge that rape occurred. Naturally, inside prison, the rape of a prisoner by an interrogator inside a solitary cell is nearly impossible to 'prove' given the aforementioned criterion. This, despite the fact that such rapes occur with the knowledge of those party to the crime- i.e., prison authorities, who are either judicial officials or law enforcement forces- who to date in this research will not speak out, or even be interviewed.

On the issue of torture, Article 578 of the Islamic Penal Code states:

If any of the juridical or non-juridical governmental authorities and employees inflicts corporal harm and torment upon an accused in forcing him to confess, he will, in addition to being subject to *qisas* (retribution) or payment of blood money as the case may be, be sentenced to a term of six months to

three years in prison. If somebody orders in this respect, only the person who has issued the order
shall be sentenced to the said imprisonment. Where
the accused dies as a result of corporal harm and
torment, the perpetrator shall be subject to the pen-
alty for homicide; the person ordering the corporal
harm and torment shall be punished for ordering an
act of homicide.[1]

Yet neither this article, nor any other article in the body of
Iran's law, considers inflicting psychological tortures such as fear
of rape or imprisonment in a solitary cell, or other forms of torture such as inflicting hunger, preventing or refusing access to
basic facilities such as a bathroom and showers, and refusal to
administer medication to sick prisoners, as crimes that are punishable by law.

It is vital to note that the majority of women who were subject often numerous times to sexual harassment and torture had
no possibility of making a formal complaint regarding what they
were subjected to. Even if there was an option, given that these
women were usually imprisoned for intending to exercise their
constitutional right to freedom of dissent and free expression,
they did not find Iran's judicial bodies legitimate or have faith in
the law to proceed with such complaints. Indeed even assump-
tions of such exercise were out of possible fathom. Family
members of the victims were subject to such harsh treatment
that they lost any hopes of a resolution to their complaint. A few
of the prisoners who did intend to complain were never given
the opportunity to do so, and in the few cases where prisoners
actually discussed their rights violations with supervisory committees while imprisoned, or with responsible officials after their
release, the actors and perpetrators never met the justice they
deserved.

The Research

The scope of the research: The initial aim of this research was
to investigate the extent of sexual abuse of female political prisoners and to undertake a more systematic documentation of

---

[1] see http://www.redress.org/downloads/country-reports/Iran.pdf

these abuses by ex-prisoners who were willing to share their experience with us. For methodological and conceptual reasons we decided to exclude from our research the sexual harassment of non-political female prisoners, although it is widely believed that such abuses are also widespread in Iranian prisons.[1] There were also repeated reports of male prisoners being subjected to rape and sexual torture, particularly after the post-2009 election arrests, and we recognize the need for parallel research on the experiences of male political prisoners as well. However, because such research would necessary delve deep into particularly personal and painful experiences of the male interviewees, its execution would require expertise that our research team did not posses at the time. Our team was trained to deal with the intricacies of the feminine perspectives in cases of rape and torture and provide the necessity psychological support for interviewees, but the project did not have the resources available to extend the necessary training for interviewing male victims. Furthermore, based on the initial readings of the memoirs of female prisoners, we had deduced that gender played a key role in the regime's rationale for perpetuating systemic sexual torture against female prisoners and thus we felt it is important to document the unique experiences of torture and abuse of female political prisoners. The logic and the goal of the regime in exercising these differential patterns of sexual abuses against male and female prisoners stemmed from their different visions of the social and moral position of women in Iranian society. Our subsequent interviews re-affirmed our initial understanding that gender played a major role in the way a political prisoner was viewed, both inside prison, and amongst family and the wider community outside. This role is not confined to the past. In the 1980s, as today, a woman political prisoner was treated as transgressor, as a person who acts out of her league, and not as a citizen who happens to disagree with the regime's political ideology. Thus a woman was to be taught a lesson, and made an example of, in order to discourage other women from engaging in public politics. Further, women's chastity was supposed to represent their families and male-kin's honor. Thus women subjected to sexual torture

---

[1] Although some of the female political prisoners interviewed for this research noted that non-political female prisoners were sexually used and abused particularly in prisons outside of Tehran,[1] researching the manner, spread, and goals of these types of harassments and sexual tortures required further resources that we lacked. Often abuses of non-political prisoners took place due to corruption of the authorities dealing with them and because the prisoners often came from poorer and less connected sections of the population.

not only suffered as individuals, but were often also burdened with the guilt of 'dishonoring' their families, particularly if they came from more religious or conventional social backgrounds. In the words of one of the former prisoners, "from the very first moment of one's arrest, with the demeaning looks they cast upon you and the *chador* they force on your head, they make you feel that you are a 'woman' and not a human being."[1]

Indeed the state's governing religious ideology is one major source of women political prisoners' unique experiences of harassment and torture within Iranian prisons. State ideology considers women subordinate to men and as potential sources of immorality. In public, the state forces them to observe *hijab* (*chador*), which covers a woman's body completely except for her hands and face. The state also deems public gender segregation as necessary, and as an 'Islamic' requirement. Women are also deemed 'naturally' suited for domestic tasks, and the prevailing state ideology certainly believes that independent political activism should not be a woman's pre-occupation.

While we had initially intended to research and document the sexual harassment that female political prisoners faced, our interviews directed us to many other forms of gender specific tortures and abuses that women were subjected to, besides the widespread physical beatings[2], lashings, and the use of sexually explicit and vulgar verbal abuse.[3] Our interviews and testimonies make it amply clear that the regime used 'motherhood inside prison' as a specific form of both psychological and physical abuse of women. Some women were either pregnant at the time of their arrest or were arrested along with their infants. About one fifth (15 out of 77) of our interviewees recounted horrific experiences during pregnancy, delivery (or abortion/ miscarriage), as well as traumas of raising their children inside prison in the 1980s. Many of the interviewees viewed the act of being deprived of basic hygienic, nutritional, and personal care products, for themselves or their children, as a form of torture. While we

---

[1] Witness Testimony of Hayedeh Ravesh, Justice For Iran.

[2] For more information, see chapter IV.

[3] Abuse of political prisoners, particularly various sexual forms of abuse, seems to be common when the authorities are not accountable to the public, as the case of Iraqi prisoners in Abu Ghraib made clear. For further information, see:
http://www.wired.com/science/discoveries/multimedia/2008/02/gallery_abu_ghraib, and http://middleeast.about.com/od/iraq/tp/abu-ghraib-complete-guide.htm.

normally consider this as 'inhumane treatment', having listened to numerous dreadful accounts of these deprivations, we determined that prolonged and consistent inhumane treatment, systematically carried out, is equivalent to torture. Accordingly, we added such cases to our documentation of gender based violations and include a section on them here.

We also uncovered the practice of forced marriages inside prison.[1] As we will discuss, a considerable number of marriages occurred inside prison, particularly between imprisoned women and male authorities. These marriages are too frequent in number to be considered exceptional cases. Taking into account the structures put forth in international legal definitions, the sexual relations that resulted from these marriages, where women did not have a real choice and were forced to accept sexual relations with prison authorities, were instances of sexual torture.

Given the lack of pervious such studies in Iran, we devoted considerable time reflect and consult with other human rights researchers to developed appropriate research methodology for conducting the research in this unchartered human rights abuses. We hope this work contribute in developing and refining methodological framework for conducting future research and documentations which are essential vehicle for social mobilization to eradicate sexual torture and human rights violations in Iranian prisons. We also hope this research will propel the realization of restorative justice for victims and survivors of these crimes.

Timeline: Our preliminary research led us to an understanding that the treatment of women prisoners in Iran depended largely on a temporal quality that was influenced by the political shifts taking place in the Iranian government. There have been significant shifts in the political climate of Iran from 1979 to present (2012). Most scholars of Iran agree that since 1979 there are three different distinguishable political eras that each indicates some ideological shifts. These shift interns have some impacted on how political oppositional groups and individuals were viewed and accordingly treated in the Iranian prisons. Our preliminary research confirmed the validity of these shifts and thus we designed our research around these political shifts and have,

---

[1] For more Information, see chapter II

therefore, divided our project into three phases. The focus of the first research phase, and of this report, is the first decade after the establishment of the Islamic Republic in 1979, where prisons were primarily under Ayatollah Khomeini's direct rule. The second phase will focus on the post-Khomeini era of 1990s to 2009. The third phase will focus on the post-2009 election protests and subsequent arrests and abuses of prisoners. Once we have concluded our interviews and have had a chance to analyze our data more closely and comparatively, we hope to identify the trends of the regime's changing policies in relation to the human rights of political prisoners.

Research questions: There were several important considerations in formulating our research question and the manner in which we collected our information. These considerations included the passage of time since the crimes were committed, the execution and death of many of the victims, and the cultural taboos on discussing issues related to sexual abuse. Furthermore, the research team had to carefully consider the potential political consequences in Iran for our would-be interviewees, the survivors of these stories and their family members for speaking out. Not all of our interviewees remain in Iran; however, many women still have relatives in the country that could be adversely affected by their participation in this type of research. Indeed, these aforementioned factors played a role in the reason many women did not come forward earlier to share their stories. Ultimately, our research sought to respond to the following central questions:

1) In what manner and to what extent were sexual torture and rape implemented in Iranian prisons against female political prisoners? Was the rape and sexual abuse widespread? Were there systematic acts of rape and sexual violation?

2) Who were the perpetrators and executors of sexual torture in the prisons of the Islamic Republic of Iran and what positions do they occupy today?

3) What were the reasons interviewees, other victims, or those aware of the abuses, did not to go public about these atrocities earlier on.

Research team: The research team was composed of eight members, whom the authors pulled together through their vast network and years of experience as human rights activists both inside and outside Iran. We believed that not only was it absolutely necessary to shed light on such an important and overlooked situation of human rights abuse, but also that we would be able to find a team who was willing to work with us to negotiate such a sensitive and traumatic topic. After the initial stage of research and mobilizing contacts, it was clear that a substantial number of ex-prisoners were willing to share their experiences. However, many lived in diverse parts of Asia, Europe and North America. This meant that the project needed an experienced team of researchers who could travel and who possessed the necessary research expertise, but, more importantly, who would be accepted by our interviewees to make this research feasible and legitimate. Thus the research team is made up of many Iranian human rights and women's rights activists who, at various political conjectures, have been forced to leave Iran due to their political activism, but who have remained engaged in the struggles for justice in Iran from their bases in Europe and elsewhere. Some of them had themselves been imprisoned during the 1980s, and as such were connected to a vast network of ex-political prisoners. They willingly shared this valuable social capacity with this investigation. Although for security reasons we are not able to provide more extensive details, without their generous support as well as encouragement, this research would not have been possible.

Methodology: At the first stage of our research, we began a literature review where we learned that most of the existing information on this subject consisted of memoirs of former prisoners, published as books, articles or on various human rights websites. Newspapers of diverse political inclinations published in the 1980s also provided very valuable insights into discussions that were current at the time.

Knowing the sensitive nature of our research and the consequences of re-counting some of the difficult experiences of torture and imprisonment for interviewees and interviewers alike, we organized several training workshops for our team to learn from experienced psychologists who had worked with victims of torture. Even though our team members themselves were experienced human rights activists, focused training in psychology greatly strengthened our ability to engage on this topic.

Our first conversations with our interviewees made explicit the potential impacts of such an interview on their welfare, and we identified social workers, psychologists, or organizations that were locally based and could provide support for them after the interview, should they consent to participate. As a rule we stay in touch with interviewees for several days to weeks after the interview is conducted, to insure we are providing the emotional support they may need. On many occasions, we also had to provide psychological support and counselors for the research team as well, who began suffering from second-hand post-traumatic stress.

We began our research by interviewing female prisoners who had, prior to our inquiry, documented instances of sexual abuse against themselves or other inmates. This enabled us to refine our questions and learn about the kind of support we needed to provide for those who were willing to share with us their painful memories. Meanwhile we had mobilized our network of human rights activists and organizations in order to contact various women who had been imprisoned during the 1980s for their political activism. We adopted in-depth interviews as our principal method of collecting primary data. We also tried to contact individuals who had occupied relevant positions of authority in the prisons in the 1980s, and might possess valuable information. However, only one person out of all those we contacted agreed to an interview. We also contacted many religious leaders to ask about the existence of the alleged instruction by Ayatollah Khomeini on raping unmarried girls before execution in Iranian prison in the 1980s; they rejected the possibility of existence of such edict or *fatwa*.

Being forewarned by other human rights researchers of the challenges to our project, we set ourselves a modest goal to document twenty experiences of rape and sexual harassment against female political prisoners imprisoned during the 1980s. However, over the course of six months, the number of interviews and cases far surpassed our initial goal (see Table 1 below). In the course of the investigation, 95 individuals were interviewed, 64 of whom were former female political prisoners. The majority of the prisoners had served more than 3 years. Thirteen (13) of the interviewees were male prisoners who were close associates of victims and survivors, or witnesses; another 13 of the interviewees were family members, or friends and acquaintances, of the executed or killed;[1] and 5 of those interviewed had valuable information and connections to the topic, due to either their own extensive research in this area, or their political roles during the 1980s that they were willing to share with us.

Table 1- Details of the interviewees (position, sex and country they live)

Country	Former Political Prisoners		Victims' Relatives		Informed Individuals*	
	Woman	Man	Woman	Man	Woman	Man
Iran	6					
Canada	11	6	1			1
Germany	18	3	4	2	1	1
The United States	6		1	1		1
UK	7			1		
Sweden	7	1				
The Netherlands	3	1				
France	2	1	1			1
Turkey	1					
Azerbaijan	1	1				
Norway	1			1		
Switzerland	1					
Denmark				1		
Sub-total	64	13	7	6	1	4
Total	77		13		5	

*The persons who either because of their political positions at the time or because of their knowledge were interviewed

[1] Mahshid Mojaverian, Mehdi Taghvaei, Mehdi Navidi, Leyli Shokati, Farhad Taghi, Shahin Nava'ee, Parvin B. Monir Khosravi, Mehran Kh. Babak Ghassemlou, Abbas Vakili, Bijan Al-e-Kanaan, and Azam, were family members of those killed or executed with whom we spoke.

Those we interviewed had the option of having their testimony published, either fully or in part, under their real name or a pseudonym, in order to ensure their confidentiality and safety. They were also given the option of withdrawing their testimonies before publication. These assurances greatly contributed to a relationship of trust and mutual respect between the researchers and our interviewees. The researchers directly interviewed all witnesses; the majority of the interviews were conducted in person, while some were conducted via telephone or Skype, due to time and financial limitations. All interviews are preserved in the form of audio files, and some were also video-recorded (see table 2).

Table 2: Methods of the interviews

	Former Political Prisoners	Victims' Relatives	Informed Individuals*	Total
Face to Face	43	2	1	46
Via Skype	5			5
By Phone	29	11	4	44
Total	77	13	5	95

In some cases, in the follow-up interviews, other methods were used.

In the course of our in-depth interviews, we collected our interviewees' history of activism, arrests and experiences in prison, including their experiences of sexual torture, as well as what happened after they were released. As such we gained vast and valuable insight into the history of Iranian political activism, particularly by women, which is a history that has remained largely unwritten.

Span of the research: Since the majority of the existing memoirs published to date by female prisoners were penned by those imprisoned in penitentiaries of Tehran Province, we made a considerable effort to include less-known stories, collecting testimonies of women imprisoned across the 9 provinces of Tehran, Khuzestan, Khorasan, East Azerbaijan, Kurdistan, Fars, Isfahan, West Azerbaijan and Gilan. We also ensured that our interviewees had a diverse range of political affiliations, in order to assess whether abuse was inflicted on female political prisoners across the board, or directed at people with particular political tendencies. Two interviewees had been arrested on the charge of collaborating with independent leftist groups, while three were arrested without specific charges. The details of four interviewees are kept confidential for security reasons (see Table 3 below).

Table 3:
the geographical and political organizational affiliation of the interviewees

	Place of arrest / Organization	Tehran	Khuzestan	Khorasan	East Azerbaijan	Kurdistan	Fars	Isfahan	West Azerbaijan	Gilan	Total
1	Mojahedin-e Khalq	9		3	2		2			1	17
2	Fadaian-e Khalq (Minority)	10	2	2	2		1	1			18
3	Peykar Organization for the Liberation of the Working Class	7		1						1	9
4	Organization of the Revolutionary Laborers of Iran (Rah-e Kargar)	4				3	1				8
5	Organization of the Revolutionary Toilers of the Iranian Kurdistan (Komala)					3					3
6	Union of Combating Communists (Sahand)	6									6
7	Communist Union of Iran (Sarbeh-daran)	1	3								4
8	Iranian Toilers Party (Ranjbaran)	2									2
9	Tudeh Party of Iran							1	1		2
10	Organization of Warriors for the Liberation of the Working Class	2									2
11	Fadaian-e Khalq (Majority)	1									
12	Toufan Marxist Leninist Organization				1						1
13	Majority - Keshtgar Party - 16 Azar Announcement					1					1
14	Forqan Group	1									1
15	Other Leftist Groups	3				1					3
	Total	46	5	6	5	8	4	2	1	2	77

At the final stage of our research we revisited the existing published material that we had consulted earlier, as well as what became available after the project was launched. Through this process we were able to confirm facts that arose from interviews, ensuring data such as names, dates and places were correct, in order to complete the legal files on the perpetrators of sexual torture.

Major Challenges of the Research

We experienced many challenges in conducting our research, only some of which we were able to negotiate successfully. As mentioned, the social and cultural taboos around discussing sexual abuse have stopped many from speaking out about their experiences. Although sexual violence is considered a heinous crime, the stigma is attached more readily to victims and survivors and their families- particularly when they are women- than to the aggressor. While many of our interviewees had repeatedly spoken out in public and private settings about other forms of torture that they experienced while imprisoned, the majority of our interviewees stated that this was the first time they were discussing their experiences of sexual violence in prison with others. These experiences were too painful and dehumanizing for them to recount without having emotional support in place, even years later.

One common reaction to sexual violence in Iranian society is the feeling of shame. Ironically, instead of the perpetrators of violence, who should feel shame and lose respect if the matter becomes widely known, it is the victims and their families who feel they will lose face by going public. The victims and their families are made to feel that they must have done something wrong to bring such an ill fate upon themselves; that they are somehow responsible. This deep fear of losing respect amongst their friends and families causes many raped women and their relatives to seek the path of silence and denial. They often set aside their desire to bring the perpetrators to justice. Unfortunately, this makes perpetrators the real beneficiaries of such silence, since they gain a sense of security that they will not be punished for their crimes, and that they can continue to commit the same crimes with impunity. We hope that by helping to break this silence and by bringing these crimes to greater public consciousness, this research will open new frameworks for engagement on this issue and go a long way in preventing the unchecked perpetuation of sexual violence as torture.

Respect for victims' memory: Another reason for silence on the topic is a fear of tainting the memory of victims and distorting their images as brave heroines. Some female prisoners expressed their deep and utmost respect for the resistance of their fellow inmates- some of whom are now deceased- as well as the bravery of the women inside Iranian prisons as a whole. One might imagine that discussion of the suffering these women went through in their support for freedom of expression and principal of justice, would add to the merit of their resistance, however within the cultural setting of Iran, out of fear that their testimony and the final research results would distort the important history of women's political struggles and challenge the definition of resistance and bravery, our interviewees tread this path with care. Some fear that stories of rape and sexual torture will reduce the status of women to that of sexual objects. Others, including a few women activists, feel such stories may be used to discourage other women from becoming politically active. These hesitations demonstrate a need for broader cultural shifts in understanding sexuality- particularly a need to examine and expel internalized forms of oppression that insist a woman is defined only, or above all, by her sexuality.

We hope the public discourse on this matter would begin a nationwide soul searching and questioning of reasons behind their willing silence on matters of sexual abuse, not just in relation to of the political prisoners, but also in the wider society from family to streets and other institutional levels. The public silence in this matter has meant that the victims of sexual torture had to find individual strategies to re-build their lives. Understandably, many victims focus their energies on coping with the psychological and physical trauma, which often has meant adopting strategies of saying little on what went on behind the wall of Iranian prisons. This reluctance to go public caused serious impediments to our research, particularly in regards to the rape of virgin girls prior to execution. In these cases, since all the victims were executed, the only ones who could attest to such acts are the detainees who shared a common cell with these women or their families. However, the majority of them have so far been resolved to silence. Other witnesses, although motivated by the necessity of bringing the truth to light and perpetrators to justice, remain concerned about inflicting even more pain and suffering to their families and those of the victims. Therefore, most of the victims either keep their silence or are unwilling to use their real names. These are challenges one has to face whenever research confronts deep social and cultural taboos.

Lack of security and trust inside prison: Even within the prison walls and amongst cellmates, the silence pervaded. Those we interviewed recounted the actions and behaviors of cellmates that suggested they were either afraid of being raped, or already had been, but it was not openly discussed. Some interviewees explained that most conversations amongst inmates touched on small talk because there was little or no trust established between them. There was a persistent fear and threat that an inmate's closest confidant in prison could be turned into an informant under torture, and therefore give up any confidential information that they had been trusted with. Inversely sometimes inmates choose not to know, because they were worried about being able to keep the secret under physical and psychological torture and then lose their self-dignity and carry the guilty conscious for the rest of their lives.

Fear of losing respect: Fear of losing respect, or of not being believed, is another reason why most female prisoners refuse to speak of the sexual torture they were subject to. Particularly in prisons in smaller cities, where everyone knows everyone, female prisoners took to silence out of fear that the news of what happened to them might travel through the grapevine and reach the ears of their family and community. Some women who broke the aforementioned taboos and spoke of their experiences of sexual harassment and rape prior to our research discussed how they faced an unexpected and harsh reaction from the wider community. For them it was particularly tormenting to have the political organizations they were affiliated with, as well as their communities, react with disbelief and denial. In fact most women who openly spoke of being raped were considered 'liars' and in some cases 'psychotic', by the political and intellectual

Iranian community.[1] Our scholarly research shows that writers have often sought to find, and aggrandize, errors in prisoners' narratives, thereby heavily discrediting accounts by female political prisoners. While there was little doubt about cruelty existing in Iranian prisons, the suggestion of sexual immorality and abuse towards political prisoners was hard to digest for a great majority of the population, including the opposition forces.

Need for gender-sensitive analysis: Another challenge that became apparent during the process of research was the 'gender-blindness', or lack of gender-sensitivity, of the activists and prisoners of the 1980s. Some of the individuals interviewed viewed rape as a form of torture that carried no more weight than other forms of torture. This view was particularly prevalent amongst supporters of leftist groups who were heavily influenced by the book *The Epic of Resistance* by Ashraf Dehghani. Dehgahni was a member of the *Fadaian-e Khalq* and was arrested by the Pahlavi regime prior to the revolution. In her book, that came to be the source of inspiration for many female activists of the time, Dehghani clearly states that she sees no difference between rape and lashing:

> He tied me face down to a bench and shamelessly, in front of his colleagues, pulled his pants down and lay on top of me. This was, as they say, incomplete raping and was done to belittle me and get on my nerves. I was angry because of his despicable action but tried to pretend that I was indifferent and calm so as to bring shame and disgrace to him. I wanted them to understand that their boorish and contemptuous behavior was not important to me. In fact, what importance could it have had? How was this act any different that being lashed? Both were torture and committed with the same intentions and goals.[2]

For this reason, many prisoners who were entangled in the whirlwind of detention and severe torture did not recognize that the specificity of the violence they were experiencing was gen-

---

[1] Indeed even when male prisoners spoke out on sexual rape, the initial reaction was that of disbelief that such things happened in the Islamic Republic jails.
[2] The Epic of Resistance, Ashraf Dehghani, P. 71, available in Persian at:
http://www.siahkal.com/publication/Hemaseh/contents.pdf.

der-based. Similarly, although they might have been seriously disturbed by certain sexually charged words and actions, many prisoners did not categorize, or recognize, them as sexual harassment and torture. As such, some of the former prisoners we approached for interviews initially stated they did not have much to contribute to our research. However, by the end of the interview, they had told us shocking narratives, which they came to understand were experiences of sexual torture and harassment.

Post-traumatic stress disorder: Understandably, discussing experiences of harassment and torture was not always easy. Listening to narratives filled with layers of violence and injustice, and hearing stories that for the most part had been kept untold until that moment, certainly had deep effects on everyone involved in this project. In recalling extremely bitter memories, many interviewees succumbed to post-traumatic stress disorder (PTSD) the day of the interview and the days following it. But not only the interviewees were affected; many interviewers and researchers also suffered from secondary PTSD during the process.

Time, memory and the nature of organized political activism: The negative effect of time on witnesses' memories presented another challenge. Those interviewed testified to events that transpired 20 to 30 years ago. Many had also made great efforts to erase all memories from their mind, either to protect the stability and their mental health, or for security reasons. Even amongst those who had excellent memories, remembering many of the names or events was impossible due to the nature of political activism of the 80s. The prevalent use of pseudonyms in political organizations, as well as limited and confidential contact between members and supporters of organizations, resulted in closed circles. These uncertainties will forever mask the true identity of some of the victims.

Identifying perpetrators: Another goal of the research was identifying the perpetrators of the sexual abuse and torture, which proved extremely difficult. In fact, aside from high ranking judicial officials, such as religious magistrates, and the heads of the prisons where torture and abuse were documented, the identities of other actors involved in sexual torture have been hidden. Prisoners were often forced to wear blindfolds, and interrogators and low-ranking officials often went by pseudonyms in prison. For example, an individual with the pseudonym of 'Hamed' (Brother Hamed, Interrogator Hamed) appears in different testimonies of female prisoners as one of the actors in sexual harassment and torture of prisoners. He was the head interrogator of Branch 6 of Evin Prison's Revolutionary Prosecutor's Office, where the leftist prisoners' case files were processed. Some of the former prisoners state that Hamed had a Turkish accent, but none of those interviewed by us were able to see Hamed's face. That he would unbutton the clothes of prisoners who had lost consciousness from being lashed and touch their breasts, speak of sexual relations with female prisoners, and make suggestive comments such as "it has been a while since I slept with someone", unjustly interrogate young women at desolate hours of the night, commenting on their 'beautiful bodies' and so on, are just some of the actions that have been recounted about Hamed in former prisoners' testimonies. To this day, his real identity and position in the Iranian government structure is unknown to us.

Although we had hoped that former officials of the Islamic Republic who are now amongst the opposition to the regime would collaborate with us on this research, none that we contacted were willing to offer detailed information to our questions. Unfortunately without insight from former officials, accessing the identities of the actors involved in sexual harassment and violence in prisons remains a persistent challenge.[1] While we have managed to gather more information critical to identifying many of the perpetuators of the sexual crimes in 1980s, a clearer picture may only be revealed after an all-encompassing public discussion on the topic.

To sum up: In spite of the various challenges and areas for further research, the results of our study have far surpassed our initial expectations. Many agreed to share with us their experiences despite it not being easy for them and given the repetition of the many similar stories indicted that sexual abuse was a systematic

---

[1] To answer some of the questions, we reached out to Mohsen Makhmalbaf and Akbar Ganji. Neither were willing to speak to us regarding the events of 1980s. Also, our correspondence with Ayatollah Yousof Saanei was left unanswered.

policy. Our data indicates that certain forms of torture and sexual harassment against female political prisoners in the 1980s were absolutely systematic, with some forms more widespread and prevalent than others. Based on our first hand documents and witness statements the research indicates, for example, that imprisoned virgin girls were raped prior to being executed and that the actions were 'legitimized' by the manipulation of *shari'a* laws relating to marriage. As will be discussed in the proceedings chapters, our research also shows that, whatever the 'justification' used, the majority of rapes and sexual harassment against female prisoners were performed with the explicit political intention of breaking women's resistance and forcing political prisoners to give up their political activism. This project has also made clear that the deepest and most painful effects on the psyches of prisoners subjected to sexual harassment and torture were never given appropriate attention. We hope that this report will shed light on the need for increased social and psychological support for the victims, the need for public discourse in order to transfer the shame from the victims to the perpetrators, and the need to stop these abuses from continuing.

I- Women's Political
   Activities after the
   Revolution of 1979:
   A Historical Review

I- Women's Political Activities after the Revolution of 1979:

A Historical Review

While resistance to Mohammad Reza Pahlavi's regime was long brewing, it was the months leading to the revolution of 1979 that brought millions of Iranians to the streets and incited them to political activism. A very diverse set of political forces rose in opposition to the Shah, from religious clerics to Marxists, from liberal nationalists to constitutional monarchists. These forces employed different methods to fight against the Shah's regime. Some, such as the leftist *Fadaian-e Khalq*, Islamist-leftist *Mojahedin-e Khalq*, and smaller religious groups,[1] included armed operations against the state institutions and leaders of the Shah's government as part of their mandate, while others such as *Nehzat Azadi* (the Iranian Liberation Movement) never condoned or promoted armed struggle. This divide was also present amongst the followers of Ayatollah Khomeini. Some of them were terror groups following the path of the religious *Fadaian-e Islam* who assassinated more than five leading figures in Shah's regime between 1945 and 1979; while others used mosques and religious organizations to fuel the flames of people's dissatisfaction and mobilize them against the Shah.

Other than the small religious groups who were unanimously male- dominated, women participated as members or followers of various groups and political organizations, including the religious groups, which did not advocate armed struggle. Women aligned with pro-Ayatollah Khomeini clerics used mosques and women's religious gatherings to organize and mobilize the masses. Meanwhile the *Fadaian-e Khalq* and *Mojahedin-e Khalq* attracted women members in universities and workplaces, and also mobilized their female relatives to join their groups.

---

[1] This refers to smaller groups such as *Mansouroun*, *Ommat-e Vahedeh*, *Badr* and others. After the revolution, these groups merged together and formed the *Mojahedin* of the Islamic Revolution Organization.

The Shah's regime made full use of prison as one of the most important tools for crushing opponents. The number of women political prisoners-very few in the early 70s-soon grew exponentially in the years leading up to the 1979 revolution. However, all such activists were released from prison several months before the Shah was overthrown, due to a number of factors, including, public pressure and considerable public outreach by the political dissidents to Europe and North America, a very active confederation of Iranian students who mobilized locally, and international pressures after the election of President Carter who was elected on a foreign policy platform of democracy and liberalism. Some of those released re-engaged in political activism, participating in the 1979 revolution, only to be reimprisoned for many years, and sometimes executed, when they opposed the new regime under Ayatollah Khomeini.

Despite diverse actors participating in the revolution, as February 1979 drew to a close, religious forces took an increasingly dominant role in the leadership of public demonstrations. Even though *Mojahedin-e Khalq* and the *Fadaian-e Khalq* raised banners and shouted their own slogans in protests, over time, the pro-Khomeini clergy used a vast network of mosques to influence and educate a large portion of the public, ultimately shaping the dominant slogans and demands of the revolution according to their vision. Ayatollah Khomeini was promoted as the future leader of the revolution to such an extent that for fear of losing support, all the political groups and organizations avoided directly criticizing him, even if they did not endorse his leadership. Soon men and women were demonstrating in separate groups and even secular women began wearing the veil to show support for the general atmosphere of the demonstrations.

On February 1, 1979, under both internal and international pressures, the government of Shapour Bakhtiar, the Shah's last prime minster, consented to permit Ayatollah Khomeini to return from exile to Iran. Once back inside, Khomeini began preparing the scene to form his vision of Islamic government.[1] On January 12, 1979, he ordered the creation of the Revolutionary Council, which was tasked with assessing the domestic political

---

[1] Bakhtiar Prime Mistrial period last only 36 days.

situation and preparing for the establishment of the Interim Government.[1]

Some of the most important activities of this council included: suggesting Mehdi Bazargan for Prime Minister of the Interim Government, approving the statute of the *Sepah-e Pasdaran-e Enghelab-e Islami* (Islamic Revolutionary Guards Corps), nationalizing the banks, establishing and structuring the Revolutionary Courts, holding a referendum about the nature of the Islamic Republic regime, reviewing the draft constitution, ratifying the procedure for the National Council, nationalizing large industries, passing the Procedural Code for the Assembly of Experts, and holding presidential and parliamentary elections.

Establishment of the Interim Government

On February 4, 1979, Mehdi Bazargan, a long time political dissident and a member of *Nehzat Azadi* (the Liberation Movement) who had begun his political activities by engaging in the nationalist movements during the nationalization of oil in the 1950s, was appointed as Prime Minister by Ayatollah Khomeini. While the first interim government comprised members of *Jebhe Melli* (the National Front) and the Liberation Movement, blocked the entry of the leftist organization and *Mojahedin-e Khalq* members into the government was blocked. Yet, the Islamists still did not demonstrate any obvious opposition towards the activities of political organizations who were not part of coalition that formed interm government. Almost all of the parties and political organizations, including *Mojahedin-e-Khalq*, *Fadaian-e Khalq*, and various other leftist organizations and nationalist parties, were allowed to operate freely, barring minor restrictions. Organizing through offices in Tehran and elsewhere, their followers openly distributed flyers and promoted their opinions,

---

[1] The first members of this Council consisted of Ayatollah Motahari, Ayatollah Beheshti, Ayatolla Mousavi Ardabili, Dr. Bahonar, Hojatolleslam Hashemi Rafsanjani, Ayatollah Taleghani, Ayatollah Khamenei, Ayatollah Mahdavi Kani, Ahmad Sadr Haj Seyyed Javadi, Mehdi Bazargan, Dr. Yadollah Sahabi, Mr. Katirayi, Major General Valiollah Gharani, and General Ali Asghar Masoudi. After the victory of the revolution and the creation of the interim government, Dr. Hasan Habibi, Ezzatollah Sahabi, Dr. Abbas Sheibani, Abolhassan Bani Sadr, Sadegh Ghotbzadeh, Mirhossein Mousavi, Ahmad Jalali, and Dr. Habibollah Peyman were also added to the list. See: Formation of the Revolutionary Council, Islamic Republic Documentation Centre, available at:
http://www.irdc.ir/fa/calendar/77/default.aspx.

especially in schools. From February 1979 to March 1980, scores of women, particularly young women, joined political parties and organizations. Most of them were supporters or low-ranking members, and did not hold leading roles. They engaged mostly in administrative and organizing activities such as selling publications, writing slogans in public spaces, engaging in street debates, recruiting forces, participating in demonstrations, advertising and spreading their organizations' ideologies and political positions, collecting provisions and soliciting donations, and even participating in self defense classes that were offered by the political organizations. For example, the *Mojahedin-e Khalq's* militia[1] was open and free to all.

However, it was only a month after the Shah was deposed that leaders of the revolution turned and began imposing controls on women. During the 'Spring of Liberation'- an expression used at the time to refer to the period immediately following the revolution- Keyhan Newspaper published a decree by Khomeini declaring that women, including female employees, could not appear in governmental places and offices without an Islamic *hijab*. This meant that they had to cover all of their body except their faces and their hands and feet below the wrists and ankles. This decree ran counter to Ayatollah Khomeini's earlier statements made while living in exile in Neauphle-le-Chateau, France. When asked about his plans for the future of Iran by a foreign journalist, Ayatollah Khomeini had stated that in his future regime, women would not be forced to cover themselves. [2] Thousands of women poured into the streets of Tehran in protest against the *hijab* ruling. The demonstrations continued for several days in spite of the violent crackdown by Ayatollah Khomeini's supporters. Women finally ended their street demonstration with the promise of Ayatollah Taleghani, a moderate religious leader that there would be no compulsory *hijab*. However, *hijab* did gradually become compulsory over the next couple of years.

Before this event, with another order from Ayatollah Khomeini, all of the rights bestowed upon women through the

---

[1] Militia, a branch of the *Mojahedin-e Khalq*, was formed on November 23, 1979. Although Militia forces were given military training, they were mostly unarmed. In 1987, Militia changed its name to National Liberation Army of Iran (NLA).

[2] "Women are free in the Islamic Republic in the selection of their activities and their future and their clothing." -Ayatollah Khomeini (in an interview with The Guardian Newspaper, Paris, November 6, 1978)

Family Protection Law- including the right to divorce and have child's custody- were ruled as contrary to the regime's under-standing of *shari'a*, and subsequently annulled. However due to the tumultuous political events of the time, the matter received only scattered attention, even amongst the thousands of women who in the course of the Revolution had become more politi-cized. On the other hand, the Islamic Revolution Party, founded by clerics and officials close to Ayatollah Khomeini, mobilized a group of their own women supporters to hold a demonstration in front of the Radio and Television Building to protest against the covering of the women's demonstration against the compul-sory *hijab* by the national Radio and Television. All this indicates that new regime had a clear gender policy at work and was de-termined to implement it without any delay despite the fact that there were no constitution written and at the time no election has yet taken place.

The Islamic Republic Party also involved women in its other activities. One important example was marking the birthday of Fatima Zahra, the daughter of the Prophet Mohammad, as Women's Day in the Islamic Republic and holding a ceremony for it in May 1979. This later became an official celebration of the Islamic Republic's calendar.

Meanwhile, religious forces close to Ayatollah Khomeini re-invigorated the *Komitehs* (Revolutionary Committees), which had been formed in neighborhoods and mosques to organize pro-tests and provide social assistance in the face of shortage in the months prior to the revolution. Ayatollah Khomeini appointed Ayatollah Mahdavi Kani to chair the *Komitehs* and Hojatolislam Nategh-Nouri became his deputy. In the new structure, a cleric was elected chairman of each *Komiteh*. In close cooperation with Mahdavi Kani, some of the armed religious groups that later formed the *Mojahedin* of the Islamic Revolution took charge of organizing and directing the *Komiteh*s. Among the members of the Central Cadre of the *Komiteh*s who worked with Ayatollah Mahdavi Kani were Saeed Hajjarian, Seyyed Bagher Zolghadr, Mohammad Atrianfar, and Khosrow Tehrani.[1] As a result *Ko-miteh*s took on the roles of police and security forces; their mem-bers were armed and allowed to carry and use weapons.

---

[1] Interview with Mohsen Sazegara, Justice For Iran.

Despite the power vested in *Komiteh*s by religious and conservative forces, they were not considered 'official' by ordinary individuals or members of political groups. Instead the *Komiteh*s were viewed as pressure groups, thugs, or rogue forces. People referred to them as '*chomaghdar*' (club wielders). This was somewhat accurate, since the *Komiteh*s used their mandate to 'protect' and ensure 'security' to attack oppositional locations, including the political parties' offices and newsstands, especially those of *Mojahedin-e-Khalq*.

As mentioned earlier, apart from the Revolutionary Committees, in early 1980, another armed group by the name of *Sepah-e Pasdaran-e Enghelab-e Islami* (*Sepah*) or Islamic Revolutionary Guards Corps was created. This paramilitary force was created by a group of Ayatollah Khomeini's supporters, who for various reasons were either not willing to cooperate with the *Komiteh*s, or did not consider the *Komiteh*s' range of power to be sufficient to protecting their dominance. The first constitution of *Sepah* proposed the creation of '*Sepah* Intelligence'. Later this unit became responsible for the arrest, interrogation and torture of political activists. In all Iranian cities, *Sepah* seized the former Organization of Intelligence and National Security (SAVAK) headquarters, and used the detention centres to hold detainees. Some of the pre-revolutionary religious armed groups known as the right wing of the *Mojahedin* of the Islamic Revolution Organization who later split from this organization- entered *Sepah*'s Intelligence. Mohsen Rezaei was the most well-known person amongst them who went on to become the head of *Sepah*'s Intelligence Office. Later, with the resignation of Morteza, Ayatollah Khomeini appointed Moshen Rezaei as *Sepah*'s commander.

In addition to *Sepah* and the *Komiteh*s, at least two other intelligence and security agencies began operating between 1979 and 1981. Hashem Sabaghian, the Interior Minister, founded the first Prime Minister's Intelligence Unit. In an interview with Ayandegan Newspaper on August 7, 1979 he outlined that the Intelligence Agency's duties would be to collect intelligence, both locally and internationally, that would affect Iranian government policies, under the supervision of the prime minister's deputy.[1] This unit began its work under Prime Minister Raja'i

---

[1] Ayandegan Newspaper, August 2, 1979, P. 3.

and later, when Raja'i began his career as president after the dismissal of Bani Sadr, the unit continued with the new Prime Minister Bahonar. As discussed below, one of the original plans to crackdown on oppositional political forces was formed at a meeting in this unit during the presidency of Bani Sadr and Prime Minister Raja'i.

The Information Unit under the direction of the head of the military court Hojatolislam Ray Shahri, was also active in investigating political cases. Ray Shahri was responsible for cases of Ghotbzadeh, Nojeh Coup, Muslim Nation Party (*Hezb-e Khalq-e Musalman*) and the military leaders of the Tudeh Party.

Officially the old regime fell on 10 Febrary 1979, though the old regime had been losing power since January 1979. Ayatollah Khomeini, on the other hand had been assuming power ever since he arrived in Iran. Even before organizing armed intelligence and security forces such as the *Komiteh*s and *Sepah*, Ayatollah Khomeini had taken control of the Iranian judiciary, through the establishments of the Revolutionary Courts. Two days after the overthrow of the Shah's regime, on February 13, 1979, Ayatollah Khomeini officially appointed his former student, and then unknown cleric, Hojatolislam Khalkhali, as the religious magistrate of the Revolutionary Court to oversee the 'trials' of leaders and supporters of the past regime. Khomeini's regime sought to maintain control by use of fear and intimidation, seeking to execute all opposition and threats as quickly as possible. Indeed, executions began on February 11, when the Shah's regime was actually overthrown. According to Amnesty International, by March 1980, 709 people were executed, mainly under Khalkhali's orders. They were given 'trials' that were mostly very short and denied access to a legal counsel.[1] The executed individuals included the heads of the previous regime, the leftist Kurdish dissidents and members of opposition movements in Turkmen Sahra, as well as prostitutes, drug-dealers and traffickers deemed 'immoral' influences and a scourge on society.

The crackdown on Kurdistan began when popularly elected municipal councils refused to follow orders of the central gov-

---

[1] Amnesty International Seeks to Send Mission to Iran in Effort to Stop Executions, AI INDEX MDE 13/13/81, 12 October 1981, available at:
http://www.iranrights.org/english/document-174.php.

ernment, expressing dissent by taking control of various barracks and fuel distribution centres. During the Persian New Year in 1979, military forces and Revolutionary Committees attacked the Kurdish cities of Sanandaj, Paveh, Marivan and Baneh. In September 1979, in an attack on the village of Gharna, which was claimed to be a hiding place for Kurdish *Peshmerga* (armed Kurdish fighter) forces, almost the entire civilian population, including women and children were massacred.[1] These attacks were carried out with the guidance and support of the central government, and mostly targeted the Kurdish Democratic Party, *Komala*, *Fadaian-e Khalq* and Sheikh Ezzedin Husseini's forces. The number of civilian deaths and military casualties on both sides of these conflicts is not known to this day. On August 19, 1979, the conflict heightened as the army tried to occupy Sanandaj with tanks and aircrafts. The defeat of the less-equipped Kurdish force was inevitable. Six months after the start of the conflict in Kurdistan, Sadegh Khalkhali travelled to this province to, as he claimed, "end the Kurdistan issue". He held several trials and executed approximately 80 people in Sanandaj, Paveh, Marivan, Mahabad, and Saqqez, most of whom were members of the Kurdish Democratic Party.[2]

Another similar struggle took place in Turkaman Sahra. Mobilized largely by the teachings of the *Fadaian-e Khalq* Guerilla Organizations, peasants in Turkaman Sahra villages created their own Peasant Councils, taking over and cultivating land that had

---

[1] Gharna is a Kurdish village in the environs of Naghadeh, West Azerbaijan Province. Located seven kilometers southwest of Nagahdeh, the village was attacked on September 2, 1979 by forces loyal to Hassani, Friday Prayer Imam of Orumiyeh. In the armed conflict that ensued, nearly the entire village was massacred. In his report, published in Ettelaat Newspaper on September 17, 1979, Mehdi Bahadoran who was sent by Ayatollah Montazeri to investigate the massacre of Gharna writes, "After extensive research through the reports and available tapes of the chivalrous employees of the Gendarmerie, Mojahed pretenders of Naghadeh, led by Mr. Ma'budi and Major Najafi, massacred 45 innocent people at their place of residence in Gharna in the environs of Nagahdeh and then relocated the corpses to the wilderness to pretend that they were killed in battle. Then they looted the village and set it on fire. Sergent Biglari killed five people in Kupelku. Such actions were done due to inability or treachery and conspiring of the Gendarmerie commanders on the one hand, and the inciting of anti-Kurdish tendencies on the other, which led to the awakening of vengeful desires against the innocent Kurds. Unfortunately although the actors of this massacre are known, due to the protection provided to them by Zahirnejad (Commander of Corps 64 of Orumiyeh) who is a local corrupt, their arrest and punishing is not possible."

[2] Haunted Memories: The Islamic Republic's Executions of Kurds in 1979, Iran Human Rights Documentation Centre, available at:
http://www.iranhrdc.org/english/publications/reports/3508-haunted-memories-the-islamic-republics-executions-of-kurds-in-1979.html

been abandoned by the feudal landowners of the Shah's time. They began their own production and distribution cooperatives. Similar to the case of Kurdistan, Turkaman Shahra officials' failure to obey orders of the central government and fear of losing power in the region compelled the government to send in their armed military forces once again. In the spring of 1979, the first conflict in Gonbad resulted in many casualties on both sides but was unsuccessful in destroying the Councils of Turkmen Sahra. However, the second conflict of Gonbad in February 1980 dealt the final blow to these councils. Vahedi, Toumaj, Makhtoum, and Jorjani, four of the leaders of the Central Committee and Cultural-Political Centre of Turkmen Nation were sentenced to execution by the religious magistrate of the Revolutionary Court, Khalkhali. At the same time, internal disagreements amongst the *Fadaian-e Khalq* split this organization into two groups, Majority and Minority, and forever destroyed the possibility of united oppositional mobilization against the central government in this area.[1]

Continuous and vocal opposition to the regime led to increasingly harsh tactics for control. The government shut down independent print media, and acquired from control of radio and television. There were also severe restrictions placed on foreign journalist and human rights activists. Iranian Bar associations were dissolved and several lawyers were detained. Even harsher reprisals were enacted against oppositional forces and political prisoners already in captivity. The regime embarked on many summary prosecutions, by officials who neither had experience or legal training. Those 'tried' were condemned to long years or imprisonment or execution. Khomeini soon appointed at least one religious magistrate per province, with courts and prosecution offices being set up across the country. Khalkhali was no longer the primary prosecutor. The case files were sent to the religious magistrates from prosecution offices as well as security offices, like *Sepah*. Spaces to hold political prisoners expanded as well. In addition to *Sepah* detention centres, former SAVAK headquarters and other local *Komiteh* detention centres, the prisons of Tehran and other cities were expanded. In Tehran, Evin Prison was the first to be devoted solely to political prisoners.

---

[1] Second war of Turkmen Sahra, interview with Abbas Hashemi (Hashem), Fereidoun, Arash Publication, available at: http://www.arashmag.com/content/view/476/47.

When Evin was filled to the limit, officials prepared a section of Ghezel Hesar Prison for political prisoners as well. Officials also accelerated the process of building Gowhardasht Prison, for which construction had begun during the time of the Shah, to hold only political prisoners. Revolutionary Prosecutors across Iran- the most important of whom was Asadollah Lajevardi in Tehran- were responsible for and supervised the interrogation, torture, obtaining confession, imprisonment, and execution of prisoners. According to the Procedural Code of Revolutionary Courts, ratified on August 1979 by the Revolutionary Council, Revolutionary Courts were responsible for trying the following crimes:

1) Murder and killing as a means to fortify the Pahlavi regime and crushing Iranian people's opposition, ordering and cooperating

2) Imprisonment and torture of Iranian combating people, ordering and cooperating

3) Major financial crimes such as stealing from the nation's coffers or wasting country's money in the interest of foreigners

4) Conspiracy against the Islamic Republic of Iran with armed action, assassination, destroying institutions, and espionage to the benefit of foreigners

5) Armed robbery, rape, and production, import or distribution of drugs.

It appears that the first interrogations and 'trials' conducted by Revolutionary Prosecutors other than Khalkhali, were those of members of the *Forqan* Group, an armed religious group that assassinated more than 15 officials of the Islamic Republic. Most of the members of this group were arrested in the second half of 1979 and some were executed, including its leader Akbar Goudarzi. According to Ayatollah Nategh-Nouri's memoirs, as a religious magistrate, he was made responsible for the trial of the *Forqan* Group members at the request of Ayatollah Beheshti, head of the Supreme Court and a member of the Revolutionary Council. In turn, he personally invited Asadollah Lajevardi, to supervise the case as the Revolutionary Prosecutor. The memoir also notes that members of the *Mojahedin* of the Islamic Revolution Organization, such as Mohammad Bagher Zolghadr[1], and Mohammad Atrianfar, were among the main interrogators of members of *Forqan* Group.[2] It was under the guidance of Ayatolla Beheshti, Ayatollah Nategh-Nouri and Asadollah Lajevardi that torture was used to extract 'confessions' from political prisoners that would then be publicly broadcasted and televised. This became a common and widespread practice, repeated systematically on political prisoners, especially Tehran's prisons under Lajevardi.

Despite the considerable number of executions that were conducted by the Revolutionary Courts, there was little demonstration against them.[3] The executions of high-ranking officials of the Shah's regime were accepted by political organizations that had opposed the Shah. Executions of prostitutes and smugglers did not excite a serious reaction by the public either. The leftist political groups only seriously protested against the actions of religious magistrates and Revolutionary Courts when the aforementioned began executing leftist activists in Kurdistan and Turkaman Sahra and detaining large numbers of these organizations' members and supporters in Tehran and other cities. Even though until the beginning of May 1981, over 1810 of the members and supporters of *Mojahedin-e Khalq* were imprisoned in various prisons,[4] it was only after Bani Sadr was dismissed from office and thousands more were detained in the 20 June 1981 demonstration that *Mojahedin-e Khalq* protested against the violations of detainees' basic rights, short trials and speedy executions. Even the killing of 71 members of this organization in a street conflict with supporters of Ayatollah Khomeini did not excite the leaders into seriously protesting the violations of the rights of the political dissidents.[5]

---

[1] Memoirs of Hojjatolislam Nategh-Nouri, Compiled by Morteza Mirdar, Islamic Republic Documentation Centre, 2005, p188.
[2] In an interview with Shahrvand Emrooz, he vaguely points to the fact that he was involved in the detention and interrogation of members of *Forqan* Group. A complete text of the interview is available at: http://www.fardanews.com/fa/pages/?cid=50960.
[3] Amongst those excused was Dr. Farrokhrou Parsa, who was Minister of Education and Culture, and the first female Minister.
[4] Ervand Abrahamian, Radical Islam: the Iranian Mojahedin, 1989, I. B. Taurus & Co, P.270.
[5] Ibid, P. 272.

Documents that were later released show that various organizations founded by Ayatollah Khomeini and those around him had planned the suppression of opposing political forces months prior to 20 June 1981. During this time, however, political organizations spent a great deal of time and energy destroying and criticizing each other. Internal disputes in political organizations also increased. For example, the disagreements between the Kurdish Democratic Party and *Komala* had a serious impact on the events in Kurdistan. The bisecting of *Fadaian-e Khalq* into Majority and Minority groups weakened the organization, especially since the Majority part of the organization supported the government and its policies, practically removing itself from the opposition front.

In May 1980, Ayatollah Khomeini also set up the Supreme Council of the Cultural Revolution, to carry out policies that restricted the potential use of public spaces for opposition activism. Among those he appointed to lead the Supreme Council were Hojatolislam Rabbani Amlashi, Dr. Mohammad Javad Bahonar, Jalaladin Farsi, Shams Al-e Ahmad, Dr. Hasan Habibi, Dr. Abdolkarim Soroush, and Dr. Ali Shariatmadari. Part of this policy was closing universities, which was a major setback to groups who used campuses as their main political organizing and recruiting space. Within four days, this council closed all the offices of critical student organizations in universities of Mashhad, Karaj, Tehran, Shiraz, Jahrom and Babolsar, destroying the students' and professors' resistance movement. According to published statistics, while many conflicts erupted from the 'cleansing' of universities, it was only during the conflict of 17 April 1980 in Tehran that over 700 people were injured and dozens were killed.[1] Many of these students who participated in the resistance were later arrested and many of them were executed and others were excluded from universities

Additionally, the start of the Iran-Iraq war in September 1980 made it possible for the state to use the excuse of 'protecting national sovereignty and independence' to crush and heavily punish any dissenting voices. The state argued that any internal disagreements could potentially weaken the Islamic Republic and serve the enemy.

---

[1] "A report of the players of the Cultural Revolution + Image: Occupying the strong hold of the Marxists and closure of universities", Raja News, available at: http://rajanews.com/detail.asp?id=85511.

Coordination amongst Interrogation Agencies

As mentioned above, in the early years after the 1979 revolution, both before and after the widespread suppression of political opponents, there were a variety of agencies participating in the identification, arrest, interrogation, torture, prosecution, imprisonment, and execution of political opponents. Although there was no formal or public division of responsibilities amongst these agencies, it is clear that there was a measure of planned coordination amongst them. We know that the coordination occurred at least during two consecutive confidential[1] meetings held in February of 1981, exactly two years after the Shah's regime collapsed.[2] In these two sessions it was decided that the Interior Ministry would not permit any parties or groups to hold political meetings and rallies without a permit. This action extended their arm of control, enabling them to declare even small, informal gatherings illegal. The Revolutionary Prosecutor was mandated to implement a policy of arms amnesty, urging all political groups to turn over their weapons to the *Sepah* and *Komiteh* offices by a certain date. After this deadline, if weapons were not submitted, the organization would be declared illegal and dealt with accordingly. In the minutes 'being dealt with' is defined as:

> All the leaders and cadres of the organization would be arrested forcefully and given maximum punishment [execution] and all the sympathizers who were arrested while selling newspapers, distributing flyers and placards and other activities to benefit the groups will be punished in hopes of guiding them.[3]

After this meeting in late March 1981, Ayatollah Qoddusi, Iran's Revolutionary Prosecutor, who was later assassinated by the *Mojahedin-e Khalq*,[4] issued a statement declaring from that moment onward that only print media that obtained official permission from the Ministry of Culture and Islamic Guidance

---

[1] The resolutions of the two meeting were published in Kar magazine, the official publication of the *Fadaian-e Khalq* - Minority, No, 112, June 3, 1981.
[2] List of the attendee are: .Ayatollah Mahdavi Kani, Bagher Kani, Ayatollah Mousavi Ardebili, Morteza Rezaei, Ayatollah Qoddusi, Bijan Namdar Zangeneh, Mostafa Mirsalim, Behzad Nabavi, Mohsen Sazgara, Ali Foj Kanlou, Nasrollah Jahangard, Safar Salehi, Hossein Ghafari, Asadollah Lajevardi, Mohammad Kachouei, Khosrow Tehrani and Jazayeri
[3] Ibid.
[4] Text of the announcement is available at Justice For Iran.

could be published. Moreover, parties and organizations would no longer be allowed to open offices without first consulting the Interior Minister. This statement also gave permission to all judicial authorities in Iran to treat the members and supporters of groups that refused to relinquish their weapons as *muharib* (enemy of God), or 'anti-revolutionaries'. Punishment for being a *muharib* under *shari'a* laws is death or life imprisonment.

The Prosecution Offices and Revolutionary Courts later used ayatollah Qoddusi's statement as the basis for the treatment of all political opposition. Many young women who were members or supporters of organizations like *Mojahedin-e Khalq*, *Fadaian-e Khalq* (Minority), *Komala*, Kurdish Democratic Party, and others, as with their male counterparts, were tried and convicted as *muharib* and sentenced accordingly simply for supporting the organization, even if they themselves had never personally used arms or participated in an armed operation. These punishments even affected members and supporters of organizations like *Peykar* and *Rah-e Kargar* that had never endorsed armed struggles. Some years later, in 1983, even members of *Tudeh* Party and *Fadaian-e Khalq* (Majority) who had shown support for the Islamic Republic's policies were imprisoned, tortured, or even executed under the title of *muharib*.

Though the arrest and torture of political opposition had started months before, the issuing of the statement by the Prosecution Office led to a wave of increased repression in the first months of 1981. While supporters of political organizations openly continued their activities, distributing flyers and selling publications, there were widespread attacks on the individuals or teams who manned the publication stands by the group known as *hizbullahi* or *chomaghdar* (club wielders), who as mentioned, were mainly connected to the *Sepah* or *Komiteh*. Young women were a primary target in these types of attacks. Banoo Saberi, one of the Tudeh Party's active supporters was attacked by unknown individuals connected to the *Komiteh*. They kidnapped her on her way home, raped her in a desert near Isfahan, and in this manner removed her from the political scene for a long time.[1]

---

[1] For more information, see complete text of Banoo Saberi's testimony in Appendix I.

Denial of Torture in Prisons

In a speech made during a March 1981 demonstration -a demonstration that like other rallies of the time was violently suppressed by the *chomaghdars* -then president Bani Sadr mentioned the occurrence of torture in prisons and reminded the public that the premises of the Islamic Revolution were against torturing political prisoners. This speech incited a direct reaction by Ayatollah Khomeini, as the leader of the revolution. He delegated a group to investigate the condition of prisoners and to look into whether torture was occurring. The group consisted of Hossein Dadgar (Public Prosecutor of Tehran), Dr. Goudarz Eftekhar Jahromi (Member of the Guardian Council), Ali Akbar Abedi (Inspector of the General Prosecution Office of Tehran), Ali Mohammad Besharati Jahromi (Majlis Representative), and Mohammad Montazeri (Ayatollah Khomeini's representative). The group, titling itself 'The Committee to Investigate the Rumors of Torture'[1], received 3,620 complaints of torture from prisoners. However, in its final report it announced that not even one case from amongst the 3,620 cases offered proof for the occurrence of torture and thereby, the occurrence of torture in Iranian prisons is an absolute farce.[2] The statement was made despite the evidence presented by numerous witnesses who had managed to leave the prisons alive during 1980 and the years following and had attested to the various forms of torture inflicted upon them and other prisoners.

Suppression of political dissent took on a new and unimaginable shape following the organized protest- or riot- of the *Mojahedin-e Khalq* on June 20, 1981. On June 18, *Mojahedin-e Khalq*, disenchantment with continuous undemocratic action of the regime, announced that they had entered into armed struggle phase.[3] At the same time, president Abulhassan Bani Sadr's lack

---

[1] The appearance of the term "rumor" in the name of the committee is an indication that the committee, prior to having performed any probing into the occurrence of torture, had decided that it is in fact merely a rumor.

[2] To read the complete report of the committee, see Ettelaat Newspaper of April 19, 1981, No. 16406 p. 15, and Ettelaat Newspaper of May 19, 1981, no. 16431, Pp. 3 and 13.

[3] Part of the announcement reads, "The *Mojahedin-e Khalq* of Iran protests such anti-revolutionary and anti-*shari'a* and illegal action and hereby, request permission from the heroic people of Iran to, henceforth, with the aid of God, take the most decisive measures in protecting the lives of its members, particularly the central cadre of the organization that are in truth the heart of the nation and revolution. Obviously, pursuant to this announcement, all responsibilities of what might happen during a revolutionary act lays entirely on the shoulders of the reactionaries and club wielding thugs who have set to finish what the treacherous →

of competence in office was being assessed in the Majlis, primarily because he was *Mojahedin's* most important political ally. As a result of the two events, hundreds of thousands of members and supporters of the *Mojahedin* were mobilized to participate in the June 20 mass protest. Some observers suggest that in Tehran alone, 500 thousand people protested in the streets that led to Enghelab Square. However, the protest was effectively squashed in its early stages. Some of the protesters were injured and even killed in the streets while a larger number were arrested in Tehran and other cities on that day and the days, weeks and months following.

Based on numerous reliable reports, in those days, lashing on the soles of the feet was a prevalent and common method used to extract information from prisoners.[1] The punishment was cloaked in the *shari'a's* acceptable concept of *ta'zir* (discretionary punishment) so as not to conflict with constitutional principles banning torture in the constitution. Although no statistic exists on the number of prisoners arrested post June 20, 1981, witness accounts describe the prisons as overflowing with detainees. They were kept handcuffed and blindfolded for hours and even days in the hallways leading to the interrogation rooms until their turn for interrogation would arrive. Even when relocated from hallways to wards, the prisoners' conditions did not improve.

Farzaneh Zolfi, arrested at the age of 16 in Karaj for supporting the Communist Union of Iran, describes how more than 40 prisoners were stuffed in a room built to hold three people:

> We usually slept in shifts. The third bunk bed on top was where ten or twelve of the girls had to sit until the morning. In the first and the second bunks a bunch of people were sleeping on top of one another. On the side of the bed where it was very nar-

---

← shah and the hated SAVAK started through squashing the *Mojahedin*. Therefore, we are resolved that whoever the aforementioned are and whatever post they may have, they are deserving of the harshest and most severe form of revolutionary punishment. The *Mojahedin-e Khalq* reserves the right to, when not possible to execute the punishment of the criminals in the process of carrying out a revolutionary act, do so in a compounded manner as soon as possible to serve the related actors and agents their just due." *Mojahed* Publication, No. 127, June 23, 1981.

[1] Law and Human Rights in the Islamic Republic of Iran, Amnesty International, MDE 13/003/1980, 1 February 1980, at:
http://www.amnesty.org/en/library/info/MDE13/003/1980/en

row, a few people would hang to the bars. Then we would switch places between [those sleeping and] those sitting on the top bunk or even the window ledge. There was a small window that we used a lot. Many times, in the middle of the night, we would wake with a very loud noise; someone had fallen from the third bunk or the second bunk had broken because it could not handle so many people.[1]

According to the names published by Abdorrahman Boroumand Foundation website (Omid: A Memorial in Defense of Human Rights), between June 20, 1981 and June 20, 1984, at least[2] 3895 people were executed inside Iran, 580 of them women. The height of the executions was in the fall of 1981. As a result of widespread suppression, all political groups disbanded their public presence and resorted to continuing their activities in clandestine or semi-clandestine conditions. Many of the members and supporters of the various political groups who, prior to June 20 and due to the openness of the activities of the parties, were recognized in their schools, neighborhoods, or places of work had to leave their public life and resort to living in hiding. Harboring these individuals would have brought detention or dismissal from jobs for their families, friends or acquaintances. Men could spend their nights sleeping in parks and public places, particularly during the warm seasons, but many of the young female supporters of political groups who had left home because they were being pursued had a harder time finding a place to sleep or to spend their nights. At times, situations became so difficult that these women, left with no other option, returned home and were arrested shortly after. Inside prison, there was an extreme amount of pressure on members of different political groups to expose the safe houses where other members of their group would be hiding; so much so that some people lost their lives as a result of lashings and others sustained permanent damage to their feet, kidneys and other body parts. In most cases, extreme torture was successful: addresses and groups' rendez-vous[3] locations were handed to the officials of the Prosecution

---

[1] Witness Testimony of Farzaneh Zolfi, Justice For Iran.

[2] We say at least because many of the executions were never officially announced, and in spite of the restless efforts of Boroumand Foundation in collecting the various lists of different political groups and completing them, there are still many, particularly in smaller cities, whose names are not in the list.

[3] A group's rendezvous dates were coordinated by a few particular members or supporters of that political group. In a rendezvous, the work matters relating to two people were assessed and decisions were made in a short period of time. After the illegalization of the activities →

Office, *Sepah* and *Komiteh* and the affiliates of that particular political group were arrested one after the other. Some prisoners even helped the officials by accompanying them in their street sweeps to identify their friends and associates. The need to leave home to evade arrest forced some political groups to prepare safe 'team houses' for their higher-ranking members and cadres. Sometimes in the team houses, male and female members pretended to be married, in order to escape the scrutiny of their neighbors, who might otherwise report them to security forces. As such, women arrested in team houses faced increased pressure from security forces, as they could be accused of having uncustomary sexual relations with their male friends in the house.

The implementation of the 'Landlord-Tenant Plan' from September to November of 1982, made housing political opposition members in team houses virtually impossible in Tehran. Based on this Plan, executed by Tehran's Prosecution Office, *Komiteh* forces and local Revolutionary Guards (*pasdars*) were to report any and all houses that seemed to have suspicious residents. On the other hand, all landlords and tenants had to register their information with the local *Komiteh* offices.[1]

The coalescing of these various policies enabled the Islamic Republic to consolidate the most severe and widespread system for suppressing political opposition, within just three years of ascending to power. With virtually no checks and balances, the suppression resulted in executions, mass imprisonment, and the disengagement from political activity by those who survived prison and were released. It also hastened the forced exile of political dissidents, and increased the number of political prisoners across all cities, large and small.

As testified by most witnesses and corroborated by historic accounts and documents, during the three years between June 1981 and mid-1984, the pressure and torture inflicted upon prisoners was at its worse.[2] But increased international pressure by human rights groups and the United Nations on the Islamic Re-

---

← of political groups, in order to show up at a group rendezvous, individuals had to use code signs to show the situation was safe. The signs were called health dictum.
[1] For more information about Landlord-Tenant plan see http://www.psri.ir/mojahedin/18-3.pdf.
[2] IRAN: BRIEFING PAPER, Amnesty International, MDE 13/008/1987, 30 April 1987, at: http://www.amnesty.org/en/library/info/MDE13/008/1987/en

public regarding the condition of political prisoners, as well as the wave of criticism from within the regime, particularly by Ayatollah Montazeri and his associates and others such as groups rivalling Lajevardi, did lead to some reform inside prisons. Various supervisory committees were sent to assess the situation in prisons. One such committee, comprised of Hojjatolislam Mahmoud Doa'ee, Hojjatolislam Mohammad Ali Hadi Najafabadi, Ali Mohammad Besharati, and Hojjatolislam Hadi Khamenei, was sent by Ayatollah Khomeini to visit the prisons. Witnesses attest that some of the female prisoners discussed their being subjected to rape and sexual harassment with this committee and yet the visit did not result in any effective action. However, outside pressures and internal conflicts resulted in the eventual removal of Lajevardi in January 1985 from all judicial positions. Pursuant to that, in other prisons, individuals such as Haji Davoud Rahmani,[1] an appointee of Lajevardi at Ghezel Hesar, were removed from their positions and the prison conditions in heavily populated Evin and Ghezel Hesar improve by a small increment. Some prisoners were also released.

This improvement however, was short lived. A few days after Ayatollah Khomeini announced a seize-fire and the end of Iran-Iraq war in August 1988, visitation was halted for prisoners in most prisons across the country. Following that, over 5000 prisoners were hanged in secret within a two month span from the time of their sentencing by judicial and intelligence authorities and prison officials. None of those executed had been previously, during their first round of trials, sentenced to execution. In fact, they were executed without an official execution sentence and merely as a result of the order issued by Ayatollah Khomeini, quoted below. Of those executed in 1988, over 300 were women who had initially been sentenced to few years imprisonment for supporting the *Mojahedin-e Khalq*. Some of them had even completed their imprisonment terms yet were not released because they refused to give official statements denouncing their former political beliefs.

The text of the order and questions surrounding it were published in Ayatollah Montazeri's memoir:

---

[1] For more information about Haj Davoud's role in widespread and severe violation of prisoners' rights, see:
http://justiceforiran.org/human-rights-violators-individuals-databank/hajdavud/?lang=en

In the name of God the compassionate the merciful,

Since the treacherous *munafiqin* do not believe in Islam and what they say stems from their deception and hypocrisy, and since as per the claim of their leaders they have become apostates of Islam, and noting that they are *muharib* and are engaging in classical warfare in the western, northern and southern parts of the country with the collaboration of the Baathist Party of Iraq, and also their spying for Saddam against our Muslim nation, and since they are tied to the World Arrogance and have inflicted foul blows to the Islamic Republic since its inception, it follows that those who remain steadfast in their position of *nifaq* (hypocrisy) in prisons throughout the country are considered to be *muharib* (enemy of God) and are condemned to execution. In Tehran, the matter would be decided by majority vote of Misters Hojjatolislam Nayyeri, may God extend his benefits (religious magistrate), Mister Eshraghi (Tehran's prosecutor), and a representative from the Ministry of Intelligence. It is prudent to reach consensus. Likewise in the prisons of provincial capitals, majority vote of religious magistrate, Revolutionary Prosecutor or his assistant, and representative of office of intelligence is necessary to obey. It is simple-mindedness to have clemency on *muharibih*. Decisiveness of Islam in the face of the enemies of god is an undeniable principle of Islamic government. I hope that you are able to draw God's contentment by unleashing your revolutionary rage and rancor toward the enemies of Islam. These gentlemen who are making the decision must not hesitate or show any doubt or concerns and try to be '*Ishda' ala-al-kuffar* (be severe towards the infidels). Uncertainty in judicial matter of revolutionary Islam is to deny the pure and holy blood of the martyrs. *Wa Al-Salam.*

Ruhollah Al-Mousavi Al-Khomeini[1]

---

[1] Memoir of Ayatollah Montazeri, Hossein-ali Montazeri, Ketab publication, winter 2000, pp.351-352.

On the back of the letter, Ahmad, son of Khomeini wrote,

> Eminent Father, his Excellency the *Imam* (May God extend his shadow),
>
> With greetings, Ayatollah Mousavi Ardebili had ambiguities regarding Your Eminence's recent decree about the *munafiqin* that he expressed in three questions over the phone:
>
> 1. Is the decree for those who have been in prison, who have already been tried and sentenced to execution but have not changed their stance and their verdict has not yet been carried out, or are those who have not yet been tried also condemned to execution?
>
> 2. Are those *munafiqin* who have received limited jail terms and who have already served part of their sentence but continue to hold fast to their stance of *nifaq* also condemned to execution?
>
> 3. In reviewing the status of the *munafiqin*, is it necessary to refer the case files of those *munafiqin* who are in cities that have an independent judiciary to the provincial capital or can the [judicial authorities] act autonomously?
>
> Your son Ahmad[1]

Below the letter, Khomeini wrote,

> In the name of the exalted,
>
> In all the above cases, if the person at any stage or at any time maintains his position on *nifaq*, the sentence is execution. Annihilate the enemies of Islam immediately. With regard to the case files, use whichever criterion speeds up the implementation of the verdict that is the intention.
>
> Ruhollah Al-Mousavi Al-Khomeini[2]

---

[1] Ibid.
[2] Ibid.

Those detainees who survived this mass execution campaign spent another few years in harsh conditions inside prisons. They were slowly released, particularly after the death of Ayatollah Khomeini in June 1989. A small number of them remained in prison until the early 1990s.

To sum up: Thousands of Iranian women participated in the revolution. However, the post revolutionary regime's gender policies eventually disheartened the majority of the women and many of them subsequently become members or supporters of political opposition groups. Not only did women lose many of their rights in the spheres of public and family life under the Islamic Republic, but they also when arrested suffered severe and widespread suppression as members of political opposition groups. The fast paced political changes of the first decade of the revolution dramatically changed the lives of women in unprecedented ways. For the democratic forces which included large segment of the female population who had participated in the revolution in the hope of freedom and democracy, the fruits of the revolution was the imprisonment of thousands of girls and young women who lost their youth to prison, and were tortured, or executed. For those who weren't imprisoned, they lost much of the rights they had as well as loosing close friends and relatives to torture and execution, and were often forced to abandon their political activism, or escape from Iran out of desperation.

These women entered politics with dreams of improving lives for everyone. They were imprisoned in the heat of the political battles and were eventually released with unforgettable signs of torture on their bodies and souls. They are permanently scarred and emotionally distraught and remain, now and forever, in bondage.[1]

---

[1] This sentence was inspired by a witness Sarah L. where she spoke of being in prison with her child.

II- Raping of Virgin Girls before Execution

II- Raping of Virgin Girls before Execution

Mass Arrests of Youth from June 20, 1981

20 June 1981 marked the onset of widespread arrests of the followers of different opposition groups across the country. Various governmental forces, in particular, *Sepah-e Pasdaran's* Intelligence Office and the Islamic Revolutionary *Komiteh*s arrested thousands of people during this wave of detention. Those targeted were mostly members and supporters of the *Mojahedin-e Khalq* and leftist communist organizations, with the exception of the *Tudeh* Party and the *Fadaian Khalq*. There was no clear division of labor between *Sepah* (the Revolutionary Guard) and *Komiteh* Revolutionary Committees) who assumed the role of the police and security and almost freely had defined the extent of their issues under their jurisdiction. Both of these organizations conducted the arrests of citizens and interrogated them. In the end, however, all those arrested by the two organs were 'tried' in the Revolutionary Courts, which are governed by religious magistrates. The trials were convened in private, and adjudication took place without the presence of an attorney and without the prisoner's right to appeal.

Almost immediately after the arrests on June 20, 1981 the executions began.

There are no (valid) reliable statistics available of the number of people who were detained on 20 June or the days and weeks following. Some detainees were executed a few days after 20 June without any confirmation of their identity. On 24 June, Ettelaat Newspaper published a notice from the Revolutionary Prosecution Office of Tehran with the photos of 12 young women who were executed by a firing squad, asking their families to refer to the central office of Evin prison in order to identify their children and claim their corpses (see picture next page).

In the years immediately following the 1979 revolution, a large number of the supporters of various political groups and organizations were comprised of youth. Almost every organization had a student branch to mobilize youth throughout schools. Another significant source for mobilization was the creation of neighbourhood branches directed by youth and unemployed high school graduates who were given the opportunity to participate in political activism during the revolution. *Mojahedin-e Khalq* had the highest number of youth and young adult supporters amongst the opposition organizations. Because *Mojahedin-e Khalq* announced a policy of armed struggle in fighting the Islamic Republic, they were deemed *muharib* (anti-revolutionaries) by the Islamists in charge. *Mojahedin-e Khalq* members and followers effectively became subject to the sentence set forth for *muharibih*, even if they had not physically taken-up arms.

Mojahedin-e Khalq supporters were not the only ones sentenced to execution as *muharib* (enemy of God). Based on Ayatollah Qoddusi's (Iran's Revolutionary Prosecutor) announcement on July 12, 1979,

> All the groups and parties who had taken arms against the Islamic Republic of Iran will be allowed to remain politically active only if they officially denounce their current stance and surrender their arms to the *Sepah-e Pasdaran* (Revolutionary Guard) or military officials. Otherwise, they will be tried in the Revolutionary Courts and will be dealt with in accordance with the Islamic laws pertaining to *muharib*.[1]

---

[1] Ettelaat Newspaper, No. 16475, 21 Tir 1358 [July 12, 1979], P2.

In effect, other organizations that were categorized as 'hostile' by government officials, such as Kurdish Democratic Party, *Komala*, *Peykar*, *Fadaian-e Khalq* (Minority), *Rah-e Kargar*, *Fadaian-e Khalq* (Ashraf Dehghani group), *Arman-e Mostazafin*, and *Razmandegan* were all considered to be *muharib* and their supporters possibly subjected to the execution sentence based on the decision of the jurists[1] and Ayatollah Khomeini's famous *fatwa*.[2]

In Tahrir al-Wasilah, Ayatollah Khomeini describes *muharib* as such:

> A person will be called *muharib* if she/he draws her/his weapon with the intention of threatening and scaring the people, or intending to spread corruption on earth, either on land or sea, either in city or village, either at night or day. The punishment for *muharib* will be carried out once these conditions are met. In verifying the conditions the suspicious character of the individual, meaning if he is a villain, holds no merit and also there is no difference in verification between men and women.[3]

As per the decision of the jurists: "The strongest punishments which religious legal terminology referred to as *hadd* for the *muharib*, are at the disposal of the magistrate to choose from depending on how serious he considers the case to be. The ultimate punishment is a death sentence, either by hanging him/her, or other methods; a lesser sentence is cutting off the hand and foot of opposing sides (for example right hand and left foot), and third is exiling him/her."[4]

Given the political activity occurring throughout schools and neighbourhood teams, the majority of those arrested after 20 June facing the charge of *muharibih*, were youth or young adults. Of these young arrestees, a large number of them were young women and adolescent girls. A quick look at the execution lists offers a glimpse into the age bracket of the prisoners at the time.

---

[1] At the time, the Islamic Penal Code had not yet been ratified and the Islamic Revolutionary Courts tried the accused based of *shari'a* principles.
[2] See Announcement of Ayatollah Qoddusi, Revolutionary Prosecutor of the Islamic Republic of Iran, Ettelaat Newspaper, No. 16475, 21 Tir 1358 [July 12, 1979], P 2.
[3] Ruhollah Khomeini, Tahrir al-Wasilah, Vol 4, available at:
 http://www.hodablog.net/files/obook/tahrir4.htm.
[4] Ibid.

Based on names published by Boroumand Foundation (Omid: A Memorial in Defense of Human Rights), within the six months between 20 June and 21 December 1981, at least[1] 2,241 individuals were executed, of which 223 of them were female. From amongst those executed women, 34 were under the age of 18 and 120 were between 18 and 29 years of age.[2]

Raping of Virgin Girls before Execution: Logic and Justifications

The subject of raping young women in prison and specially raping of the unmarried women were circulating as rumors, which the authorities had categorically denied, claiming that such rumors were the work of enemies of the revolution. However, later the issue was reframed by the authorities as 'marrying' young women a night before their execution. This new turn was presented these rapes as a religiously sanctioned action of the judiciary. The general public, and particularly the religiously inclined sections of the public, however, were convinced that even if the Islamic regime committed other kinds of cruelty, they would not engage in such morally and ethically unacceptable actions. Due to a lack of concrete evidence and the lack of an appropriate and safe platform for the victims' family to come forward, these debates on the stories of raping virgin girls remained inconclusive. An important goal of our project was therefore to examine the extent to which such rumours reflected the realities of what went on behind prison walls during the 1980s. Below we outline what our investigation has elucidated.

The controversial order of Ayatollah Khomeini and its interpretation: In 1981 and the years following, unconfirmed reports of torture and sexual violations of women political prisoners began to surface on a large scale, both inside and outside prison walls. The reports, often spread through word of mouth, detailed the systematic rape of virgin girls before execution. It was said that according to Islamic laws, a virgin girl is considered to be innocent, and therefore upon execution she will go to

---

[1] Search results in Boroumand Foundation Website, available at: http://www.iranrights.org/farsi/memorial-about.php.
[2] Memoir of Ayatollah Montazeri, Hossein Ali Montazeri, Winter 2000, P. 350.

heaven. Therefore the prison authorities, in order to prevent prisoners' entry into heaven, decided to forcibly 'marry' (*siqih*) girls sentenced to execution to a *pasdar* (Revolutionary Guard) or other prison employee, so that they could be raped, rendering them no longer virgin, and then executed the day after. A leftist activist, who was herself 16 years of age at the time, recounts:

> We had heard that when they killed girls they would then take flowers and sweets or sugar cones to the homes of their families and tell them that their daughter was married off to a Revolutionary Guard the night prior and executed on that day. We also heard some families were forced to pay for the bullets the girls were shot with. This news spread so extensively that one of my father's greater sensitivities towards my political activism was that if I were to be arrested, they would cause a 'tragedy' to happen to me in prison.[1]

Although most of the former political prisoners interviewed for this report were most certain that a '*shari'a*-based' *fatwa* existed that called for raping virgin girls prior to their execution, no such *fatwa* has so far been cited or found in any of the available literature. Through our research we were able to uncover how the policy of raping imprisoned young women prior to executing them actually stemmed from a particular interpretation of an order banning the execution of 'girls' and had no basis in *shari'a*.

In his memoir, Ayatollah Montazeri recounts being asked the following question: "The publications of the *munafiqin* (referring to the *Mojahedin-e Khalq* publication *Mojahed*) outside of the country wrote that you issued a *fatwa* to marry off the *munafiqin* girls on death row prior to carrying out their execution. Please explain what this fabricated affiliation is based on." He responds,

> ...at the time many of the people arrested in affiliation with the *Mojahedin-e Khalq* were girls and they were executed as *muharib*. One day I complained to *Imam* (referring to Ayatollah Khomeini) and said,

---

[1] Seyyed Mahmoud Hashemi, "Who is a *muharib* and what is *muharibih*?" a diagnostic discussion, Part 2, Fiqh-i Ahl-i Bayt, No. 13, available at:
http://www.hawzah.net/fa/articleview.html?ArticleID=85967.

"Sir, as the *fatwas* of the jurists state that a female *murtad* (apostate) should not be executed, some jurists believe that a female *muharib* should not be executed either. There is a disagreement about it between the jurists. If the person is a murderer, well of course the sentence for such crime is execution and there is no difference between a female and a male murderer. But in cases that are unrelated to murder, it is not as such for female *murtad* or *muharib*. Please order that these girls not be executed. They are mostly misguided; they have been given a flyer to read and taught strongly worded slogans to chant. Most of them do not possess discerning power and so have been influenced. They should be given an imprisonment term so that they will realize their folly and then be released."

Imam stated, "Alright, tell the gentlemen not to execute girls."

He continues in his memoirs to say,

…So, on behalf of *Imam*, I told the judicial officials and officials of Evin prison and other locations not to execute *munafiqin* girls. I also told the judges that they are no longer permitted to issue execution sentences for girls. This is what I said to them. Later on, here and there, they pretended like I had said that girls should not be executed but instead first married off and then executed. The *munafiqin* outside of the country were using this [story] as well. But the real story was what I told you. I was trying to prevent the execution of women and girls, other than those who had committed murder… over all, my opinion was that women should not be executed, but because most of the female *Mojahedin* imprisoned were girls [unmarried young girls], I refer to them as such, but the devils at play misinterpreted my words. [1]

---

[1] Montazeri, Memoirs. Ibid.

Ayatollah Montazeri is pointing to the opinion of jurists such as Ibn Junayd (830- 910 CE) Abu Hanifah (699 - 767 CE), and Ibn Idris ((1760- 1837) who, in contradiction to the general consensus, considered the *hadd* of execution only administrable for *muharib* men.[1] Their argument is that since *Koranic* verse 33 of the Ma'idih Surah- the basis for describing *muharibih* and its *hadd*- refers to men, the sentence cannot be extended to women as well. The opinion does not in any way discuss whether or not the female *muharib* is a virgin and instead, as a general rule, excuses a female *muharib*, and female *murtad*, from death sentence

However it was Montazeri's use of the term '*munafiqin* girl' that was focused on. *Munafiqin*, the plural of *munafiq* (meaning hypocrite), is an expression the Islamic Republic officials had adopted for the members and followers of the *Mojahedin-e Khalq*. Although according to Ayatollah Montazeri, his intention was a general ban on execution orders for female members or supporters of *Mojahedin-e Khalq*, because the general understanding of the term 'girl' pointing to a woman who is unmarried (and hence a virgin). He suggests those lower officials interpreting his order deemed that 'women'- the married ones- are automatically disqualified from being subject to the order of amnesty issued by Ayatollah Montazeri and the lower officials misinterpreted his words to suggest that virgin girls must be deflowered before execution. In the context of Iran, this interpretation indicates ingenuity on the part of those who had vested interests in twisting the words of the Supreme Jurist 180 degrees to produce exactly the opposite result. That there was no follow-up to ensure that Montazeri's order to stay executions was being followed, however, also demonstrates that the regime was more focused on securing the loyalty of its supporters than on ensuring that justice was served.

Hence a rumour was spread claiming that Ayatollah Montazeri had issued a *fatwa* to rape virgin unmarried girls before execution. Yet the regime's authorities initially claimed that there was no raping of girls in prison, and that the *Mojahedin-e Khalq* was the source of these 'unfounded' rumors. Re-examining many of the documents, it is clear that the *Mojahedin-e Khalq* did publicize these cases to show the morally corrupted nature of the re-

---

[1] See decision of Ayatollah Montazeri in this regards, available at:
http://amontazeri.com/farsi/frame4.asp.

gime and its abuse of human rights. Once these raped became publicized the prison authorities placed the responsibility on Ayatollah Montazeri, despite Montazeri's claims that he was morally opposed to such actions. What is important here is recognizing the fact that these rapes and practices were known, to both Montazeri and other high officials in the regime according to his memoirs, and yet no concerted action was taken to stop them.

The execution of girls in fact continued from 1981-84 in Tehran and other cities.[1] In 1985, after nearly everyone who had received a death sentence was already executed, the heightened wave of internal complaints regarding prison conditions resulted in some reforms that stymied executions. This was short-lived however, and during the Prison Massacre of August and September of 1988, over 300 female *Mojahedin-e Khalq* members were executed; 157 of them were under 29 years of age.[2]

Indeed accounts from interviewees below demonstrate that judicial and prison officials explicitly promoted the idea of raping virgin girls before execution, publically speaking on their 'religious' justifications for it. The only religious text which seems were used as a justification for raping the virgin girls prior to execution is a *hadith* from Prophet Mohammad, published in a few sources which said: "if a virgin girls dies, she will go to heaven."[3]

Witness accounts of the authorities' exercise of rape before execution: Mohsen Makhmalbaf, a movie director who had close relations with judicial authorities during the 1980s, affirms the occurrence of rape before execution in an interview with Deutche Welle in 2009. According to multiple interviews given by former female prisoners, they were forcibly taken out of their cells and wards into the common areas of the prison to watch Makhmalbaf movies. Moreover, with the collaboration of relevant judicial and security officials, in 1984 he used the Adel Abad prison in Shiraz, one of the most notorious political prisons, as

---

[1] According to the list available at Boroumand Foundation's website- which is not complete and is particularly missing executions that took place in the cities due to the absence of sources- at least 322 female political prisoners were executed in 1981, 122 in 1982, 100 in 1983 and 60 in 1984.

[2] Analysis of the data provided by Boroumand foundation.

[3] Abolfotouh Razi, Rozoljanan o Rouholjenan fi Tafsire Alquran, the 10th volume, Moasses Tahghighat va Nashr-e Maaref-e Ahl-e beit, P. 128.

the location for shooting the movie 'Boycott' and used political prisoners as extras.[1] He said:

> It has been 30 years since such acts have been taking place in the Islamic Republic and in certain cases they have given it legal and shari'a-based justification such as raping of a virgin girl who is to be executed the following day merely because a virgin girl goes to heaven.[2]

Parvaneh Aref, a supporter of *Peykar* (a small left organization), was arrested when she was 17 after school officials reported on her. She remembers a night in the latter half of 1981 when students were taken to the *Hosseiniyeh* (the religious chapel) of Evin prison. Some nights, there were varying programs carried out at the *Hosseiniyeh*, such as *Komeyl* prayer (a particularly long prayer) and religious mourning processions, speeches given by prison officials, as well as interviews with the *tavvabs* (prisoners who recant their political opposition and express their support for the regime). On that night Asadollah Lajevardi (who was then head of prisons, the Revo-

Asadollah Lajevardi

Lutionary Prosecutor of Tehran, and the Head of the Prosecution's Intelligence Office), gave a speech to prisoners, during which he discussed the issue of raping virgin girls before execution. Parvaneh Aref says:

> It was roughly the end of fall or winter of 1981. We were staying at 'Evin apartments'. The wards were still filled and they had brought us to a location they referred to as apartments. It was clear that it wasn't used as prison before. Prisoners who were under heavy interrogation were taken to the apartments.

[1] Jahangir Ismailpour, "Adel Abad, A Lasting Grief," Baran Publication, Sweden, P. 106.

[2] Makhmalbaf: Sexual raping in Iranian prisons is a certain matter, Fariba Valiat, Behnam Bavandpour, Deutche Welle, August 16, 2009, available at: http://www.dw-world.de/dw/article/0,,4575831,00.html. Justice For Iran was unable to conduct an interview with him, due to his unwillingness to respond to our inquiries.

The girls would return every day after being heavily tortured. I remember it was a Thursday, and Thursdays were *Hosseiniyeh* days. They hadn't yet made it mandatory to be present at the *Hosseiniyeh* but we accepted to go, probably because we felt like we were in a tight cage and had no contacts. We thought this was an opportunity to go outside and see what was happening. The visitations had not started yet. *Hosseiniyeh* was a place where the girls who had completely lost it and become *tavvab* would speak. After the *tavvabs* spoke, as always, Lajevardi started speaking. He started threatening us in order to weaken our spirits. The war had just started and they used to play battle marches in the beginning of the program at the *Hosseiniyeh*, like they were starting a show. Lajevardi used military lingo too. He said, "You are our captives, you are war captives… we can do as we please with a war captive…" Then he started to give examples. First he started with the guys. I don't recall the part about the guys anymore but I remember the part about the girls very well because I was a girl myself. He said: "don't assume that we send you for execution a virgin…" then he laughed a horrendous laughter. I had pushed my blindfold up and saw it. As he was standing, he said: "you think we will execute you a virgin so you can go to heaven? You will not be executed a virgin…" I think he even recited a verse of the *Koran*.

When I returned [the speech] was weighing heavily on me. Silence had taken over the ward; it was hard to accept. It became something that each of us thought about, every moment of our interrogations. I was tortured heavily too and was lashed with cables many times. But I can say about myself at least that I thought the worse possible scenario is if such acts would happen. Of course one thought about it. As a nightmare it was always something we expected to happen. But when Lajevardi said such it felt very unusual… at the time, the executions were horrible. Two days a week on a constant basis, the prisoners were taken for execution. Therefore, when we returned to the apartments from *Hosseini-yeh*, we realized that the girls sitting next to us who awaited executions were the topics of [Lajevardi's] blunt speech. It felt heavy for us to look at one another.[1]

Mersedeh Gha'edi who was arrested in 1982 for supporting *Peykar* Organization, says "One of Lajevardi's expressions was that we are war captives, meaning the guards have complete power over us."[2]

Nasrin Nekubakht, a supporter of *Forqan* who was imprisoned at Evin from October 1981 to October 1984 explains that in the seminars on ideology set up for *Forqan* members and supporters, one of the topics discussed was supposed *shari'a*-based justifications for raping virgin girls before execution. She says,

> I remember very vaguely that this discussion took place in prison; in the ideological classes [set up for] the girls. Different groups had ideological classes. We had teachers sent by the religious seminary, by the *pasdars* [Revolutionary Guards], to teach us the Islam. The ideological analysis for raping the girls before execution stemmed from the *Koranic* verse '*bih ay danab qutalt*'. The meaning of the verse is "for what crime are you being killed". The history of this verse is that Arabs used to bury their daughters alive and Prophet Mohammad was against it. When he came to power and brought Islam to the Arabs, this verse was revealed and Prophet Mohammad faced his own society and said, "Why are you killing your virgin girls?" In effect he called the girls innocent. However in the Islamic prisons of Iran, in order not to go against this verse, while yet insuring that they would not be questioned by God for executing virgin girls, they would 'marry' off virgin girls on the night of their execution and rape them because they wanted to make sure everything was being done correctly and Islamic.[3]

---

[1] Witness testimony of Parvaneh Aref, Justice For Iran.
[2] Witness Testimony of Mersedeh Gha'edi, Justice For Iran.
[3] Witness Testimony of Nasrin Nekubakht, Justice For Iran.

Shayesteh Vatandoust was a *Mojahedin-e Khalq* supporter who was held in various prisons, including Bandar Anzali Prison, for two terms totalling 18 years. She remembers a day in March 1982 when female prisoners made a written inquiry on the issue to the head of Bandar Anzali Prison, Hossein Moayed Abedi. Below is how she remembers the exchange:

> I think it was spring of 1982 when one of the Friday prayer *imams* proposed the idea that a female prisoner is akin to a war captive and *halal* to them. Around the same time, the head of the prison Hossein Moayed Abedi[1] came for a supervisory visit and asked us what issues we wanted to discuss. He was talking and telling us that we are making a mistake and the *Mojahedin-e Khalq* is such and such, when we complained and asked about executions. We wrote the question down and gave it to him. We wrote, "Why do you say that you don't execute virgin girls, when virgin girls have been executed?" He said, "You have heard correctly that we don't execute virgin girls. If someone is going to be executed, before execution, she has to be wedded to one of the brothers[2]..." We discussed this matter for a few days amongst ourselves. Each person expressed her opinions, and what they would do if they were to be taken for execution. My opinion and that of 2-3 others was that we would rather die than undergo such an act, but some said that since they are going to be killed anyway, this was a small matter...[3]

Simin Behrouzi was imprisoned from age 16 until 22 at Shiraz' Adel Abad prison. She remembers that the prison officials and the clerics who would come to give sermons to prisoners would repeatedly, either explicitly or indirectly, point to why raping virgin girls was 'necessary':

---

[1] Ibid.

[2] In the vernacular of the government officials in the early years of the revolution, 'brother' was a general term that was used to describe any of male government affiliate or supporter (*hizbullahis*). When used by the prison officials, it usually referred to the guards, *pasdars* or other prison or revolutionary prosecutor's officials.

[3] Interview of Shayesteh Vatandoust, Justice For Iran.

In their speeches they referred to the fact, saying that someone who has committed sin should not go to heaven. Then they would say that those who are virgins go to heaven. In fact, indirectly they were saying: "you have committed sin and are also virgins. You should not go to heaven. Therefore, we will remove the virginity from you so that you can go directly to hell".[1]

Mojdeh Arasi, a *Fadaian-e Khalq* (Minority) supporter, was imprisoned at different prisons in Tehran province from October 1982 to July 1990. She describes how in conversations between interrogators and prisoners, as well as those between prisoners who held on to their beliefs (*sar-e moze*) and the *tavvabs*[2] in Evin prison, the same pattern arose. The raping of virgin girls was repeatedly discussed, and those behind it continued to present the practice as being based in religious responsibility:

This wasn't an issue that they denied at all, neither the interrogators nor the *tavvabs*. I was shocked when I was out of the prison and left the country and noticed that people were not aware of the situation or that the issue of raping of girls before execution was not proven. For me, it was as clear as daylight. For example, my own interrogator told me the very first night of my interrogation: "as a Marxist, either you stand by your belief, defend it, and get executed immediately, or you become straight and a *tavvab*. And it is not just death for you to simply die. Before death, more will happen to you." I mean they said it with a threatening tone. They wouldn't say "we'll do this to you", but would make a general statement that a virgin girl will be married to a *pasdar* brother before execution. They never discussed raping; they called it marriage. I remember I argued with the *tavvab* and said, "what do you mean marriage? Marriage is when you say you love someone and he loves you and you want to be married. This isn't marriage; it is rape!" The *tavvab* defended the

---

[1] Testimony of Simin Behrouzi, Justice For Iran.
[2] For more explanation of *sare moze* and *tavvab* look at Prison Marriage under Chapter 3 of this report.

act and said, "No it is legal. They are married and *mahram*; permissible to one another". *Tavvabs* wanted to break our spirits and tried to convince us to switch sides and become *tavvab* within 24 hours. Then we would insist that this is in fact rape but they would say, "No it is not rape because they become married to the *pasdar* brothers".[1]

According to some female prisoners' witness testimonies, the interrogators and prison officials ideologically justified the raping of female prisoners under Islamic laws dealing with 'war captives' that mostly stem from verses 23 and 24 of Surah An-Nisa of the *Koran*, which outline which women Muslim men can and cannot have sexual relations with. Verse 24 states: "Also (prohibited are) the women already bound in marriage, except the bondwomen you come to own". (Translation of Mufti Taqi Usman)[2]

It is important to recognize the era in which the Surah were written; a time when slavery was common. As such, interpretations of Verse 24 and other verses relating to female slaves (*kaniz*), resulted in laws that gave male slave owners (*malik*) complete control over their relations with their slaves. Hence a *malik* was not bound to recite marriage vows in order to have sexual relations with a woman he purchased or took captive in war. This translates to a modern ideology underpinning warfare, in which infidel men, women and children, or those of idolaters, are put at the disposal of their governor.[3]

---

[1] Witness Testimony of Mojdeh Arasi, Justice For Iran.
[2] A few other translations include: *Abdul Daryabadi*: And also forbidden are the wedded among women, save those whom your right hands own; *Dr. Mohsen*: Also (forbidden are) women already married, except those (slaves) whom your right hands possess; *Yusuf Ali*: Also (prohibited are) women already married, except those whom your right hands possess.
[3] Visit the Elmiyeh Seminary of Qom's website to see laws regarding *kaniz* and war captives. Some such laws are available at:
http://www.hawzah.net/fa/questionview.html?QuestionID=9894&ListQuestionSubject=True&List KeywordAlpha=True&SearchText=%DA%A9%D9%86%DB%8C%D8%B2;
http://www.hawzah.net/fa/questionview
.html?QuestionID=10932&ListQuestionSubject=True&ListKeywordAlpha=True&SearchText=%DA%A9%D9%86%DB%8C%D8%B2;
http://www.hawzah.net/fa/questionview.html?QuestionID=63593&ListQuestionSubject=True& ListKeywordAlpha=True&SearchText=%DA%A9%D9%86%DB%8C%D8%B2;
http://www.hawzah.net/fa/ question-
view.html?QuestionID=63593&ListQuestionSubject=True&ListKeywordAlpha=True&SearchText=%DA%A9%D9%86%DB%8C%D8%B2.

Sanam Ahmadi, a *Peykar* Organization supporter was a student of 16 years when she was imprisoned for the ten months at Seyyed Ali Khan detention centre in Isfahan. She says,

> One of the *pasdars* was named Hamid- I later found out his last name was Ghorbani. He has since been killed at the front line. He was a young man of 24-25 with a long chin and face that looked like a fox. This is all I could see from behind the blindfolds… he told me, "Listen! There is no one in this room aside from you and me. I can easily do anything I want to you and wouldn't have to answer to a single soul because you are amongst the plunders of the war between Islam and the *muharibih*."[1]

Nazli Partovi was detained for ten months from November of 1982 in the Joint Committee Detention Centre for the charge of collaboration with the Union of Combating Communists (*Sahand*)[2]. She recalls, "One night, two of my interrogators were talking to each other after torturing [me]; they were talking so loud that I could hear. They said, "They are *halal*- permissible to us." They were saying that and laughing."[3]

Farkhondeh Ashna spent the years between 1982 and 1990 in various Tehran province prisons for her activism with leftist labour associations. Her judge was Hossein Ali Nayyeri, one of the individuals responsible for the mass execution of political prisoners at Evin in 1988. She says, "[Nayyeri] said, "We were really merciful to you. Islamic Law states that an infidel is fully permissible to Muslims [to do with her as they please]. You are permissible to our brothers to do whatever they want to you but we took mercy on you"… basically he was indirectly pointing to the matter of the rapes."[4]

External accounts of rape of female political prisoners: The topic of raping virgin girls prior to execution can also be investigated from the aspect of external publicity and the effects it had on the female prisoners and their families outside of prison. In

---

[1] Witness Testimony of Sanam Ahmadi, Justice For Iran.
[2] Her total imprisonment lasted eight years.
[3] Witness Testimony of Nazli Partovi, Justice For Iran.
[4] Witness Testimony of Farkhondeh Ashna, Justice For Iran.

one of its documents published in 1987, Amnesty International states:

> Amnesty International has also received reports of various kinds of sexual abuse of both male and female prisoners, including rape. Amnesty International has noted the well-publicized reports that young women prisoners have been forced into temporary marriage contracts with members of the *Sepah* and have subsequently been raped the night before their execution, and has been told of cases in which IRGC members approached the families of young women who had been executed to present the bride money. Amnesty International has noted also reports that IRGC members have boasted about such acts to male prisoners, or threatened to enter into temporary marriage contracts with their female relatives. While Amnesty International has not been able to substantiate such reports it seems clear that, irrespective of whether this practice does exist or has existed in the Islamic Republic of Iran, many former prisoners who have testified to Amnesty International believed these reports were true and themselves suffered the anguish, while in prison, of fearing that they or their female relatives were liable to receive such treatment.[1]

Mina Farzi, supporter of *Fadaian-e Khalq* Guerrilla Organization (Minority), was arrested as a 'suspicious person'. Between 1981 and 1991, she was held in various prisons in Tehran Province. She says, "every time, they spoke of execution to me, I was filled with worry about rape."[2]

Many of those interviewed had either heard about the raping of virgin girls prior to their own arrests, or else they came to realize it very soon after they were imprisoned. Moreover, they realized that the logic of who was a potential target for rape by prison officials was based on ensuring that no living survivors could recount the atrocity. Thus, only people who were about to

---

[1] Amnesty International Document, MDE 13/09/87-mde130081987.
[2] Witness Testimony of Mina Farzi, Justice For Iran.

be executed and thereby killed or those who had become insane as a result of the prison treatment were subject to rape.[1]

In the numerous books and articles written about the prisons, many prisoners discuss cases where in the days following the execution of a young woman, one or more *pasdars* would show up at their family's door and give them money or sweets or flowers, presumably as the *mahr* (a gift that according to Islamic marriage groom pledge to give to bride at the time of religious marriage ceremony) of the their daughter and 'condolences'. The groom/rapist would tell the family that the night before her execution; their daughter was married off to him sometimes using the word of *mahr* (often understood as temporary marriage). It appears that such cruel behaviour towards the family who had just lost their young daughter, intended to punish the families as well as discourage other women from engaging in political activism. Many of the prisoners interviewed in preparation for this report remember such accounts, although only a small number of them could identify families who had such or similar experiences. Furthermore, some of the former prisoners refused to provide the names of such families for security reasons or to prevent bringing further and unnecessary pain and grief upon the families of the executed girls. Therefore, a large number of unspecified accounts, or those without accurate or detailed identification, were put aside with hopes that future research may find a way to uncover the truth about those cases.

We were lucky however, to access other documented accounts, which explain the various manners through which families came to understand what transpired in the final hours of their daughters lives. Prisoners were sometimes given a pen to write their final will in the hours before their execution. Some prisoners used these pens to write on their bodies or clothes that they were raped (Elaheh Daknama, Adel Abad Prison Shiraz and Sima Matlabi, Vakil Abad Prison of Mashhad). Some families saw signs of torture on the bodies of their executed daughters (Mahnaz Yousef Zadeh) and others had a *pasdar* show up at their door with a box of sweets (Shahin Sami, Bandar Anzali Prison; Mitra and Mandana Mojaverian, all were executed at the Vakil

---

[1] For example, see witness testimony of Mitra Haghighat Lager, Taraneh and Sanam Ahmadi with Justice For Iran.

Abad Prison in Mashhad). Some of the Families of victims in Isfahan received few Imam Zaman Coins as a price of *mahr* of their daughters (Fariba Ahmadi, Dastgerd Prison of Isfahan)[1]. In one case, while handing over the property of the prisoner, the officer pointed to the sweets and money in the bag and stated that they were the *mehriyeh* of the family's daughter (Afagh Daknama).

The Statute of the International Criminal Court considers rape or sexual violence, if is it widespread or systematic, to be a crime against humanity. Therefore, random acts of violence are excluded from being categorized as crimes against humanity. In fact, the very essence of the term 'systematic' highlights the organized nature of the act. In *Prosecutor v. Katanga and Ngudjolo Chui*[2], the International Criminal Court's pre-trial Chamber voted on its jurisdiction to preside over the case due to the systematic nature of the action. It then defined the meaning of systematic as:

> The term 'systematic' has been understood as either an organized plan in furtherance of a common policy, which follows a regular pattern and results in a continuous commission of acts or as 'patterns of crimes' such that the crimes constitute a 'non-accidental' repetition of similar criminal conduct on a regular basis".[3]

There is no certainty that the regulated plan of forcibly marrying virgin girls before execution was carried out for every single girl who was executed in the 1980s. However, given the widespread accounts and witness testimonies and keeping the ICC's definition in mind, it can be deduced that raping virgin girls prior to their execution was a systematic occurrence, and should be considered a crime against humanity perpetuated by Iranian authorities. We recognize that there are still many ambiguous details surrounding the rapes that need to be probed further; who were the perpetrators of the rapes prior to the executions? Was the interrogator of each prisoner also her rapist, or

---

[1] For more details about Fariba Ahmadi's case, see Appendix II.
[2] For further details about the case, see footnote page 18.
[3] Prosecutor v. Germain Katanga and Mathieu Ngudjolo Chui, "Decision on the Confirmation of Charges", 30 September 2008, International Criminal Court, Decision No. ICC-01/04-01/07, para 397. Decision available at: http://www.legal-tools.org/doc/67a9ec/.

would the act circulate randomly amongst the *pasdars* in prison and even amongst their close associates outside of prison? Was the rape merely a 'fulfilment of duties' or was it also considered to be a reward? Even without those details, it can now be said, without a doubt, that the raping of girls prior to their execution was a 'pattern of crime' that became regularized through various ideological means, including the interpretation of the *fatwa* issued on behalf of Ayatollah Khomeini by Ayatollah Montazeri, as well as interpretations of the *Koranic* verse '*bih ay danab qutalt*' and the Surah relating to war captives (*kaniz*). It was acted out and repeated through the crime of enforced marriage of girls awaiting execution.[1] Below we discuss more detailed case studies of this crime.

Case Studies of the Rape of Virgin Girls before Executions

1. Mashhad - Events in the Second Half of 1981

In August 1981, Hojjatolislam Seyyed Reza Kamyab, Mashhad representative in the Islamic Consultative Majlis, was assassinated by the armed forces of the *Mojahedin-e Khalq*. In an interview, Ayatollah Hashemi Nejad announced the reasons for this assassination to be the shortcomings and negligence of the Office of Justice and the Revolutionary Court. Hashemi Nejad, who had famously stated in an interview that "the *Mojahedin* are more dangerous, and filthier, than the Marxists"[2] was himself assassinated by the *Mojahedin* in October of the same year. Shortly after the harsh interview of Hashemi Nejad, the make-up of the Revolutionary Court and Revolutionary Prosecution Office completely changed. Rasoul Shokati, a political prisoner who was arrested shortly after this event, believes that the changes in the prosecution office as well as the heightening of suppression of dissent in Khorasan province were carried out at the behest of Ayatollah Va'ez Tabasi, Ayatollah Khomeini's Representative in

---

[1] It appears that the policy of giving information to the family was dismissed due to extreme reactions on the side of some families. Mojdeh Arasi says, "I remember a *Mojahed* mother whose daughter was executed was in prison. She was arrested along with her son and husband because they beat up the *pasdar* who went to their door introducing himself as their groom and giving them 200 bucks." There are also other cases the witnesses point to, on file with Justice For Iran.

[2] Khorasan Newspaper, August 2, 1981, No. 9294, P. 1.

Khorasan.[1] Changes included the appointment of Mirfendereski as the Revolutionary Prosecutor of Mashhad, Mostafa Pour Mohammadi as the General Prosecutor of Khorasan province, and Ali Razini as the religious magistrate of the Revolutionary Court. In their testimonies, former inmates recall that the new officers of the Revolutionary Prosecution Office began their work from September of 1981 and oversaw another wave of executions of political prisoners.

Khorasan magazine, a publication of the Mostaz'afin Foundation- a foundation formed order of Ayatollah Khomeini to process the confiscated property of *taquti*[2] individuals after the revolution by- affirms this claim. The editorial published on August 25 titled, "Mr. Prosecutor, Boldly, Boldly" speaks of a new prosecutor that arrived in Mashhad who vowed to exercise 'revolutionary boldness'.[3] A response by Mirfendereski 10 days later reads "…with reliance in God and the support of the martyr nurturing people of Mashhad, and the responsibility of each and every one of the dear citizens, I intend to, at first, boldly deal with all the inauspicious conspiracies of the wayward and anti-revolutionary and anti-Islam political groups …"[4]

From right: Ali Razini (religious magistrate of Mashhad), Ayatollah Mousavi Tabrizi (Member of the Supreme Judicial Council), and Mostafa Pour Mohammadi (Prosecutor of Khorasan)

In the Friday prayer sermon of October 2, Mirfendereski announced that within the last 10 days, over 70 members of the

---

[1] Witness Testimony of Rasoul Shokati, Justice For Iran.
[2] Individuals referred to as *"taquti"* were a diverse group comprising from government officials to venture capitalists, factory owners, farming land owners and private and commercial property owners.
[3] "Mr. Prosecutor, Boldly, Boldly," Khorasan Newspaper, August 25, 1981, No. 9294, P. 1.
[4] Response of the Revolutionary Prosecutor of Mashhad to the article "Mr. Prosecutor, Boldly, Boldly," Khorasan Newspaper, August 31, 1981, No. 9298, Pp. 1-2

Mojahedin-e Khalq had been executed. Political prisoners who had either been held at Vakil Abad Prison (Mashhad) at that time or who were arrested shortly thereafter affirm that this wave of executions only targeted male political prisoners.[1] Eventually, some younger women were executed after 22 December, 1981 According to official statistics, on December 22nd and 23rd alone, respectively 4 and 6 young female prisoners were sent to the gallows labelled as *munafiq*. Immediately following these executions, family members of the executed girls began reporting that they had been raped prior to execution. In this manner, the news of raping girls before execution in Mashhad quickly

circulated around amongst the political activists and their families. Accordingto the witness testimonies of two political prisoners, one tried in September of 1981 and another in December of 1981, Ali Razini was the religious magistrate who issued the execution orders of the young women.

The persecution of the Mojaverian family: It is unclear how the executions of women began in Mashhad, but Sepideh Farsi who was arrested in November of 1981 and tried in January 1982 for hiding a fellow classmate who supported *Mojahedin-e Khalq* says:

> Before arrival of the Razini as religious magistrate of the Revolutionary Court there was almost no death sentences issued for women in Mashhad. When Razini arrived, he started issuing execution orders for girls who had really done nothing, like they had distributed flyers in school. Razini was famous for being cross with women and giving them heavy sentences. It wasn't just execution; he issued life sentences for a lot of people who weren't really even political. His sentences were so heavy and meaningless that later, in 1982, they reduced some of those sentences or even gave prisoners clemency.[2]

---

[1] Witness Testimony of Rasoul Shokati, Justice For Iran; Witness Testimony of Amir Mirza'ian, Justice For Iran; Witness Testimony of Taraneh, Justice For Iran.
[2] Witness Testimony of Sepideh Farsi, Justice For Iran.

Sepideh Farsi says, "those who received execution sentences did not return to Vakil Abad but remained at the [Revolutionary Prosecutor's office's] location." Having been tried by Razini herself, she says, "My trial was very short. I remember he asked me, "will you do an interview or not?" I knew that if I responded negatively right out, I would receive a heavy sentence so I tried to close the subject by saying things like, "I am only a high school student and ashamed of speaking in front of the camera."[1] The 'interview' meant a forced televised confession and often a recantation. Eventually, Sepideh was given a two-year prison term. According to her, a few of the young women who had been transferred from Vakil Abad in the morning alongside her were handed execution sentences from Razini and never returned to the women's ward. Executions were usually carried out on the same day or within 2-3 days from the day of the sentencing.

Mandana and Mitra Mojaverian (18 and 19 years old when they were arrested) were amongst the first group of young women who were sentenced to execution in Mashhad. Their family members shared their story with us. Between mid-December and early January, everyday a group of female prisoners was taken from Vakil Abad prison in Mashhad to the Revolutionary

Mandana Mojaverian

Prosecutor's Office adjacent to the *Sepah-e Pasdaran* base so that they could be tried by Ali Razini,[2] the religious magistrate. The newsof Mitra Mojaverian's execution, along with four other women and two men, was published in Khorasan Newspaper on 22 December, 1981. The news on Mandana Mojaverian's execution, along with 6 other women and 2 men, was published the following day in the same newspaper. Sima Matalebi[3] was reported to be one of the 6 women executed along with Mandana.

Mahshid Mojaverian returned to one of the team houses of *Mojahedin-e Khalq* on a November day in 1981. The house had been discovered and occupied by the *Sepah* forces. They staged an ambush and everyone who returned to the house on that day

---

[1] Witness Testimony of Sepideh Farsi, Justice For Iran.
[2] Presently, Razini is the Prosecutor of the Iran's Government Employees Court.
[3] Her full story is narrated below.

was arrested, including Mitra Mojaverian. Mahshid Mojaverian says, "The day after they arrested Mitra, they arrested my father. His only crime was that he was Mitra's father. They had nothing against my father. They kept my father for a year after they executed Mitra. This was because he refused to pray while in prison. They did everything they could, even confining him in a solitary cell, and he still didn't pray."[1]

Immediately after the arrest, Mitra Mojaverian was transferred to *Sepah* Detention Centre on Malekabad Boulevard. Mehrnoush Mojaverian says, "She was probably in the detention centre for two weeks and then transferred to Vakil Abad prison. [I guess this] because when she was transferred they gave visitation permission to the family. However, she was tortured

Mitra Mojaverian

so much [lashed with cables] that she couldn't walk herself and so they would grab her from her underarms and bring her for visits."[2]

One day during her detention, Mitra Mojaverian was taken from the *Sepah* Detention Centre to the adjacent Office of the Religious Magistrate. Mitra's mother, who had stationed herself outside to follow up on her daughter's affairs, noticed that Mitra was brought back to the Detention Centre shortly thereafter. Later during visitation, she noted that Mitra's sentencing occurred during those few minutes. Mehrnoush Mojaverian says, "My mother asked her, "How were you tried in 5 minutes?" Mitra laughedand said, "I entered the room and saw that the religious magistrate had removed his slippers and placed his feet on the table. I looked at him and said, "This is a court and you are a judge?" The religious magistrate said, "Take her! Execution!"[3]

According to the witness testimonies of two former prisoners, it can be deduced that Ali Razini was the religious magistrate that Mitra spoke of to her mother. The two prisoners who bore witness against Razini state that in their respective trials, the principles of due process such as presence of an attorney and

---

[1] Interview of Mahshid Mojaverian, Justice For Iran.
[2] Ibid.
[3] Ibid.

procedural integrity concerning crimes and punishments were not respected. The 'trials' were rushed, often only minutes long, and the sentences were issued and carried out immediately without granting the accused the right to appeal.

Arrested in the streets in November of 1981 for supporting the *Mojahedin-e Khalq*, Mandana Mojaverian was Mitra's cousin. Like Mitra, after passing the interrogation phases at *Sepah* Detention Centre on Malekabad Boulevard, she was transferred to Vakil Abad Prison. Mehrnoush Mojaverian, Mitra's sister and Mandana's cousin, says, "Mandana was not tortured as much as Mitra was because at the time of visitations, her physical state was fine."[1]

Mehrnoush Mojaverian, who herself was a supporter of the *Fadaian-e Khalq* (Minority), remembers that Mitra and Mandana were in the same school. The *Mojahedin-e Khalq* had an office at the beginning of the street where they lived and Mitra and Mandana passed by it every day. In the early days of the revolution, filled with the passion and excitement of youth, they joined the office and began distributing their flyers. At that time, neither of them ever imagined that the activities of the *Mojahedin-e Khalq* and *Fadaian* would soon be declared illegal. Nor could they possibly foresee that they would be forced to separate from their families and live in hiding, or else face imprisonment and execution.[2]

Mehrnoush Mojaverian speaks of the events following the execution of Mitra and Mandana Mojaverian:

> One day they brought flowers and sweets to our door. It was a few days after the execution of Mitra and Mandana. The mourning ceremonies were in process, and friends, family and neighbors were coming and going from the house to give us their condolences for the unbelievable calamity. It was very crowded. In fact because they had executed a lot of people at once, the family members of those prisoners would hold joint mourning sessions at our house. Anyway, a car from the *Sepah* came to the

---

[1] Ibid.
[2] Ibid.

door; the door was open and one of our close relatives was standing there. They told her, "these are
flowers and sweets for your family because your
kids married our *pasdar* brothers prior to execution".
This lady, our relative, takes the flowers and candy
and dumps them in the trash can right there and
doesn't say anything to anyone about it. A few years
after that incident, she told me this herself. My father was in prison at that time and didn't find out
about this. In fact, even today, my parents don't
know about it. I never told my family anything
about this because I think they won't be able to bear
it. One time, many months later, my mother asked
me, "do you think they did such things with our
daughters too?" I said, "I don't know. What do you
think?" she said, "No, I don't think so." It meant
that still her hopes and desires were that they had
not done such thing to her children. She must have
heard from other families that their girls were raped.
Every Friday, many of those whose children were
executed used to visit the grave sites of their beloved together.[1]

Taraneh, a former supporter of the *Mojahedin-e Khalq* who
was arrested six months after the execution of Mandana and Mitra along with her husband, also remembers the news; "… At
that time I heard through my husband that they took money and
sweets to the home of Mojaverian family and told them that
their daughters were married to the brothers the night before
their execution."[2]

As previously mentioned, news of the raping of girls the
night of their execution spread around Mashhad rapidly in the
winter of 1981. The Mojaverian family was not the only family
who had a *pasdar* show up at their door. The same story has been
told about a number of other families.

The bodies of Mandana and Mitra Mojaverian were returned
to their families so that they could be buried in *La'nat Abad* (land
of the cursed), a section of Behesht-e Reza cemetery in Mashhad
which was reserved for those who had turned against Islam.

[1] Ibid.
[2] Interview of Taraneh with Justice For Iran.

The Matlabi family: Leyli Shokati was a member of the Graduates Association of Mashhad along with the mother of Sima Matlabi. Sima was executed in January 1981. Leyli Shokati speaks of what she had personally heard from Sima Matlabi's mother and father:

> We went to Mrs. Matlabi's house to visit her. They couldn't hold a ceremony but we would go anyway. Mr. Matlabi said that he was called to prison and so he went. They told him to speak to his daughter and advise her to repent. So Mr. Matlabi tells his daughter, "Listen to everything they tell you." His daughter says, "They told me if I marry one of the *pasdars*, I won't be executed." Mr. Matlabi told us that he turned around and told his daughter to do as she deems fit. Then [when he left the visitation] they slapped Mr. Matlabi in the face. He was a weak man too, poor soul, and he fell. They kicked him out of the prison and told him, "We called you here to advise her, not to tell her to do what she wants. We know what she wants!" He said it was a long way from where he was to the entrance of the prison and by the time he reached the entrance, he heard the sounds of shooting. Mrs. Matlabi said that they later called and told them to go and take the corpse. When they took the body and took it to the morgue where the body was to be washed, she said, "I touched her hands; I touched her feet! And then saw that she had written under her feet that she was raped." Meaning the night before they called her father they had done the deed and they later wanted to have a formality wedding too so they could give an Islamic colour to the story.[1]

No clear information is available about Sima's age at the time of her execution. On their website, the *Mojahedin-e Khalq* report she was about 20 years old at the time of her execution, but Leyli Shokati believes that she was a high school student and around 16-17 years old.

---

[1] Interview of Leyli Shokati with Justice For Iran.

Taraneh, who was transferred to Vakil Abad prison six months after these executions, remembers:

Sima Matlabi

There was a terrible feeling. Mentally, the friends of these girls had been messed up They said many people were executed and all the names were not published in the newspapers. At the time, the law at Vakil Abad prison was 'interview or execution'. They said, "Either you give an interview or we will take you for execution." It had also become evident to everyone that any virgin girl who was taken for execution was raped the night before she was killed.[1]

2- Incidents in Bandar Anzali and Rasht Prisons (1982-1988)

In 1981 there was a need to build a new prison in Bandar Anzali for the large number of political prisoners. The former Boy Scout building in Bandar Anzali that was used as a recreational centre before the revolution was modified and extensions were built to turn it into a political prison. Both male and female political prisoners were housed there. Although in the female ward there were female guards, in the solitary cells the only guards female prisoners were in contact with were male. At that time, the head of the prison was a man by the name of Hossein Moayed Abedi.

Shayesteh Vatandoust was detained for 18 years for supporting *Mojahedin-e Khalq*. She was held in Bandar Anzali between 1981 and 1985. She states that in one of his visits to the female ward in 1982, Hossein Moayed Abedi answered a written question from prisoners and affirmed that virgin girls were married to one of the 'brothers' prior to their execution.[2] Clearly this was

---

[1] Interview of Taraneh with Justice For Iran.
[2] The details of this incident have been described in the introduction to this section.

systematically carried out with full knowledge of prison officials at Bandar Anzali Prison.

Shayesteh Vatandoust testified about Mahnaz Yousef Zadeh who was executed at the age of 20 on 29 November, 1982:

> Mahnaz was beautiful. We were in the ward and she was in solitary. When we had a breather, I took the opportunity and spoke to her. Mahnaz told me this herself; the prosecutor had propositioned her. He had told her to fake a recantation; "I like you and want to marry you." But she rejected him. The man Mahnaz loved and wanted to marry was executed before her in May."[1] At that time, the prosecutor of Bandar Anzali was a man named Abutaleb Kusha.[2]

> Later when I was released, I saw a photo of Mahnaz's corpse. Right in the middle of her legs was fully bruised. It was clear from the photo that the corpse showed signs of beating and injuries, being tied with a rope and that she had resisted. A friend who saw the body said that she was shot in her genital area. They gave her body to the family because her mother, who did not know Mahnaz was executed, went to the prison for visitation. Someone called her inside the prison, gave her a box of sweets and told her, "Wish me well. I married your daughter." Her mother said, "I will wish you well when you hand me her corpse." After a few days they showed them the body.[3]

Ahmad Mousavi, a former political prisoner who was jailed both in Gilan and Tehran from 1981-1992, writes of Mahnaz Yousef Zadegan in his memoir.[4] Remembering his time in a mixed ward, he writes, "Once we accidentally saw each other in the bathroom and spoke a few words. She was a very small, resistant and strong girl. Prior to her execution, she spent most of her prison term in solitary cells, or with another person. To force

---

[1] Witness Testimony of Shayesteh Vatandoust, Justice For Iran.
[2] He is presently a professor of law at the Judicial Science University.
[3] Witness Testimony of Shayesteh Vatandoust, Justice For Iran.
[4] It appears that Ahmad Mousavi made a mistake in registering the name of Mahnaz Yousef Zadeh. Her name has been listed as such in all the existing prisoners' lists.

her to recant, they put a lot of pressure on her but did not succeed. Later on I met and got to know her father in Rasht prison when we were in the same ward for a period of time. He said, "After her execution, they did not allow her body to be buried in the city cemetery and so we were forced to bury her in our house's yard."[1]

After a few years,[2] Hossein Moayed Abedi was replaced by Seyyed Reza Rouzan who went by the pseudonym of Mousavi. He was transferred to Bandar Anzali from Fouman Prison.[3] Moayed Abedi in turn was appointed head of Gilan Provincial Prison. In 1988, he was the head of the Gilan Office of Intelligence.

Mass execution of 1988: In the summer of 1988, thousands of political prisoners were executed throughout Iran, on the orders of a *fatwa* by Ayatollah Khomeini. All of them had either been in the process of serving their imprisonment term or had finished their term, but would not be released because they refused to do an interview to recant and express their disgust regarding their political stances.[4] None of those executed were officially sentenced to execution in court. According to Ahmad Mousavi who was imprisoned at Rasht prison at the time, 95 of the 120 male political prisoners in ward 1 of Rasht prison were 'called for' by prison officials on various days in August 1988. Save for two of them, the rest never returned.[5] There was also a group whose sentences had been reduced just two weeks before the massacres began; they were waiting to be released, but never were.[6]

According to Shayesteh Vatandoust, a supporter of *Mojahedin* who from the thirty female political prisoners in Rasht prison only four survived. The rest were executed over two sessions. Neither they, nor the other prisoners, knew they were to be executed. Shahin Sami was one of them. At the time of her arrest in 1986, Shahin Sami was 17 years old. She was called from the

---

[1] Ahmad Mousavi, Goodnight Comrade, Baran Publication, Sweden, 2005, P. 23.
[2] The exact date of this appointment is unknown.
[3] Ahmad Mousavi, Goodnight Comrade, Baran Publication, Sweden, 2005, P. 175.
[4] Prisoners referred to this group as "*melli-kesh*".
[5] Interview with Ahmad Mousavi regarding the prison massacre of 1988 in Rasht, Monireh Baradaran, June 5, 2008, Bidaran, available at http://www.bidaran.net.spip.php?article152.
[6] Ibid.

ward on July 31, 1988 at the age of 19. Prior to that, she had been sentenced to a 20-year imprisonment term.

Shayesteh Vatandoust narrates the massacre of July-August 1988 at the female ward of the Naval prison of Rasht:

> They only called two people for questioning, or 'court'- Faranak Tavousi[1] and Maryam Vahedi.[2] They took them at 9 am and 10 am on July 30. When they returned they told us that Abedi[3] and two other men whom they didn't know asked three questions of them- they were not blindfolded and assumed the questions were for the purpose of releasing them. The questions were:
>
> What is your opinion about the *munafiqin* organization? What is your opinion about the Islamic Republic? And are you willing to do an interview?
>
> They didn't call either of them back until later that night when they came with a list. Faranak had a month left of her prison term and was supposed to be released on September 7. Mahnaz had recently been arrested and had a 10-year prison term. The two were executed along with another 24 who went before this court, or rather death committee.
>
> Twenty people were called out of the ward in the afternoon of July 30 and the rest around 2 am on July 31. Shahin was one of them.
>
> In fact, I spoke with Shahin in those last moments, while she was wearing her *chador* next to the window. I asked her where they were being taken. I was worried but wasn't thinking about execution at all. Mostly I was thinking that they were being taken away and I was being left alone.[4]

---

[1] Further information about Faranak Tavousi can be found at http://www.iranrights.org/farsi/memorial-case--3439.php and http://www.mojahedin.org/pages/martyrsDetails.aspx?MartyrId=19680.
[2] Further information about Maryam Vahedi can be found at http://www.mojahedin.org/pages/martyrsDetails.aspx?MartyrId=19940.
[3] Hossein Moayed Abedi.
[4] Witness Testimony of Shayesteh Vatandoust, Justice For Iran.

According to Ahmad Mousavi, the death committee of Rasht was comprised of local officials. Four people were on this committee: a representative of the Prosecution Office, a representative of the Intelligence office, the Interrogator of the case, and Abdollahi,[1] head of the prison.[2]

Shayesteh Vatandoust believed that Shahin Sami was executed that very night- on July 31. However, she is not certain whether Shahin and the other ladies from Bandar Anzali were executed in Rasht or in Bandar Anzali. She says that the family members of Shahin and the other women from Bandar Anzali were shown unmarked graves in the Cemetery of that city and told that it was the location of their children's burial. Some families never believed the graves to be the final resting place of their daughters.

Shayesteh Vatandoust recounts from a reliable source[3] that "someone brought a box of sweets for Shahin's mother and told her that he married her daughter before she was executed."[4]

To sum up: Documents and testimonies offered in this section clearly establish the fact that the raping of virgin girls, arrested for political activism, prior to their execution took place systematically inside Iranian prisons during the 1980s. The rapes, rooted in a twisted misunderstanding of one of Ayatollah Khomeini's orders, were justified under the religious term of *siqih*. As stated by Ayatollah Montazeri, deputy leader of the time who went on to become an opponent of Ayatollah Khomeini, he was able to convince the leader of the revolution that girls (young women), who were on the forefront of the execution lines in those days, should not be executed as there are Islamic interpretations stating that they should be given imprisonment sentences as is prescribed for female apostates. However, the judicial and security officials who had no intention of halting the execution of women interpreted the order as a dictate to kill as long as the

---

[1] Ali Abdullahi Aliabadi. He is currently the Security and Law Enforcement Deputy of the Ministry of Interior.
[2] Witness Testimony of Shayesteh Vatandoust, Justice For Iran.
[3] Information about the source is kept confidential at Justice For Iran.
[4] Witness Testimony of Shayesteh Vatandoust, Justice For Iran.

girls were to lose their virginity prior to their execution. While, as our research demonstrates, this was one reason behind the raping of a large number of female political prisoners prior to their execution, different prison officials of the 1980s tried to find or create so-called *shari'a* based justifications for this action. According to the interpretations of the International Criminal Court, such acts can be construed as crimes against humanity. However, due to our inability to extend our research to encompass former judicial and security officials, the scope and spread of retributive justice against these officials, has not yet become clear to us.

As we have attempted to demonstrate, rape before execution was a systematic action. The fact that it continued for so many years also means it could not have been unknown to higher officials within the government, and thus the entire regime is implicated in this atrocity, not just those committing these crimes. The officials that sanctioned such cruel treatment of women prisoners should be brought to justice as well. A thorough, public discussion of the government's misuse and manipulation of religion to excuse or legitimize violence against women would enhance the public consciousness, which is the foundation for development of humane political culture and society, denounces such actions, and demands it should never again be repeated. It is an ethical duty upon all humanity and in particular human rights activists to make an issue of these uncivil developments and unethical practices, in this case carried out in the name of ethics and religion, to prevent them from happening again.

III- Prison Marriages

III- Prison Marriages

Consent and Rape according to International Law

From amongst the testimonies acquired and the interviews conducted with political prisoners of the 1980s, many have reported the prevalence of marriage between interrogators or other prison officials and the female prisoners. In most, but certainly not all cases, the female prisoner was a *tavaab-* prisoner who had recanted her political opposition and expressed her support for the regime. In the interviews, statements such as, "the girl became a *tavvab* and then married her interrogator" is very prevalent. The prisoners rarely considered the marriages in the prison to be 'forced' and the sexual relationship resulting from it to be akin to rape.

However, according to the International Criminal Court's definition of consent, and those of other bodies of international law, it is clear that in the case of these marriages, the consent of the women prisoners is very questionable.[1] 'Consent' which sets apart a willing and free relationship from that of rape, effectively ceases to hold merit when the woman is in prison and under threat, enforcement or harassment. This holds true even if she is not directly threatened, forced or harassed but is in an atmosphere where enforcement and dominance reign. Based on these definitions, even if the victim expresses her consent in having sexual relations or entering into a marriage, this consent is not 'genuine'[2] and cannot be a justification for denying the occurrence of rape.[3]

---

[1] Here we define consent as an act of reason and deliberation. A person who possesses and exercises sufficient mental capacity to make an intelligent decision demonstrates consent by performing an act recommended by another. Consent assumes a physical power to act and a reflective, determined, and unencumbered exertion of these powers. It is an act unaffected by fraud, duress, or sometimes even mistake, when these factors are not the reason for the consent. Consent is implied in every agreement.

[2] genuine consent.

[3] Amnesty International, Rape and sexual violence: Human rights law and standards in the International Criminal Court, Index No. IOR 53/001/2011, 1 March 2011, available at http://www.amnesty.org/en/library/info/IOR53/001/2011/en.

When it comes to 'rape' as a criminal offence, the only sexual relation that is considers legal by the international human rights law is a consensual and voluntary one which results from a free desire on the side of the participants in an atmosphere where such freedom is possible. Contrary to the local laws of many countries, the International Criminal Court considers 'lack of consent' to be the necessary element to prove rape. Therefore, any form of sexual relation, even a consensual one, if proven that it took place under coercive conditions, is considered to lack the necessary consent to disprove rape. International legal practices have established that when force and threat of force, coercion or a coercive environment exists, consent has no meaning. Any invasion that takes place with force, threat of force or coercion, such as what is done using fear of violence, enforcement, detention, physical suppression or abuse of power, or taking advantage of a coercive environment, is a crime.[1]

The aforementioned definition of rape is best exemplified by the International Criminal Court (ICC) case against Kunarac (Dragoljub Kunarac was the commander of a special unit for reconnaissance of the Bosnian Serb Army in the area of Foča between June 1992 and February 1993). Kunarac was accused of having Serbian soldiers and police under his command rape Bosnian women in detention centres and military bases. In the appeal court, the judges explained that although the discussed sexual relations were suggested to be consensual, they are considered a crime because the women were coerced. Under conditions of duress the assumption is the absence of 'consent'.[2] These ruling can easily applied to the case of Iranian female political prisoners who had agreed to marry their interrogators during the 1980s. Therefore, it can be deduced that the marriages that took place inside the prison, as well as certain marriages outside of prison between former female prisoners and officials- as is discussed later in this section- were non-consensual, even if prisoners used the word consent. As such prison marriages must be considered forced marriages and thereby, any sexual relation that stemmed from such a marriage should be recognized as rape. While investigating the occurrence of rape and sexual tor-

---

[1] Ibid.
[2] Ibid.

ture in Iranian prisons during the 1980s, we adhered to the definition and framework of rape per international law standards and have therefore dedicated a section of this report to prison marriages.

Context of Prison Marriages in Iran

The information compiled from witness testimonies show that forced marriages inside prisons, or even marriages that happened between prisoners and prison officials, employees or their close associates, and male *tavvabs*[1] after the prisoners were released, served different functions. Some marriages were proposed as a condition for freedom. In other cases, marriages were the condition for escaping execution. There were also cases in which marriage, the promise of marriage- temporary or permanent- as well as sexual abuse were used as a tool to prove faithfulness and complete and irreversible conversion from previous political beliefs. Still, in other cases marriage was used as a method to control the beliefs and actions of the female prisoner outside of the prison upon release. Some prisoners were able to escape harsh punishments and relieve pressure on themselves and their families through accepting marriage. Many others who were offered the same proposal never accepted it and often faced death as a result of it. Within the group that accepted marriage, the acceptance caused maladies and agonies that remained with them for the rest of their lives.

Below, we investigate the various functions served by prison marriages and the manner in which this form of torture was implemented. It must be noted that a marriage- or its proposal- could have served one or multiple functions simultaneously.

Marriage as a condition of release: There is a general assumption that once a woman marries, due to the responsibilities of upkeep of her husband and child, she will not have a lot of time for political activism. At least in one case, Mitra Haghighat Lager, who was in Shiraz Adel Abad prison twice during her imprisonment sentence, speaks of the 'chain of marriage' that was proposed as condition for release:

---

[1] Mehri Elghaspour spoke of a woman in Ahvaz prison who was a supporter of the Communist Union and married one of the *tavvabs* of that group by order of the prosecutor.

It was 1982 and a new religious magistrate had arrived at Shiraz. He forced a 'marriage sentence' on many female prisoners. Even though their crimes were not even heavy, they were forced to remain in prison and would only be released if someone would come to prison, marry them and take them. Many of them accepted and their families found them suitors so they did not have to remain in prison. The sentence did not have a rationale other than the religious magistrate's opinion that married girls would abandon their political activities.[1]

In other cases, as Simin Behrouzi recounts, "Marriage had to be with one of the *pasdars* or war veterans." She speaks of a *Mojahedin-e Kahlq* supporter, Maryam Ansari,[2] and says:

Maryam was from Isfahan and had not been exposed yet. One day, a visitation took place and a *pasdar* from Isfahan was amongst the committee visiting the prison. He saw Maryam and recognized her and told her, "Your sentence is execution. You can come with me and marry me and then you'll be released or you will be executed." Maryam told me this herself. She was executed within a month's time. But there was also another prisoner who had a marriage sentence and was unwilling to marry a cleric but she was released immediately. I have a friend who now lives in Iran. She had a five years' imprisonment sentence and was unwilling to accept the marriage sentence so she served her five years.[3]

Consequently, some of the prisoners who married prison employees in order to get released from prison were shunned from their families for years. One case recounts a female prisoner who was offered a marriage proposal by one of the *pasdars* in her prison. By marrying him she was released from prison. Yet for years none of her family members were willing to speak to

---

[1] Witness Testimony of Mitra Haghighat Lager, Justice For Iran.
[2] For more information about Maryam Ansari, see:
http://www.mojahedin.org/pages/martyrsDetails.aspx?MartyrId=1611.
[3] A complete list of this group of prisoners who had marriage sentence is kept confidential at Justice For Iran archives.

her or re-establish relations with her.[1] Some prisoners believed that this imprisoned girl was first raped by her interrogator and then accepted the marriage condition.[2] Others believed that she became a *tavvab* and so married her interrogator.[3] In any case, after her marriage and release from prison, she never returned to Sanandaj where her family lived.

Marriage as a condition of escaping execution: Tuba Kamangar, a supporter of *Komala* who was married and pregnant at the time of her arrest, was placed under heavy pressure and threats immediately upon entering prison. Officials told her that either she would marry one of the brothers or she would be executed. Although she never accepted to be married, the threat of rape was constant throughout her detention in Nashur village and Sanandaj *Sepah*'s detention centre.[4]

While pregnant, Mehrangiz was imprisoned along with other female prisoners in a container in the Yard of Gachsaran prison. She tells of an instance when Va'ezi, the religious magistrate of Gachsaran, told a girl that if she accepted a temporary marriage, her execution sentence would be commuted to life imprisonment and that she would be released from prison in a few years. She says:

> Homeira[5] tricked him and presented that she accepted his offer, and then asked him to allow her to leave prison to get her matters straightened out with her family. So he gave her three days leave. She left and in those three days married her fiancé and then returned to the prison a married woman. The religious magistrate sentenced her to execution and really harassed her, but her husband and family were finally able to rescue her through Gachsaran's representative in the Majlis. She was transferred to a Isfahan prison and later released after 5-6 years.[6]

---

[1] Name of the witness and the prisoner is confidential with Justice For Iran.
[2] Witness Testimony of Kobra Bane'i, Justice For Iran.
[3] Witness Testimony of Azar al-e-Kanaan, Justice For Iran.
[4] Complete text of the testimony of Tuba Kamangar can be found in Justice For Iran web site: http://justiceforiran.org/documents/tuba-kamanger/?lang=en.
[5] For security reasons, a pseudonym was selected for this prisoner. Her name and identity is archived and confidential at Justice For Iran.
[6] Witness Testimony of Manijeh, Justice For Iran.

In March 1981, Bahram Tajgardun, Gachsaran's representative in the first and second post revolutionary parliament demanded the removal of Va'ezi from his post as the religious magistrate of Gachsaran, Kohgiluyeh and Buyer Ahmad areas because of various violations he had committed. Indeed Va'ezi was tried and sentenced to one-year exile and his property confiscated for "illegal arrests, fabrications of evidence, and other violations." However, he was eventually transferred to Sistan and Baluchestan province where he continued his work.[1]

Shayesteh Vatandoust tells of a similar tale in Bandar Anzali prison:

> Mahnaz Yusof Zadeh was a supporter of the *Mojahedin-e Khalq*. She told me herself that the prosecutor propositioned her to get married. He had told her to fake a recantation. He said "I have fallen for you and want to marry you!" but she did not accept and [she was executed].[2]

Farzaneh Zolfi remembers a *Mojahedin-e Khalq* supporter in Karaj who was sentenced to execution. The religious magistrate fell in love with her and commuted her sentence so that she was released after marrying him.[3]

It appears that marriage for the purpose of commuting the sentence, particularly execution sentences, was quite commonplace during the 1980s. Recently, during a political argument, Tehran's mayor, Mohammad Bagher Ghalibaf, exposed that Rahim Mashaee, head of Ahmadinejad's presidential office and a former interrogator, had married his wife, who was a former supporter of the *Mojahedin-e Khalq*, in prison. Ghalibaf indicated that Mashaee had used his authority in prison to marry his wife, who was not in a position to give full consent at the time of their marriage.[4] The use of prison marriages in return for a lesser sentence, including commuting executions, has remained an open secret and few have engaged in discussing it.

---

[1] Complete text of the deliberation of the Islamic consultative Majlis, November 17, 1983, Session 501.
[2] Witness Testimony of Shayesteh Vatandoust, Justice For Iran.
[3] Witness Testimony of Farzaneh Zolfi, Justice For Iran.
[4] Ghalibaf: Rahim Mashaee Was a Supporter of the *Munafiqin*, Site-e Islam (reprinted at Peiknet) available at http://peiknet.net/09-juli/news.asp?id=39528&sort=Iran.

Marriage as a condition to relieve harassment and threats:
Based on some of the testimonies, while prisoners were undergoing serious and extreme harassment and interrogation, marriage was proposed as a measure to alleviate some of the prisoner's emotional stress. Nevertheless, the proposal itself was an
act of pressure and coercion. Nasrin Nekubakht was sentenced
to three years of imprisonment for membership in *Forqan* although the accusation was never substantiated. Her first interrogator was killed in a traffic accident and a new and much kinder
interrogator took over her case:

> He kept talking about making an in-person visit
> possible for me so that I could go home and visit
> my parents. Every time I was called for interroga-
> tion I thought that he is going to rape me and call it
> something else, like marriage! I thought that he will
> sit me on the chair and say, "I want to marry you,
> are you willing or not?"[1]

She then describes the coercive conditions of the prison:

> A prisoner knows who she's dealing with inside the
> prison… for me, this meant that either I would
> marry him or that he would pass a sentence for me
> that would either mature to become a death sen-
> tence or life imprisonment… particularly since the
> possibility of it was there! I was called into a room,
> behind closed doors with a blind fold, talking to a
> man who had suddenly become so nice. I could tell
> from behind the blindfold that the room was really
> small. I was alone and the interrogation was point-
> less because I had been sentenced and there was no
> reason to be called back for interrogation.
> Unless…[2]

These experiences indicate of wide spread practice of authorities and prison officials using their position to forced their
suggestion of advancement to their female prisoners. Mojdeh
Arasi speaks of a friend of hers who after the 1988 prison massacres was interrogated and pressured for marriage numerous

---

[1] Witness Testimony of Nasrin Nekubakht, Justice For Iran.
[2] Ibid.

times by the representative of the Ministry of Intelligence, a man who introduced himself as Zamani. She says:

> She was a beautiful, tall girl with dark hair and eyes. She was a member of the [*Fadaian-e Khalq*] Minority.[1] She was constantly called for interrogation and knew that it was out of the ordinary. He really worked on her psyche and pretended that he had fallen for her. He put all his efforts into convincing her to go with him [and accept a relationship with him]. Each time she went for interrogation her whole body shook. When she returned she would tell us, "He asked me to go with him again..." He threatened her with execution. But soon thereafter they started giving vacation time to political prisoners[2] and she was granted vacation, left prison and then left the country.[3]

Marina Nemat recounts one of the most detrimental experiences of forced marriage in prison. She was accused of collaboration with leftist groups and arrested at age 16. Due to her interrogator's threats about arresting her father and fiancé, she accepted to change her faith from Christianity to Islam and marry her interrogator. In her testimony, Marina describes her sexual relation with her interrogator as 'painful' and speaks of the negative effects of the relationship on her life henceforth. She explains, "After I was released from prison, I lost all ability to enjoy sexual relations with my own husband, whom I love and married of my own choosing."[4]

Marriage as a mental reaction to continuous torture (Stockholm Syndrome): One of the most controversial occurrences inside the prison discovered within the testimonies of this report is the marriages between officials and the *tavvab* prisoners. Witnesses repeatedly speak of women who established emotional

---

[1] Name of this prisoner is archived and confidential at Justice For Iran.
[2] After the 1988 prison massacre, in late February and early March of 1989, a group of political prisoners were given vacation and allowed to leave the prison. Most of them were never called back to complete their sentence.
[3] Witness Testimony of Mojdeh Arasi, Justice For Iran.
[4] Witness Testimony of Marina Nemat, Justice For Iran.

relations with, fell in love with and married officials in different prisons.

The majority of the prisoners interviewed for this report were *sar-e moze* (those who refused to repent) and clearly they disliked the *tavvabs* who had given in and changed their ideological position.. Prisoners generally dissociated with and boycotted *tavvabs* in prison, due to the fear that any conversation with *tavvabs* would result in new reports against the prisoner in question. Witnesses attest that even when they were kept in the same wards as *tavvabs*, they would not speak to them unless it was absolutely necessary. Many of the prisoners have affirmed that during the 1980s, particularly at Evin prison, women *tavvabs* left the ward every morning to work in different parts of the prison, including the interrogation chamber, and returned late at night. Some of the *tavvabs* were even called out at night.

However, as discussed above, numerous former prisoners have testified that 'unusual relations', meaning sexual relations, existed between some of the *tavvabs* and the interrogators and prison authorities. The prisoners used expressions such as "she had hooked up with the interrogator", "she was promiscuous", "was in love with her interrogator", and other such phrasing, all of which describes a sense of active behaviour on the part of the female *tavvab* in her relationship with her prison official. This is despite the fact that, as discussed earlier, the female *tavvabs* were in a coercive environment and prison authorities had power over them. As such, it is difficult to speak of personal agency or sexual autonomy on the part of the *tavvab*.

As expressed through the testimonies of prisoners, the abnormal or sexual nature of the relations between the interrogators and *tavvabs* was almost never expressed directly by the *tavvabs*. Other than in one case, where two witnesses attest that a *tavvab* openly declared in the ward that she had married her interrogator and that Assadollah Lajevardi, head of Evin Prison, had conducted the marriage ceremony,[1] the majority of the cases are based on observations by the prisoners.[2] Repeatedly being called

---

[1] Although we were not able to interview this person, based on the testimony of one of her close associates, either no marriage took place or if one did take place it was a temporary marriage and short lived. Name of the prisoner and witness are archived and confidential at Justice For Iran.

[2] In her testimony, Marina Nemat spoke of the shame of speaking to other prisoners about marrying the interrogator.

for interrogation at odd hours, particularly at night and returning in the morning, going for interrogation with gladness and returning without hurt and with a refreshed mood, obtaining points and forbidden items such as tweezers and shoes are some of the main signs and evidence of an existing relationship between a *tavvab* and her interrogator. One prisoner who was held at Evin speaks of a *tavvab* who would be called for interrogation at nights; when she returned to the ward in the morning she would tell the other prisoners that she must perform *qusl*, a ritual washing that Muslim are expected to perform after intercourse .[1] This *tavvab* was from Mashhad and was arrested for supporting the *Mojahedin-e Khalq*.[2]

Expression of love and fondness by the *tavvabs* towards their interrogators was also proposed as evidence of the existence of a sexual relationship between them. In a few cases, the witnesses said that they were informed by the *tavvab* prisoners that they had been given promises of marriage; however, there is no information available about whether or not such promises were fulfilled. Yet the reason why the witnesses did not consider this type of marriage to be a subset of prison marriage was the close and friendly relation the *tavvab* prisoners had with their interrogators and the feeling of hatred that such relations incited in the hearts of other prisoners. These expressions are also reasons why the witnesses deduce that if a marriage took place between the *tavvabs* and the prison authorities, it was based on love, choice and consent. While it is possible that *tavvabs* expressed love and affection for their interrogators, as we will discuss, such fondness and love can also be analyzed within the context of a psychological reflex towards a person who possesses absolute decision making power in a relationship; i.e. the power of the interrogators in regards to the fates of the *tavvabs*. This psychological reflex is called Stockholm Syndrome.

Stockholm Syndrome is an expression that became popular in the early 1970s and describes the sense of belonging expressed by victims of violence towards individuals who had treated them with extreme violence that was offset with periods of brief kindness. Based on this syndrome, in conditions of sensory deprivations, such as sight and hearing, and emotional deprivations,

---

[1] Witness Testimony of Violet, Justice For Iran.
[2] Name and information of this *tavvab* prisoner is archived and confidential at Justice For Iran.

such as undergoing belittling and solitude, a victim can form strong bonds with his/her torturer.[1]

Such psychological conditions occur when "someone threatens to kill you but does not do it". The relief caused by the removal of the threat of death causes a deep sense of gratitude mixed with fear in the victim that prevents the victim from showing negative feelings or reactions to the person keeping him captive.[2]

Monireh Baradaran speaks of a very young girl named Hamideh who was detained for supporting leftist groups and was infatuated with her interrogator:

> Close to Nowruz (Persian New Year), they brought her and another girl into our cell. She walked around the cell all the time deep in sorrow and grief that since it was during the Nowruz holiday and the interrogator was on vacation, she would not be going for interrogations. When they finally called her for interrogations, her cheeks were flushed.[3]

Mitra Tahami witnesses another case of infatuation with the interrogator:

> She was a lovely and beautiful girl. I met her at Evin. She would say that she misses brother Meysam [Joint Committee's interrogator]. I told her, "Do you know the kind of villain Meysam is? He is an animal. He is lashing people from morning to night. How can a person miss someone like this?" But she continued speaking in a manner as if she was a lover separated from her beloved. She said, "I hate Evin. I don't want to be at Evin. I want to return to Joint Committee". Now, what had Meysam done, you ask? Apparently this girl had seen Meysam without a blindfold. Meysam had taken her home from Joint Committee! When we were at the Joint Committee we didn't even have visitations for a year![4]

---

[1] Cognitive Dissonance, Nouriman Ghahari, Arash Magazine, available at: www.arashmag.com/content/view/676/47.
[2] Ibid.
[3] Witness Testimony of Monireh Baradaran, Justice For Iran.
[4] Witness Testimony of Mitra Tahami, Justice For Iran.

Doubtless, the actions of the interrogators were pivotal in creating such reactions. Mitra Tahami, Tahmineh Pegah, Mojdeh Arasi, and Parvaneh Alizadeh recall moments in their imprisonment experience when they were alone with their interrogator and he tried different ways to establish an emotional relationship with them. They also attribute a prisoners' young age and lack of experience as a cause of some prisoner's infatuation with their interrogators and torturers.

Mitra Tahami who had been arrested for supporting *Tudeh* party) explains the difference between male and female prisoners, particularly during the most uneasy and difficult part of interrogation and torture:

> Every prison has a good interrogator and a bad interrogator. However, a defining characteristic of the Islamic Republic prisons was that they weren't only after information, but also after total altering of a prisoner's personality; you had to become a new person. Even if you were to give information, they would still bother you until you would deny yourself. It wasn't over until you would say "I was a terrible person, a filthy person…"

> Under such condition, a male prisoner would start handing over his information when he had made the decision to establish relations with the good interrogator. Eventually, based on his ability [to withstand pressure] either he would cease all activity or recant and become a first class, second class or third class *tavvab*.

> Now, what would happen to the women? A female under extreme pressure would want to establish a contact with the good interrogator. He spoke kindly to her and no doubt enjoys it himself. Generally when people are in a very limited sexual structure, such occasions are both business and pleasure for them. Majority of the female prisoners were high school students. At maximum they were asked to expose those in school who were politically active. They would have to give a few names. When one reaches the point of resistance, there are two

choices. Either you are lashed or you escape it. How? You have to comply with their demands. There are different types of people [in prison]; they can both beat you or exchange pleasantries and take you home to your parents. It is your choice which you want to deal with. Their tactic is that they tell you about the two paths you can take; "either you comply with me or not." After all you are a prisoner and the same person who can beat you can in turn provide you with the best of facilities. For example, these girls were taken out of the prison. They used to tell us that they were taken to a Kebab restaurant.[1]

Parvaneh Alizadeh says,

Although I was only 23 at the time, I was amongst the older crowd. A majority of the girls were either in high school or had just graduated. I felt like they were my little sisters. Once they brought in a girl who was heavily tortured and was extremely beautiful. She was 19 or 20 and her feet were wrapped with bloody bandages. I sat next to her and asked, "Did they beat you a lot?"… She had a special kind of beauty… at that time, they used to send those who had caved in outside to bring news in. They had told her to go get news as well… once she came in the ward and told me that her interrogator had told her that he wants to marry her. This girl and I had established a friendship that the other girls found unusual. The girls who knew me faulted me and warned me not to speak to someone who has caved in. But in my eyes, this girl had not caved in. There was something between us that the others couldn't understand. She told me, "My interrogator and I, we go out in a car every day and eat sandwiches. We are supposed to get married. I leave the prison every day. At nights, we go for the coup de grâce."[2]

[1] Witness Testimony of Mitra Tahami, Justice For Iran.
[2] Witness Testimony of Parvaneh Alizadeh, Justice For Iran.

Mojdeh Arasi narrates her memory of Hamed, an interrogator who according to the female prisoners was extremely violent:

> Hamed was a very violent man. I had heard that he would take girls. Usually, he took female prisoners to interrogate and called them for interrogations at night… although he was not my interrogator, he called me one night. We were in the hallways. He told me to sit down and I did. I sat on the ground and leaned on the wall. He came and sat next to me facing the opposite direction with his back to the hallway as if we were sitting there chatting amicably. He brought his mouth near my ear and spoke in a manner as if he was trying to give his voice an erotic undertone. Everywhere was silent and he was trying to create a certain mood. I kept responding very loudly and saying that he wasn't even my interrogator. I tried to interrupt the mood he was trying to create. He kept trying and trying. They tested us this way. At that moment, when a person is under pressure, any human interaction, any signs of life and kindness, of human relations, anything can act as a window to safety, a cord to hold a person from collapsing. Many people grab unto such cords. Some of the *tavvabs* were in love with Hamed and really collaborated with him. They were with him; had a relationship with him. We knew! There was this one girl, every time they called her for interrogation, they would ready the bath for her and she would take a shower and then go for interrogation. Then, when she returned, she would *qusl* as well.[1]

Contrary to the cases where establishing relations with interrogators, in forms of temporary and permanent marriage, brought forth certain comforts, there were other instances where such relations had irreversible, negative consequences. Fariba Sabet says, "The first case I saw with my own eyes was a beautiful girl named Azam. It was around 1983-84. We were in the ward at Evin and she constantly repeated that a *pasdar* named Ali wanted to marry her. According to her, he was with her and she

---

[1] Witness Testimony of Mojdeh Arasi, Justice For Iran.

was pregnant. She kept repeating this until she became completely mad."[1]

Marriage as a tool to control the mental and physical behaviour of the prisoner: Forced marriage as a mean of controlling the thought and action of the female prisoners ensured that she was under control even outside of the prison. In fact, marriages conducted with a male prison employee or his close associates offered an iron-clad assurance that the female prisoner would not step out of line, even after her release from prison.

Somayeh Taghvaei was nine years old when she was arrested without charge in March 1982, and kept at Evin prison for five years as collateral for her parents. She was summoned to the prosecution office years after her release while she was in high school, and forced into marriage at the age of 18. Although her would-be husband was not a prison employee, he had served for many years in the war front and was from a family with close ties and relations to the Islamic Republic officials. At Evin's prosecution office, Somayeh was told that if she did not agree to the marriage she would be returned to prison. Since Somayeh's parents were outside the country at the time and the possibility of Somayeh joining them increased the likelihood of her becoming a living witness to the arrest and imprisonment of children as hostages, the decision to force marriage upon her can be defined as a means of controlling her body and mind. On the other hand, some interviewees suggest that Somayeh's case also proposes the possibility of officials using female political prisoners as a form of reward by forcing their marriage to politically adducing individuals as well as those who have been of great service to the Islamic Republic, a topic deserving of further research.

Somayeh had two daughters from her forced marriage, and died of cancer in a London hospital in 1997.[2]

A sister of one of the *tavvabs* who was rumored to be married in prison stated, "I am positive that no marriage in the real sense took place. I mean there really was no husband to speak

---

[1] Witness Testimony of Fariba Sabet, Justice For Iran.
[2] See Somayeh Taghvaei's biography in Appendix II.

of. But my sister never wanted to tell anyone what really happened to her. Whatever it was, its pain is forever with her… and if there was a matter of rape, she kept that to herself too…"

Such emotions, especially spoken by the sister of a prisoner, demonstrate how difficult it is to understand what really took place between interrogators and prison employees and female prisoner who married them inside or outside the prison. In particular, understanding the relations and conditions governing the lives of *tavvab* prisoners will not be possible until they decide to speak of it. It would be very enlightening if future research can answer the question of whether the prison employees used the female *tavvab* prisoners as sexual workers during the interrogations, night watches. In other word they used them as free labour forces to guard, manage the internal affairs of the prison, and even conduct interrogations and executions.

To sum up: Our findings indicate that marrying off the female political prisoners of the 1980s was an issue that recurred more frequently in various prisons and thus it indicates the systematic policy. Many of the prisoners have experienced it happen to themselves or their ward mates. Placing pressure on the female prisoner to accept the marriage proposal of the interrogator or other prison or judicial officials ranged in reason from personal vendetta, controlling the female prisoner even after her release. Based on what was concluded from our interviews with former female political prisoners, pressuring the prisoner to accept marriage was often done by placing marriage as a condition for release or as a guaranteed exemption from torture or execution. On multiple occasions, young female political prisoners, particularly those who had become *tavvab*, who were psychologically pressured by the harsh conditions of the prison, including interrogation and torture, developed an attraction toward their interrogators.

Many of the female political prisoners resisted the severe and unbearable pressures and did not agree to enter into marriage in prison. However, even those prisoners who agreed to the marriages, regardless of their condition or intention behind the agreement, could not be classified as having entered a 'consensual' relationship because the conditions necessary to form real 'consent' were absent inside the prisons. Hence,, such marriages are better classified as *forced* marriages and any sexual relation resulting from them a form of sexual torture in accordance with the principles of international law.

IV- Rape of Prisoners

IV- Rape of Prisoners

Testimonies of female political prisoners have demonstrated that they uniformly agree that the raping of female political prisoners in 1980s did not extend to the majority of the female prison population. At the same time, all of them believe that rape occurred in Iranian prisons in 1980s. However, they do not agree on the reasons, goals and the category of the prisoners who were subject to rape.

Some witnesses believe that the possibility of rape increased when female prisoners resisted all other types of torture. In such cases, rape was used as a method to break resistance. There was an exponential increase in the possibility if the prisoner was beautiful, had boldly defended her stance during interrogation while refusing to provide any information- a behaviour the interrogators considered audacious and brazen- or if her or her family possessed qualities that incited exceptional hatred and desire for vengeance in the interrogator.

Meanwhile, a significant number of witnesses believe that since officials did not want any trace of the rapes to leave the prison, aside from a few exceptional cases, the only individuals raped were those sentenced to execution. This group believes that female inmates with imprisonment sentences who were not awaiting execution, even if they were very beautiful or possessed the other aforementioned qualities, were not raped.

Some of the leftist witnesses believe that the charge and political affiliation of the prisoner played an important role in whether or not she was raped. They assert that since the majority of leftist prisoners considered rape as just another form of torture, raping and lashing did not necessarily differ for them. They also neither do nor hold strong religious view about sexuality and thus some interviewees believed they suffered less from rape and sexual abuse than others. Conversely, prison authorities assessed that rape is more effective when performed on prisoners belonging to the *Mojahedin-e Khalq*, due to their religious beliefs.

Therefore, in the opinion of many of our interviewees, imprisoned members of the *Mojahedin-e Khalq* suffered rape more often than the leftist prisoners.[1]

Another some of the witnesses believe that, aside from raping virgin girls prior to their executions, all other instances of rape in prison were isolated incidents performed by rogue elements or as a result of lust or sexual desire of the interrogator. In their view, good looking women were more likely to be victims of this form of torture although any woman who might be found at the right time and place for the agents or interrogators could have potentially suffered a similar fate.

The majority of witnesses who were imprisoned in Tehran province believe that due to the ideological atmosphere of the prisons and stricter control of the prison authorities, as well as competition amongst different governmental wings for authority over political prisoners in Tehran province, rape occurred less frequently in Tehran than other cities. However, this belief is disputed by others; some witnesses believe that a number of female political prisoners who were transferred to solitary cells of Gowhardasht, one of the capital's prisons, were raped.[2] Others believe the contrary, explaining that due to social connections and associations in the smaller cities, particularly during the earlier years when the officials were from the local population, the authorities seldom dared to commit such acts.

Therefore, as a result of the different analysis of the witnesses' testimonies regarding the reasons, goals and makeup of the prisoners who were raped in the 1980s, is it difficult to achieve consensus on the manner and aims of the systematic rape of female prisoners. Indeed, the cacophonous collection of analysis and opinions regarding the occurrence of rape in Iranian prisons was a major challenge to our research goals. A further challenge was the fact that a large number of the prisoners that our witnesses referred to in their testimonies have either been

---

[1] One can also argue that *Mojahedin-e Khalq* were more numerous than the leftist groups, and they generally were a bigger threat to the regime because they were more popular with the public. At the same time those that perpetuated such crimes felt that *Mojahedin* women many of whom came from more religious and conventional backgrounds, would be less likely if they were released from jail to publicized their case of rape, given the shame it curtailed for them and their families.

[2] Witness Testimony of Farkhondeh Ashna, Justice For Iran.

executed or have committed suicide inside prison or after their release. Furthermore, getting in touch with some of the living victims of rape proved impossible due to security reasons, or the witness being unwilling to disclose where they resided due to security concerns.

Four of the witnesse - Azar Al-e-Kanaan, Sa'ideh Siabi, Banoo Saberi and Shahla Molavi - have told us their stories of being raped[1]. Most of the witnesses reported at least one incident of rape amongst their ward mates, and some reported multiple incidents. In this section, we have disregarded the second hand and hearsay narratives and have only detailed cases that had either resulted from documented knowledge of the witness or had been testified to by a number of different witnesses, complementing the original narrative. Meanwhile, during our review of the prison related literature, wherever we encountered a narrative about a case of rape, to the extent possible, we tried to contact the writer and inquire about the incident in more detail, although it was not always possible. At times writers did not have documented sources to offer and had merely reflected what they heard in their writings, which did not help us reach more conclusive evidence of rape.

Testimonies of Rape

Despite the aforementioned challenges to our research on rape, we recount some short, often second-hand, narratives here to shed light on cases of rape in prisons in 1980s and paint a picture of the dimensions of such atrocities.

At times and for different reasons, such as respecting the security of the victim and unwillingness to break the trust of the victim, witnesses stated testimonies that they directly heard from the victims using pseudonyms in place of the victims' names. Manzar Bokhara'ee testifies about a *Mojahedin-e Khalq* supporter named Farideh who was raped in 1983 at Evin prison:

> There were two sisters who were arrested along
> with their husbands in the team houses. The older

---

[1] The full witness testimonies of Azar Al-e-Kanaan, Sa'ideh Siabi and Banoo Saberi are in Appendix I.

sister was in my room with her two kids, one was 4-5 years old and the other a few months old. One day, she went for interrogation and when she came back, she was unwell. There were no visible marks on her hands or feet. Usually when the girls would arrive, if they were unwell, we would help them immediately but I could not see anything on Farideh. When she slept that night, she was moaning. I went to her and asked her what was wrong; "Tell me what is wrong with you." Then, she said to me, "I don't feel well at all." I insisted for her to tell me what was wrong with her and show me where the pain was. She showed me and it really made me sick. She said, "They used electric wires to make something that looked like a baton but its head was covered in electric wires." They had laid her on the bed, with her sister and her husband standing there too. They heated the wires on a stove-top and then raped her using that. They kept telling her that she is a *munafiq* and therefore ritually impure so they couldn't do anything to her themselves, but they were raping her in front of her husband nonetheless. I saw myself that between her legs, her private parts were all burned and was hurting really bad. It really made me sick. I started banging on the door and asked for a cream. I helped her put the cream on and change her clothes. She kept saying that her real sadness was her husband. That she didn't even feel it and was only feeling his pain because of his screams and wailings. Later I heard that her husband killed himself in prison.[1]

Soudabeh Ardavan uses the pseudonym Minou for a 19 year-old girl who was arrested for supporting *Mojahedin-e Kahlq*. Shortly before she was set to be released from Evin, she was dragged for interrogation and torture as a result of *tavvabs*' reports about her. She returned to the ward visibly distressed. Soudabeh Ardavan who spoke to Minou directly says that her reason for distress was that they tried to rape her. She was amongst the prisoners who appeared topless in front of the oth-

---

[1] Witness Testimony of Manzar Bokhara'ee, Justice For Iran.

ers including the male wardens. She was released in 1985 after giving an interview in Evin's *Hosseiniyeh* and claiming that she repented.[1]

Nasrin Parvaz uses the pseudonym of Yas for a female prisoner who was a laborer in a factory in Tehran and was arrested during the laborers demonstration at that factory in 1981. She was transferred to Haft Howz *Komiteh* in Narmak neighbourhood. Yas was raped by three *pasdars* and upon release, realized that she was pregnant. Nasrin and other friends tried to collect money to help Yas perform an abortion but due to the illegality of the procedure - and therefore exorbitant cost - they were unable to collect enough money in time. Yas, fearing that her family would find out what had happened, married one of her socialist friends as a cover up. Nasrin later heard from another friend that the couple travelled to another city for the delivery and subsequently killed the baby. Nasrin never saw Yas again.[2]

Sara Raha'ee speaks of a 19 year-old supporter of *Mojahedin-e Khalq* who had lost her mental balance. She was imprisoned along with her brother at Evin prison. She told Sara, "They are very filthy, very ruthless. Try not to stay here and use whatever means possible to leave." When she asks why, the girl says, "They don't have mercy on men or women. So you can imagine how it is. They rape everyone from a 70 year-old woman to a 14 year-old girl."[3] The name and identification of this girl, as remembered by Sara Raha'ee, does not appear in any of the execution lists published.

When interrogated in the summer of 1981 at branch 6 of Evin Prosecution Office- which specializes in investigating the charges related to leftist prisoners- Akram Mousavi heard that in another section of the branch, separated with dividers from her chamber, the branch interrogator Hamed intended to rape a 12 year-old girl Akram calls Nadim. In parts of Akram's written testimony, she states,

> Hamed asked her, "Well, tell me where your brother and sister are." She said, "I don't know, I swear. I

[1] Witness Testimony of Soudabeh Ardavan, Justice For Iran.
[2] Witness Testimony of Nasrin Parvaz, Justice For Iran.
[3] Witness Testimony of Sara Raha'ee, Justice For Iran.

came home from school and have no idea of any-thing." He laid her on the bed, tied her feet and asked the same question. His voice did not have the regular anger and wrath normal to him. He was speaking slower and softer. As I heard his manner of speech, my body began to shake. I could hardly breathe and was panting. I could feel my heartbeat in my throat. What did he intend to do with her? I had to do something but what? I could clearly hear Hamed's breathing and the image of the little girl's condition was driving me insane. Suddenly I started to scream so loud; I had never heard myself do so before. Screaming was the only thing I could do. My yelling disrupted his evil plans and Hamed attacked me like a wild animal. He had only then realized that I was in that room. He started to beat me with punches and kicks like a mad man.[1]

As mentioned above, some of the witnesses refused to men-tion the names as well as any identifying characteristics of the victims of rape out of fear that they would be exposed. Kianoosh Etemadi says the following about a leftist prisoner's rape:

She was one of the girls who went to the quarantine section with us in 1983 at Unit one of the women's prison in Ghezel Hesar. She was later separated from us, beaten heavily and dropped in the bath-room unconscious. She told us that when she sud-denly came to, she realized someone was feeling her up. She let out such a scream that all of us standing in *zir-e hasht* got goose bumps. The way she screamed I thought they killed her. She didn't yell even once as loud while they were beating her but this matter was different and she said that if she hadn't yelled the guy would have continued.[2]

Mojdeh Arasi tells a story about Nasrin Nik Seresht[3]:

---

[1] Akram Mousavi also attested to this in her in person interview with Justice For Iran.
[2] Witness Testimony of Kianoosh Etemadi, Justice For Iran.
[3] Nasrin Nik Seresht (also known as Fati) was a student of communication sciences at Uni-versity of Tehran. She met Abdulrahim Saburi, a *Fadaian-e Khalq* Guerrilla Organization member and student of the same university, during a speech he was giving. She later married

She was a high-ranking girl from the Guerrillas.[1] I was arrested shortly after her execution and everyone talked about her in the ward. One of the girls who shared a cell with her said that Nasrin insisted on telling everyone the story of her rape and had told the girls in the ward to tell others as well. I later heard the story from a few other people in the ward.

When Nasrin was arrested in 1982, she had potassium cyanide[2] with her and wanted to take it immediately or after a bit of time but they noticed and stopped her. Then they took her for torture and really beat her up a lot. Nasrin was one of the girls who had a daily quota of lashing, after her interrogations. They would take her and beat her. In the first

Nasrin Nik Seresht

moments they really beat her. Nasrin said that after it was no longer possible to beat her because her body was torn and crushed they had called a doctor in and asked to inspect her to make sure she wasn't hiding potassium cyanide anywhere in her body. Nasrin said, "Someone came. They stripped me naked on that bed…" They had raped her both from the front and back. She said, "I didn't have the power to resist any longer. Every so often I'd push the guy away with my hands but I couldn't do much else." Imagine, you have been beaten to a pulp to the point that they can no longer torture you. Then

---

him. This union resulted in her activism within the *Fadaian-e Khalq*. In 1981, along with Hormati Pour, Sabouri split off from the organization and named his new group *Fadaian-e Khalq* of Iran (Iran's People's Liberation Army). Nasrin Nik Seresht was later arrested in relation to her activities with this group and executed after heavy torture.

[1] *Fadaian-e Khalq* (Iran's People's Liberation Army).

[2] Potassium cyanide is a pill that was carried both during Pahlavi times and after the revolution by political activists who carried important information. Due to its highly toxic nature, the pill would cause immediate death of whoever had taken it, preventing the person from falling into the hands of the regime alive. The pill was usually placed under the tongue. When in danger, the activist could bite the pill and cause entry of potassium cyanide into his or hers bloodstream through the highly absorbent mucus membrane which led to poisoning and subsequent death of the activist.

they bring someone under the guise of doctor and stripe you naked to look and see if you had hid potassium cyanide anywhere. Then, in the presence of others, they did this... Nasrin herself insisted and had told everyone in her cell to speak of this wherever they went.[1]

Kianoosh Etemadi attests that she heard from her fellow inmates at ward 246 of Evin that Huriyeh Beheshti was arrested for supporting *Mojahedin-e Khalq*. Huriyeh told the committee who came for inspecting the prisons[2] that she was raped inside that very prison. Hurieyh Beheshti was executed during the 1988 massacre of the political prisoners.[3]

Shayesteh Vatandoust heard senior prisoners at Evin say,

There was a case at Evin where they had raped a girl and wrote a number on her feet to take her for execution, but mistakenly they brought her back to the ward. This had happened in Evin and the senior girls told me about it. The girl wasn't feeling well either. She constantly thought that they had dropped a bottle inside from under the door for her. They had dropped Savlon [antiseptic lotion] for her. She had that feeling all the time, thinking that someone was looking from under the door. They took her from that place and no one knew where she was taken or whether she is dead or alive. Maybe she has been released and then killed herself! [I don't know].[4]

Farzaneh Zolfi tells a story she heard from her ward mate of her experience while imprisoned at Joint Committee of Tehran. "In the cell next to her, there was a *mojahed* girl who spoke to her when the *pasdars* weren't around- they would leave food for her and leave. That girl, who was sentenced to execution, told my friend that she was raped. The girl was always crying and was in a lot of pain for what happened to her."[5]

---

[1] Witness Testimony of Mojdeh Arasi, Justice For Iran.
[2] For more information about this committee see chapter I.
[3] For more information about Huriyeh Beheshti see her page in Boroumand Foundation's website, available at http://www.iranrights.org/farsi/memorial-case--2816.php.
[4] Witness Testimony of Shayesteh Vatandoust, Justice For Iran.
[5] Witness Testimony of Farzaneh Zolfi, Justice For Iran.

Nasrin Parvaz spoke of a young girl in 1983 who was arrested at the age of 12 along with her cousin who had a publication in her bag. She was told that her cousin was raped in one of the cells at Evin during her interrogation and subsequently committed suicide.[1]

In 1984, Niloufar Shirzadi was imprisoned at Ghezel Hesar when she met a Kurdish girl who was imprisoned for activity with one of the Kurdish opposition movements. She says,

> She had a two year-old son. Suddenly the word spread around the ward that her release was nearing and her family did not want to accept the child because they considered him a bastard. So they were unwilling to submit a guarantee for her release. Prison Officials claimed that she was raped by the Kurdish forces, and the Kurdish girls were saying that she was raped in Sanandaj prison. She had delivered the baby in prison too. Later there were talks of giving the baby to an orphanage when one of the leftist girls who was married but had no child spoke to the officials and convinced them to adopt the baby in prison.[2]

Sanam Ahmadi says, "While at Isfahan Prison, the girls were saying that Jamileh, who knew martial arts and had fought with the *pasdars* when they wanted to arrest her, was raped severely. Jamileh was a student who was arrested in 1981 for supporting the *Mojahedin*. She was executed later that year."[3]

Furthermore, Sara Raha'ee says, "There was a girl that everyone said was Ghashghai and had gotten accepted to the university. She was in prison and the girls said that she was raped. At that time, people didn't personally speak of being raped."[4]

About a *mojahed* girl, Violet says, "For a period, I was in the same ward with a *mojahed* woman who was a mother. She said that when she was arrested she was in the *Asayeshgah* [sanitarium-where the doors were locked at all times] and they were held be-

---

[1] Witness Testimony of Nasrin Parvaz, Justice For Iran.
[2] Witness Testimony of Niloufar Shirzadi, Justice For Iran.
[3] Witness Testimony of Sanam Ahmadi, Justice For Iran.
[4] Witness Testimony of Sara Raha'ee, Justice For Iran.

hind dividers. There was a semi-conscious girl lying next to her in a pool of blood. When she regained consciousness she called for her mother, and passed out once again. She told this woman that she was raped and was told not to tell anyone. They had said that if she doesn't tell anyone she would only be given a ten years' sentence, otherwise, she would be executed."[1]

Ashraf Adelzadeh who was imprisoned in Tabriz between July 1981 and September 1988 for supporting *Mojahedin-e Khalq* speaks of a 14 year-old girl from Ardebil who was raped by her interrogator in Tabriz prison. She says, "They had raped this beautiful girl in a solitary cell that was like a bathroom. She had told everyone about it and so they [authorities] tried to prevent more shame and proposed she marry that *pasdar*, which she promptly rejected. Later I heard she was released early."[2]

From amongst the heap of names of victims who suffered from mental imbalance in prison mentioned during testimonies, two names stood out: Nejla Ghassemlou, a member of *Fadaian-e Khalq*, and Farzaneh Amuei, a member of *Mojahedin-e Khalq*. Therefore, from amongst the female prisoners who had suffered mental disorders in prison causing their fellow prisoners to believe they were raped, we resorted to process the cases of Nejla Ghassemlou and Farzaneh Amuei. Nejla Ghassemlou committed suicide after her release from prison while had managed to flee to Paris, and the last known news about Farzaneh Amuei was that after her release from prison, she was institutionalized at Amin Abad mental hospital (Razi Educational and Therapy Centre for Specialized Psychological Care). Neither of the two can testify to what happened to them, but what separates these two from the rest is the effect they had on their ward mates in the years after they lost their mental balance. Without a doubt, we will never know if the two were raped or not, and yet in their suffering, they react the trauma of such experiences with their body movements and reactions their ward mates assumed that they were raped[3].

---

[1] Witness Testimony of Violet, Justice For Iran.
[2] Witness Testimony of Ashraf Adelzadeh, Justice For Iran.
[3] The fuller biographies we were able to collect on these women can be found in Justice For Iran web site (http://justiceforiran.org/?lang=en)

The strong belief of the prisoners that both Nejla and Farzaneh were raped created a constant shadow of fear over other female prisoners. Indeed it appears that one reason the prison authorities chose not to release prisoners such as Nejla and Farzaneh, aside from their desire to keep what happened inside the prisons in the dark, was the atmosphere of threat and fear that the presence of mentally disturbed inmates created. Prisoners such as Nejla and Farzaneh were taken directly from Evin and Ghezel Hesar to Amin Abad or sent to their homes, though in their mental status, home was no longer the sanctuary for them that it once was. For this reason, suicide or excessive loneliness was the fate awaiting most of these women. After the passage of so many

Nejla Ghassemlou

years, most witnesses still have a vivid and shocking image of the two women burned in their memories, which attests to the level and severity of psychological torture placed upon prisoners in those years.

In retelling the fate of Nejla and Farzaneh, we hope to bear witness and pay tribute to all such women who suffered similar fates in the 1980's whose pain and suffering were seldom revealed.

The Testimonies of the Infamous Solitary Cells at Gowhardasht Prison

The construction of Gowhardasht prison (currently Raja'i Shahr) had begun during the end of the Pahlavi era but it was not completed until late winter of 1984. At the time, the head of this prison was a man named Morteza Salehi who used the pseudonym 'Sobhi' to introduce himself.[1] "Also, Davood Lashkari was in charge of discipline at Gowhardasht. He would fondle women's breasts and kick them between their legs."[2] The female

---

[1] Witness Testimony of Iraj Mesdaghi, Justice For Iran.
[2] Witness Testimony of Farkhondeh Ashna, Justice For Iran.

guards at Gowhardasht were known by the names of Mrs. Naderi, Mrs. Bakhtiari (who was imprisoned during the Shah's rule, and had an Aleppo boil mark on her face) and Sa'ideh.

Based on the decisions of Evin prison authorities of the time, from mid-1982 to early 1983, some prisoners who maintained their political positions despite interrogations and tortures were sent to solitary cells at Gowhardasht as a form of punishment. The condition in Gowherdast prison was notorious for harshness and severity both physically and in terms of treatment of the prisoners. Incredibly severe conditions of Gowhardasht solitary cells clearly demonstrated the Revolutionary Prosecution Office's goal to completely and utterly break the prisoners' wills.

The stories from Gowhardasht prison presented another major challenge in dealing with the case of prisoners who lost their mental balance in prison. Indeed, in most cases, mental imbalance was believed by the witnesses to be a strong indicator of rape. Holding prisoners for long periods of time in solitary cells reduced the possibility of establishing contact between them for the purpose of extracting details and information regarding the incidents that might have occurred. The repeated testimonies were so disturbing that those interviewed, after the passage of decades, still felt haunted by their experiences and the stories they were exposed to in Gowhardasht prison. These testimonies were so consistent and came through such diverse interviewees that we felt we should dedicated a brief section to Gowhardasht due to the exceptional prevalence of testimonies associated with this detention centre.

One of the imprisoned women explains the conditions in Gowhardasht solitary cells:

> They pulled the blindfolds all the way down to the chins … the first thing that one would notice was the silence. Silence crept everywhere.

> The dimensions of the cell were 2 meters by 3 meters. A U shaped pipe was attached to one of the walls. There was a small metal toilet and sink in one corner. One window, covered with long metal shutters from between which a tiny strip of the sky was visible, was my only entry to the outside world.

According to the regulations of the ward, that we were briefed about on our first night of arrival, absolute silence was to reign at all times. If anyone had a problem or a business, they were not to call for the guard or even knock on the doors. They were to instead slide a sheet of paper under their door where there were a few centimeters of opening. Once the guard passed by and saw the sheet, he would come to the cell on his own. If anyone would break the absolute silence and thereby the regulation, he would immediately face beatings and lashings.[1]

The regulations governing the solitary cells in Gowhardasht prison, where a few female political prisoners were kept for long stretches of time (in most cases between one to two years), left horrific and irreversible effects on these women.

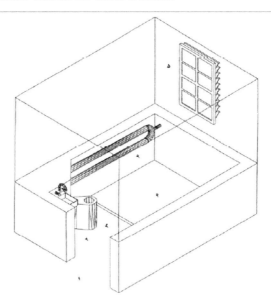

Image of a 2*3 meters solitary cell at Gowhardasht[2]

A number of them experienced such dramatic psychological effects they were no longer able to converse coherently. Other detainees committed suicide. As such, it was not possible for us

---

[1] Homa Jaberi, Islands of Torment, Amir Khiz Publication, August 2007, PP. 29-34.
[2] Plans of and Gowhardasht prison is taken from Iraj Mesdaghi, Neither Alive, Nor Dead, available at http://www.irajmesdaghi.com/page1.php?id=84.

to fully understand exactly what transpired between this group of prisoners and the guards. We hope future research will be able to get prison officials' to give testimony to shed light on this dark chapter of history. However, the testimonies of other prisoners suggest the high possibility that repeated sexual assault and rape were the factors that pushed female prisoners to lose their mental stability or become suicidal at Gowhardasht prison.

Farkhondeh Ashna says,

> In 1983, there was a *mojahed* girl who was sent for 3-4 months to Gowhardasht solitary cells. Then [after returning] she would wear her headscarf even in front of the women in the ward. She also washed her hands compulsively. She was executed in 1984.[1]

> I remember in 1985 in Gowhardasht they would take the girls for interrogations. These were the girls who were loud and making noises in the cells. They were gone for 2-3 days.... Then they would return spewing insults at the *pasdars*, insults that would suggest they have hit rock bottom. For example one of them screamed at the *pasdar*, "this filthy… Khomeini!" She told the guard, "You are a slut yourself!" or said to [the male guard], "Go and sleep with Naderi, screw up!" I mean you really could tell that the person had nothing left [to lose] and was therefore screaming obscenities in such blunt manner.

> First they screamed and shouted in that manner and then, once they returned, they cried endlessly. Then you'd see her get into scuffles with the guards. The guards would shut off their water supply because they kept washing themselves. They would take off their clothes all the time and wash themselves. Water would spill out of the cells and come into our cells. Then they would say, "I have become filthy. Your hands touched me and now I am filthy. I will never be cleansed again." They said things like that. They woke up at nights, midnights and screamed,

---

[1] Witness Testimony of Farkhondeh Ashna, Justice For Iran.

"Go away you filthy! Go away!" Things like this. It was clear they were raped.

One of them was named Demir, which means iron in Kurdish. This was a pseudonym we had given her in our Morse messages as everyone had a pseudonym. Demir was one of the girls who was really unwell when she returned from interrogations. She wouldn't enter into contacts with us. We tried a lot to ask her calmly what had happened to her but she wouldn't enter our Morse messaging anymore. She would cry and say "I have become filthy. I am a bad person." It was clear that she was unwell.

The guards would come and beat these girls. Mostly men were asked to come and do the beatings. The women lost their mental balance and would get into physical scuffles with the female guards. Their doors would seldom open. In order to feed them, they would open the doors to deliver the food when a male guard was present too because they no longer abided by any laws or regulations.

Based on our own experience we knew that someone who goes and gets lashed on the soles of her feet remains calm. Yes, her feet would become painful so she would Morse to the girls saying that she is not all right because she was beaten and for them to wait a bit so she can get better. But when these girls would return there was no communication from them at all. This is very important. Their psyche was completely messed up. For example one of the girls returned from interrogation where she as heavily beaten and her jaw were broken. In that condition, she used Morse to say that she was in a deplorable condition and thought that her jaw, as well as her arm, had broken. She asked for a few days to recuperate. Well, we understood. We watched out for her.

Also, the cells were located in a way that one could see the others, especially the ones located in front of our cells. We could see their movements and their shadows. We could see that she would drag herself on the ground to make it to the bathroom. Or that she couldn't sleep at night. We monitored the girls who went to interrogation and return from it from under our doors. We could see their manners and conditions, whether they moved or not. Those girls were completely restless. For the first few days after the interrogation they only cursed and punched and kicked, destroying the door and other things in the cell. You knew you couldn't establish contact with her, that you couldn't tell her to be calm. For example, we had a doctor named Mahvash Keshavarz. She committed suicide when she was released. In the early days, we didn't know what to do. When such situations would occur we'd ask her what to do and she would say, "Leave her alone. She is in shock." Then we'd not even speak to each other using the space under the door because we didn't want our voice to disrupt them. She was in such a condition that she couldn't distinguish between her friend's voice and the guard's voice. Any sound she heard would trigger her laps into shouting obscenities. "You are [expletive] and the other things…" She couldn't understand whether we were talking or the guards.

I saw another girl who was released in 1986 much later. She was in the psych wards of the hospitals all the time. Our families were in touch with one another. They said that the girl was released but the poor her had gone completely insane, that she couldn't sleep days or nights. Then our mothers would come to visit us and say, "For heaven's sake, don't go insane! Because so and so has gone mad, you know."

In some cases, men who were imprisoned at Gowhardasht's solitary cells heard screams and shouts from the cells opposite theirs, where women were being kept. These reports are indicative of rape and sexual torture as other forms of interrogation would not usually happen in the cell. Ibrahim Dala says, "It was September or October of 1984. I woke up with the sound of a girl screaming, saying, "Get out you filth!" Iraj Mesdaghi has a similar story: "In 1983 I was bathing when I heard the screams of a girl who was saying, "I was raped."[1]

As mentioned, Farkhondeh Ashna speaks of a girl who was known as Demir (Iron in Kurdish) and was imprisoned in the same hallway as her in 1985. Based on Farkhondeh's testimony, once when they took Demir for interrogation, upon returning, she seemed to be suffering from a psychological problem. Farkhondeh says, "she was insulting the guards and *pasdars* non-stop, using vulgar terminology. Also, she constantly washed herself so much so that water was always spilling out of her cell into the hallways." Based on the same testimony, Demir kept repeating, "Do not touch me, I have been soiled!"[2]

Farkhondeh also describes how prison authorities remained in denial or indifferent when this matter was reported to them: "I dealt with Majid Ansari[3] in person at Gowhardasht. I told him about the raping of my friend [Demir]. Her voice came from the cell adjacent to mine and she was shouting obscenities. The guard asked who it was and I gave her name and identifying information and said, "She is the one who was raped and so has lost her mental balance." Majid Ansari said, "Here in prison, you all have lost your minds! What rape? What prison?"[4]

To sum up: The Iranian officials, both past and present, have unilaterally denied the existence of any forms of torture in Iranian prisons during the 1980s- this includes the raping of women in Gowhardasht. Even still, research shows that rape was a form of torture, which was prevalent in the prisons of the 1980s. However, all the individuals interviewed are of the opinion that,

---

[1] Witness Testimony of Iraj Mesdaghi, Justice For Iran.
[2] Witness Testimony of Farkhondeh Ashna, Justice For Iran.
[3] In 1984 Majid Ansari was appointed as the representative of the Supreme Judicial Council to the Revolutionary Courts and Prosecution Offices. About this, he says, "on June 9, 1984, I was appointed as the representative of the Supreme Judicial Council in the courts and prosecution offices and later the State Prison Organization was established through efforts made. I was then appointed and the Head of SPO. In January 1987 I had to resign from my post because I intended to partake in the Third Majlis Elections. I was a member of the third Majlis from May 28 1988 when it started and so I had no role in the SPO any longer. Majis Ansari Speaks of the Prison situations at the Time of Imam, Aftab News, June 28, 2011, available at http://www.aftabnews.ir/vdcjyhevvuqe8hz.fsfu.html.
[4] Witness Testimony of Farkhondeh Ashna, Justice For Iran.

with the exception of the raping of virgin girls before their execution, raping was not a widespread and systematic occurrence in Iranian prisons.

Many reasons can be cited for the existence of rape in prisons. Some such reasons are political, such as the use of rape as a tool to break the resistance of the female prisoner. Other reasons stem from the carnal desires of the official who happened to find just the right time to carry out his act.

Prisoners have different opinions about the kinds of individuals who were more likely to be targeted for rape. For example, some believe that religious women, for whom being raped was more heavily associated with the 'dishonor' this might bring to their families, were more likely to be targeted for rape. Some think that due to a lesser political control on provincial prisons, the occurrence of rape was more likely in those spaces, while others stubbornly reject this idea and bring many examples to the contrary. Either way, no matter what the reason behind the rapes, those who perpetuated them continuously enjoyed impunity as a result of the absolute denial by Iranian officials regarding of any wrongdoing in the prisons of the Islamic Republic of Iran.

V- Other Widespread Forms of Sexual Harassment

V- Other Widespread Forms of Sexual Harassment

Nearly all witnesses experienced some form of sexual harassment, the most prevalent of which will be discussed in this section. The repeated and widespread testimonies of sexual harassment experienced by our interviewees convinced us that these experiences were extensive through the various prisons in Iran. It appears that the perpetual harassment was rooted on one side, in male prison authorities' images and beliefs of 'women' as property and captives, and on another side, in wider patriarchal beliefs and taboos in Iranian society. As Ziba Mir-Hosseini points out, there are many of the gender codes and sexual taboos in Iranian society and the expressions of sexual desire and love as well as sexual abuse and rape of both sexes are amongst them[1]. Male authorities abused these taboos, as many female prisoners say, "to break their resistance."

Interviewees all believed that the majority of female political prisoners were young women who mostly had no sexual experience. The dominating atmosphere of the political groups themselves was very puritanical and they insisted to keep their relationship in that way. One of the former female political prisoners who collaborated with *Peykar* organization speaks of the time when she was in hiding and due to necessity had to pretend to be married to a male comrade and live together in a house. Because the bedroom could be seen from outside, they worried that if the neighbors saw them sleep in different beds they may become suspicious and so they had to sleep in the same bed together. She says, "You wouldn't believe but the entire duration of those few months, I was sleeping with clothes on, with t-shirt and jeans. And he did too! We slept in a way so as to have no physical contacts with one another."[2]

---

[1] Mir Hosseini, Ziba, Broken Taboos in Post-Election Iran, Middle East Research and Information Project, December 17, 2009 at http://www.merip.org/mero/mero121709

[2] Witness Testimony of Golrokh Jahangiri, Justice For Iran.

Siba Nobari, supporter of Union of Combating Communists (*Sahand*) who later became *tavvab* in Ghezel Hesar prison during the graves[1] says, "I am sure there were exceptions but we were thicker and rougher than to think of sexual things. Personally, in the six years I was a communist, I had even crushed my passion. For three months I lived in a team house with a man who was my political and ideological ideal. I worshipped him, like an idol. Specially that I was 19 and he was 34. Because I was the only single person in our group, I was candidate for a team house under the pretext of marriage. You can't imagine how happy I was. I thought that I would be living under one roof with him and absorbing his opinions and thoughts. Not for a second did my mind wonder to sexual matter. I suggested to him that we should sleep in the same room to save on cost of fuel but he refused. Not once did we think of sexual things."[2]

Parallel to this moral and asexual atmosphere, many young female political activists were aware that they would likely be raped if taken to prison, given the rising reports that were being circulated. Ashraf Deghani's memoir of her time in prison during the Shah's regime and the rape she experienced also implied that rape occurred in prison even prior to the revolution. Hence for many, imprisonment became synonymous with rape, particularly in the minds of leftist women.

Given their own sexual inexperience as well as the fear of rape in prison, most of the witnesses who experienced various forms of sexual harassment in the early days of their imprisonment were deeply disturbed and pained by the harassment.

Fear of rape was the most common form of sexual harassment. Based on some of the testimonies, this fear was not merely

---

[1] In 1983, a group of leftist women inmates were taken to an unprecedented punishment ward in Ghezel Hesar Prison. From six o'clock in the morning until eleven o'clock at night prisoners were forced to sit, blindfolded and motionless, in small wooden cubicles, to which they were later referred as *tabootha* (coffins or graves). The head of this prison called it *kark-haneh-ye-adamsazi* (a human manufacturing factory). Covered in chador, with no movement permitted- the space was so tiny that there was no room to move anyway- while any sound, even coughing or sneezing, was punished by beatings, the inmates felt frozen in an eternal time. The overwhelming silence was broken only by the sounds of beatings and the recantations, religious hymns, or recitations of Qur'an broadcasted from the loudspeakers. Only a small minority of these inmates survived insanity, death by suicide, or falling into the abyss of collaboration as tavvabs. (Shahla Talebi, Who is Behind the Name? A Story of Violence, Loss, and Melancholic Survival in Post Revolutionary Iran, Journal of Middle East Women's Studies, Vol. 7, No. 1 (Winter 2011), P. 51)

[2] Witness Testimony of Siba Nobari, Justice For Iran.

one stemming from what the witness had heard outside of prison. In fact in many cases, the female prisoner was placed in a situation where she assumed she would be raped at any moment.

Most witnesses experienced verbal sexual abuse from the moment of their arrest, through phrases such as "You were only in team houses to take care of men's sexual desires" or belittling speech about covering the body and keeping the *hijab*. Some women considered the pain of being treated as a second-class creature devoid of political identity, instead of an independent human in charge of her own faculties, much worse than lashing.

The testimonies show us that the common presumption that Iranian prisons were devoid of sexual speech or action, due to the government's specific 'Islamic' ideology that moralizes about rigid separation between the sexes, is in fact entirely false. Rather, the atmosphere of prisons in the 1980s was exceptionally sexual. The overwhelming presence of men as interrogators, judges and wardens exacerbated the male dominance in the female wards in prisons. Numerous reports speak of female prisons that were entirely managed by men. In such male dominated prisons, women were subject to serious sexual harassments. For example, many witnesses say they figured out that while bathing or using the bathrooms, male wardens would 'check out' their naked bodies.

Homa Sadegh, a supporter of the *Mojahedin-e Khalq*, was imprisoned at *Sepah* Detention Centre of Torbat Haydariyeh for 8 months. She says, "*Sepah* Detention Centre looked like a motel where the bathrooms in each room had been disabled. They took us to another bathroom. One day when they took me to take a bath, from the window of the bathroom I saw that Khodadadi, the manager of the detention centre, was stripping naked so that he can enter the bathroom as well. I screamed so much that he immediately got dressed, zipped his pants and left."[1]

The matter was not exclusive to smaller prisons such as those in Bandar Anzali, Lahijan or Ahvaz where no female employees worked. In fact, in various sections of the large prisons in Tehran province, including ward 209, as well as a few wards in Ghezel Hesar, the female prisoners faced eyes that were check-

---

[1] Witness Testimony of Homa Sadegh, Justice For Iran.

ing them out from cracks of the doors and windows of the bath-room or toilet.[1] For this reason, in some of the prisons, female prisoners never fully undressed to change or wash.[2] Complaints filed by two female prisoners against prison authorities stating that they were checking the women out in the bathroom of ward 209 resulted in the women being sentenced to *ta'zir* (lashing) for falsely accusing the brothers.[3]

Aside from hearing insults and terminology that directly tar-geted their sexuality, female witnesses faced a dualistic behavior towards their body particularly while being tortured by lashing. Testimonies show that while the male interrogators or wardens refused to come into any physical contact with the women while transporting them blindfolded from the interrogations room to the torture chamber- where they led the women by pulling their *chador* or having them grab the free end of a pen they were hold-ing- they had no problem touching different parts of the pris-oner's body while torturing her. In fact, the *shari'a* based law governing the interactions of men and women who were not related to one another were wholly ignored. The interrogators touched the female prisoners' body or sat on their buttocks or on other body parts as they were torturing them. During such times, pain and torment of the female prisoner exponentially intensified. Based on the witness testimonies, being female made no concessions in the intensity and the kind of tortures they were subjected to but women also feared the sexual abuse and rape as they were subject to physical torture.

Feeling up the body of the female prisoners did not only oc-cur when they were being tortured. A few witnesses speak of being touched inappropriately by the prison officials while being transported to different part of prisons or other times when they came into contact with the male officials. For example, Nazli Partovi says, "The day we were done with the coffins at Ghezel Hesar, they asked us to get up. It had been months since we walked and we were confused. As I got up with my blindfold and *chador* a man grabbed my breasts and squeezed them. I didn't show any reaction and just ran. A large number of women were

---

[1] Witness Testimony of Shayesteh Vatandoust, Justice For Iran; Witness Testimony of Mo-jdeh Arasi, Justice For Iran; Witness Testimony of Fariba Sabet, Justice For Iran; Witness Testimony of Farkhondeh Ashna, Justice For Iran.
[2] Witness Testimony of Fariba Sabet, Justice For Iran.
[3] Witness Testimony of Nasrin Nekoubakht, Justice For Iran.

walking with me so he must have done this to others as well. I never told anyone about this because at the time I thought that it would bring the other prisoners, moral down."[1]

Below we analyze the most widespread forms sexual harassment mentioned in the testimonies:

Fear of Rape

As discussed, the dominance of male authorities, officials and guards in prisons, in and of itself instilled a fear of rape in the core of female prisoners. Even the guards at the solitary female wards were men, a fact that has been reported many times about the *Sepah* detention centres in various cities, some prisons of Tehran province (such as Ward 209 of Evin), as well as prisons of smaller towns, particularly in the first few years of the arrests. For example, within the first week of her detention at the male dominated detention centres of Salmas, Khoy and Marand, Sarah L. feared rape at all times. Mona Roshan who was the only female prisoner at the Sepah Detention Centre of Karaj for six weeks, feared being rape in her solitary cell. Even where there was a female guard working at the prison, the interrogator was almost always a man. Female prisoners state repeatedly that they were alone with one or more interrogators in the interrogation chamber. Many of them experienced alone time with one interrogator, which, even in the absence of a threat of rape, instilled the fear of it in them. Some of the prisoners were threatened with rape multiple times. The testimony of Tuba Kamangar, which demonstrates the multitudes of threats, is available in Appendix I.

When asked about the possibility of rape from a practical perspective, the majority of witnesses insist that in most prisons, the solitary cells, the closed interrogation chambers or places such as the basement of Ward 209 of Evin prison provided ample opportunity for rape.

Mehrai Elghaspour says,

It was very possible in the solitary cells. For example [it was possible] in the Operation Committee

---

[1] Witness Testimony of Nazli Partovi, Justice For Iran.

where I was held for seven months in a dark room. I was very afraid the first night. When I entered the room initially I thought the light bulb had burned out so I knocked and told them that. The guard said that's how it was! I died! I was alone too. I thought to myself that there was nothing I could do if they came for me. The *pasdars* could have easily raped me there. There was a *pasdar* named Hossein. When they transported me to different locations with an ambulance, he would put his head next to mine or stick his mouth to my ears and tell me to be careful! He said, "You know that you are our captive and we can do whatever we want with you!"[1]

Aside from factors such as male-dominated detention centres and being left alone with the interrogators, some prisoners were intentionally put in situations so as to instil the fear of rape in them.

Golrokh Jahangiri who was 21 at the time of her arrest was transferred for two days from a detention centre in the former Lahijan School of Health Care to Saltanat Abad *Komiteh* of Tehran. About her experience in the latter detention centre, Jahangiri says,

The [*pasdar*] said to me that they want to take me and execute me. At that time, I thought that resistance meant death. I didn't see them to be mutually exclusive. He took me inside a room. Although my blindfold was very wide, I know that he took me to a room. I was standing and he told me not to open my eyes. There was someone in the room who kept making a noise. The noise was similar to that of an elastic band. I kept thinking that the person who was there was taking his pants off to rape me. In fact I was positive he was going to rape me. I was only happy that because my blindfold was wide he couldn't see that I had turned yellow from fear. I was dying! It probably took about a minute. Then he left the room and told me that I could open my

---

[1] Witness Testimony of Mehri Elghaspour, Justice For Iran.

eyes as he was closing the door. When I did I saw
that it was a 4-meter by 4-meter room with two sets
of bunk beds on each side. It was probably a room
where the *pasdars* slept.[1]

Nasrin Parvaz speaks of a day in 1982 when she as alone
with her interrogator in the interrogation chamber of the Joint
Committee of Tehran,

> In my second round of interrogation, the interroga-
> tor came at nights, like 12 midnight. He would force
> me to push my blindfold up a bit and would touch
> his feet to mine. This made me think that he might
> rape me. I knew that screaming would not help me
> because no one would hear my voice. He didn't
> rape me but I kept thinking that he might.

Another factor that increased the fear of rape in prison was
hearing vulgar and sexually charged insults from the interrogators. Arrested only a few days after her caesarean operation
along with her infant daughter, Mehri Elghaspour speaks of her
experience at the Sahra *Komiteh* of Ahvaz:

> I was blindfolded and handcuffed. He asked me if I
> wanted to experience "it". I said, "Experience
> what?" He said, "Will you tell us?" I said "what?"
> He said "Your issues" [reffering to organizational
> information] and I said that I had nothing to say.
> He started lashing me on my hands and waist and
> hitting me on the head with a key. An hour passed
> like this. Then he told me to take my feet up. No
> matter what he did, I didn't put my feet up. One of
> them came and held my feet up. I was barefoot and
> was struggling not to be hit. They said that there
> wasn't any point to continue like that and I had to
> be tied to a bed. Prior to that they had spewed in-
> sults at me saying that my kinds of women are all
> whores and such things… so they took me and tied
> me to a bed. I was bleeding but didn't tell them that
> I have had a caesarean operation. I thought that
> they will beat me so much and then I'll die from

---

[1] Witness Testimony of Golrokh Jahangiri, Justice For Iran.

bleeding. I had no idea of how torture was done… when he said to tie me to the bed I thought they wanted to rape me. In my head I was thinking about the people I had lived with, the poverty I had witnesses, my student- because one of my students from Shiraz, Mohammad Shah Jahanbakhshi, was executed when he was 16 at Shiraz Prison when they arrested a bunch of them. I was thinking of these things but was very scared of rape. I was willing to be lashed ten times more than what I had already experienced but not be raped. I kept wondering what they were going to do to me. I thought they will tie me to the bed and I won't be able to do anything. When they finally tied me to the bed I tried my hardest to keep my feet together as tightly as possible… because of my delivery I was bleeding and they were lashing me, insulting me and playing funeral hymns. When they started beating me, the blows and my struggles made the bleeding worse and it started spilling off the table…[1]

Causing fear of rape for women was not limited to the use of vulgar terminology. Some witnesses state that they saw the wandering eye of the interrogator from under their blindfold. Other interrogators called the prisoners by their first name, asked personal questions and with a friendly tone discussed matters of a sexual nature using sexually charged terminology, thereby causing anguish for the female prisoner. Farkhondeh Ashna says that an interrogator with the pseudonym Hamed who was the manager of Branch 5 of the Revolutionary Prosecution Office at Evin broke the resistance of women, in particular young women, by entering their private sphere and instilling a great fear of rape in them so much so that they would accept his condition just so they could be released earlier.[2] She recalls that a leftist girl, who had received a compliment on her beautiful hair by Hamed, clipped her hair off with a nail clipper upon her return to the ward. From that moment, she was known as Cosette amongst the inmates.

---

[1] Witness Testimony of Mehri Elghaspour, Justice For Iran.
[2] Witness Testimony of Farkhondeh Ashna, Justice For Iran.

Nazli Partovi remembers the night after she was tortured in the Joint Committee where the interrogators were speaking and laughing with one another loudly so she could hear them. They said, "These girls are permissible to us. Wherever the Prophet went and fought, he took their wives from them too!" She thinks "they said such things to break our spirits and make us think that we are about to be raped and should be waiting for it."[1]

Other witnesses recount how the interrogators used their alone time with female prisoners to enter her private sphere and create an unsafe environment for her. Being felt up by the interrogators, particularly cupping of women's breast has been reported numerous times. In one case, Parvaneh Alizadeh, arrested in September 1981 in Tehran, says,

> Once a *pasdar* tied [my hands behind my back by passing one over the shoulder and another under the shoulder]. As he was checking to see if the cuffs were tied correctly, he touched my breasts. I was in so much pain that I wasn't paying too much attention to this but later I recalled that he had cupped my breasts too![2]

In this regard, Violet says, "It was common for them to treat the accused in such manners just to see how much it would affect her. They talked in a way that made you think they were on your side. They tried to instil passion in you, speak calmly and warmly. Then they would assess the responses."[3]

Although Parvaneh Alizadeh was not considered young in comparison to the average age of the other prisoners, she says that her older age did not help her feel less scared of rape. Naturally, younger girls were more fearful of rape when placed in a similar environment. Young female prisoners feared rape even after they were released.

Kobra Bane'i, a supporter of *Komala*, recalls that two of her ward mates who lost consciousness due to heavy torture, for years after they were released and before they got married, feared that they might have been raped and had not realize it. Given the

[1] Witness Testimony of Nazli Partovi, Justice For Iran.
[2] Witness Testimony of Parvaneh Alizadeh, Justice For Iran.
[3] Witness Testimony of Violet, Justice For Iran.

value placed on a woman's virginity such fear is real obstacle for women's political participation. In one of those cases, the women's entire family stood behind the bride and groom's marriage chamber for hours after the wedding to ensure no rape had occurred in prison and see the blood stain handkerchief after the intercourse that indicates she was a virgin.[1] Such demining stories indicate the kind of cultural pressure placed on women. In many ways even fear of rape seems to be a collective punishment as it implicates her family and other women in society. Female prisoners were struggling with such pressures while in prison as well as after their release.

Using Vulgar Terminology and Sexual Insults

Even though, conventionally, men were expected not to use vulgar words in front of women, Farkhondeh Ashna says, "From the moment of your entry, all you heard was vulgarities."[2]

The majority of the witnesses were unwilling to reproduce the exact terminology they heard used by the prison authorities, which was an indication of the degree to which the terminology still bothered them. Eventually some of them told us the phrases that were used.

Nasrin Parvaz says, "Before my interrogator knew how old I was, he called me "Student kid!" I was 22 but looked much younger. After two days he asked and I told him my age. Then he called me "whore."[3]

Farkhondeh Ashna speaks of the atmosphere dominating her interrogations at Evin prison: "For example they said, "These filth! These who have slept with everyone." Or when they throw you on the ground and you complain about your *chador* falling off, they say, "Oh! All of a sudden *hijab* is important? But when you are in team houses with boys, no problem!"[4]

Sara Raha'ee who was interrogated at Evin says, "They told me that they knew I was a whore. I said I was married. They

---

[1] Witness Testimony of Kobra Bane'i, Justice For Iran.
[2] Witness Testimony of Farkhondeh Ashna, Justice For Iran.
[3] Witness Testimony of Nasrin Parvaz, Justice For Iran.
[4] Witness Testimony of Farkhondeh Ashna, Justice For Iran.

pointed out that it was an organizational marriage. I said that many people came to my wedding even my father in law and they said, "Even your father in law said that you are a whore..."[1]

Mitra Tahami, detained in 1983 at Tehran Joint Committee for supporting the *Tudeh* Party, says, "They cursed like a sailor. Like 'pimp', 'cuckold' and 'worthless'. These were commonplace. My interrogator called me worthless as if it was my last name. He wouldn't call me without adding that to the end of the sentence."[2]

Mehri Elghaspour had a similar experience in Sahra *Komiteh* of Ahvaz: "The interrogator said, "You are a bunch of prostitutes. Plus, how do we know that your child belongs to your husband? You guys don't believe in such things! Is this your husband's kid? You live in a team house." When I was arrested in my mother's home, a few of our friends were there too. He said that I may have had relations with them as well!"[3]

When speaking of the actors and agents of sexual insults and verbal abuse, the witnesses use the plural tense to refer to them. Although they were blindfolded while being subject to verbal sexual harassment, from the sounds and behaviour, the witnesses are certain that there were two or even more men in the interrogation room, all of them sharing the usage of vulgar terminology. Therefore, much of the verbal sexual harassment was inflicted by a group of actors. Mahshid Mojaverian who was arrested and detained along with her mother and sister Mitra- who was later arrested and executed- tells a story of verbal abuse by a group of officials, when she was 18 and her sister was 20:

> It was June 1981. My father was arrested by *Sepah*. We were arrested in a demonstration and my father had come after us. They released us but kept my father. We went after him to Sepah, my mother, Mitra and I. There, Mitra and I got into an argument with the *pasdars*. They ordered our arrest, so the three of us were thrown in a truck to be sent to Vakil Abad

---

[1] Witness Testimony of Sara Raha'ee, Justice For Iran.
[2] Witness Testimony of Mitra Tahami, Justice For Iran. Although their meaning are not so vulgar in English translation, the insults are considered to be of vulgar nature in Persian, and not used in polite society or in the presence of women.
[3] Witness Testimony of Mehri Elghaspour, Justice For Iran.

Prison. We were in the back of the truck with around 10 *pasdars*. These men spewed the lewdest sexual insults at my sister. My sister was tall and beautiful… the worse sexual insults… "We'll come and do you"… "She's great for putting out"… or they talked about her breasts and other things. Very lewd things. I was young and had never heard such things. Their words were filthy. My mother passed out right there when they said "she is great for putting out her …" My sister and I kept slapping her until she came to. When she did she called my sister's name, "Mitra! Mitra!" like she really thought they did something to Mitra. I was very worried that they will rape her too. I was very worried for her. All my attention was with my mother who had passed out and Mitra was no longer listening but they listed every single body part of Mitra and she was wearing a manteau too! This took 45 minutes to an hour because there is a long distance between *Sepah* Prison and Vakil Abad Prison in Mashhad. They transferred us to Vakil Abad and finger printed us and other things.[1]

The barrage of sexual insults and vulgar terminology intended to be little and psychologically break their spirit was sometimes so intense that the prisoner could not withstand it. Zahra Zolfaghari's ward mates state that she was subject to such a horrifying degree of verbal sexual harassment that she committed suicide after being released from prison. Others say that she had a cardiac arrest while hospitalized for mental illness.[2] Farkhondeh Ashna says, "The girls who were imprisoned during the Shah's time or were arrested in team houses were insulted even more than the rest of prisoners. I remember when a *pasdar* came in the ward to call Zahra Zolfaghari, he said, "That tall whore should come out." They were always calling her with terrible names and belittling and ridiculing her. She responded and got in a scuffle with them too."[3]

---

[1] Witness Testimony of Mahshid Mojaverian, Justice For Iran.
[2] "Biography of a Classmate" September 18, 2009, available at: http://shivaf.blogspot.co.uk/2009/09/blog-post.html
[3] Witness Testimony of Farkhondeh Ashna, Justice For Iran.

Zahra Zolfaghari was born in Kazeroun. She obtained a degree of petrochemical engineering in 1975 from Ariamehr University. She was a supporter of *Peykar* organization and had worked with *Mojahedin-e Khalq* prior to the revolution. When various political organizations collaborated against the Shah's regime, apparently her commitment to political participation and probably her degree in a

Zahra Zolfaghari

primarily male educational domain made her even more subject to sexual harassment. Witnesses state that she was repeatedly and continuously subject to verbal sexual harassments and insults by wardens and interrogators. Many witnesses believe that the main reason for her distress was the demeaning manner of her treatment: "They had told her at interrogation, "They did you from behind in the team houses. Here we'll use a wood!" Zahra could answer their insults well. Because they could not defeat her politically, they were using insults and curses."[1]

In the drawing provided by Soudabeh Ardavan, the woman with black stockings is Zahra who had returned from the bath and was unwell due to dealing with the pasdars.[2]

Use of Demeaning Speech

Women who turned to political activism in the events that led to the 1979 revolution and the months following it comprised a diverse group. The diversity existed in the variety of organizations women had joined as well as the methods of their contact and activism with those organizations. Some women had

[1] Witness Testimony of Farkhondeh Ashna, Justice For Iran.
[2] Soudabeh Ardavan, Prison Memoirs, 2004, P. 61.

joined political organizations independently. Other women joined organizations because of family ties where their brother, sister or husband were already members our research shows that some organizations, such as the *Mojahedin-e Khalq* and *Peykar*, had more 'familial support' than others, such as the *Fadaian-e Khalq*. Even though the gender-blindness of the political organizations was a point of contention amongst the feminists of the time, an undeniable result of such political activism was that it inspired the creation of an independent identity amongst the young female members of these organizations. In fact, these young women felt that the organizations treated them as humans, not just women. In their organizational work, most of them felt a newfound identity, independence and autonomy.[1]

Under those circumstances, one of the most painful forms of sexual harassment inflicted on women in prisons was to deny their independent identity and consider them as appendage of their male folks. One that they could do without except for sexual services. Our research shows that reducing the value of female political prisoner to that of an item to relieve men's sexual needs was a prevalent theme in prisons across Iran. Some of the witnesses consider such talk more painful than being lashed. These talks and lack of recognition that women have acted as independent political agent and present their entry into politics an excuse to meet men and find a husband and yet worse other interrogators considered women entry into political organizations merely in order to relieve men's sexual desires. Monireh Baradaran says,

> Being a woman there was of dualistic nature. On the one hand you are their political enemy, just like men. On the other, in Islam and in the opinion of the fundamentalists you are a woman, a weakling and do not have the right to oppose them politically. For this reason, while being interrogated in court, suddenly you are asked if you are divorced and then belittled for it. You have engaged in political activities that might lead to your death sentence and yet they stoop you so low and transform your

---

[1] One Hundred Years of Pleasure, Sexuality and Power, Shadi Amin, available at: http://www.shabakeh.de/archives/individual/001199.html#more.

from a political enemy, into a woman conforming to their Islamic vision of woman, a sexual object. They didn't want to accept that we were their political enemies. You feel demeaned, alone. They hollow you from within.[1]

Shokat Mohammadi says,

They look at you as a slut, a whore, a woman who has been handed around a thousand times. I was willing to be lashed a thousand times but not hear such words. They would say, "So your issue was men! How many times did you sleep with them? Did you really go hiking or…? Filth! Garbage! Lewd!" This was normal for them. I was very young at that time and considered the circles I was with to be holy. The people I was with I had even slept next to in a room with 4 girls and 10 boys. They were idols to me, mythical creatures. I am not saying everything was so holy but at least what was between us was very pure. Maybe one of us liked or even loved the other. Even expressing it was difficult for us. It was even taboo for us for a guy to express his love to a girl…[2]

Parvaneh Alizadeh says,

They called us jambon [cold cut] in a sandwich [like you sleep between two men]. Or tell us that we were in the team houses to relieve men. If I would say that I had done nothing and was a Muslim to evade harassment, they would respond that when I was in the team house I was sleeping with ten men and now I remembered that I was a Muslim! This was something they told us leftist girls. In their view, we entered politics solely to relieve men sexually. They didn't even look at us as a political person.[3]

Tahmineh Pegah further affirms the widespread demeaning treatment of women:

---

[1] Witness Testimony of Monireh Baradaran, Justice For Iran.
[2] Witness Testimony of Shokat Mohammadi, Justice For Iran.
[3] Witness Testimony of Parvaneh Alizadeh, Justice For Iran.

In the opinion of the interrogators, we were the second sex because men told us what to do in the organizational structure; that we had independent opinions as individuals was not taken seriously by them. Their behaviour was basically that we should be ashamed of our femininity. This really bothered us. We were defined in relation to a man, a political man. For example if someone was married they would tell her that she wasn't really up for it to go into such political directions and her husband was the cause of it; therefore, she should hate him. Or to someone like myself who was young and unmarried they would say that the tomcats of the organization pulled me in. They saw us as an attachment to these men. And when we argued and defended our opinion and opined on things, we were 'crazy women'. Basically they could not digest the existence of a woman with political opinion. So a compounded pressure was that in prison they had the ultimate power and the women were in their hands to be demeaned for being a woman.[1]

Niloufar Shirzadi described Ghezel Hesar prison, under the management of Haji Davoud Rahmani, as significantly more demeaning than Evin Prison:

When I entered Ghezel Hesar I experienced a thuggish mentality that was not even about political issues, but other matters! He didn't even look at me as an anti-revolutionary or a corruptor. During our first contact with Haji Davoud Rahmani, as the representative of that culture in prison, it was declared that we were a group that were looking for husbands and wanted to satisfy the sexual desires of our male comrades in team houses. He easily told us many times that we wanted to get married. That little respect we had in Evin where they would recognize us [as activists], we were not recognized here[2].

---

[1] Witness Testimony of Tahmineh Pegah, Justice For Iran.
[2] Witness Testimony of Niloufar Shirzar, Justice For Iran.

Not recognizing women's political identity was not limited to single women; Mona Roshan was arrested alongside her husband while pregnant. She says,

> The first time they took me for torture I told them that I was pregnant. In a demeaning manner, the interrogator said, "Oooh you are pregnant? You should have thought about that when you entered this field. Why do you women even enter politics? Don't you have a home life? How did your parents raise you? How did your cuckold good-for-nothing husband permit you to enter such activities? You all lived in team houses…" and other such insults that basically said that women should not be entering politics. That this was not our field and our place was at home. They aimed to crush our personality.[1]

Demeaning women political activists did not only occur in the interrogation chambers. It was also done through orchestrated shows inside of the prison as well as spreading certain rumors and gossip outside. Tahmineh Pegah recalls the pressures Haji Davoud Rahmani placed on women between 1981 and 1984. One such pressure was to have them talk to other prisoners about their sexual experience with men in their organization:

> Haji had an exceptional sensitivity to crush the girls. A group of the girls went insane while in the 'graves'. It was very painful. Others would give in and repent and Haji would have them give interviews. He insisted on these interviews, less for men though. For women, he wanted them to talk about their relationships with men. Because in this manner they would be crushed and could never hold their heads high again. This method worked to some degree as well. We were in the wards and *tavvabs* would have us listen to the interviews. The interviews were very painful.

> One woman was from Kurdistan, a young woman who probably had never seen Tehran or a big city with the wider range of relations. She came from a

---

[1] Witness Testimony of Mona Roshan, Justice For Iran.

traditional city and when she would repent Haji wanted her to speak of sexual relations. She would lie and say that there were always birth control pills available in the bases in Kurdistan because there were few men to many women and they wanted sexual relation. Haji would pull them towards that issue because he knew once the girl goes back to Kurdistan she can't look anyone in the eyes again. She is crushed in her own society and will never again become a member in a combating group. This never happened to men. Women were coming from a society with traditional pressures in their core and Haji could keep those pressures alive.[1]

Insisting that politically active women were merely sexual objects was propagated in different ways even outside the prison. For example, the biography of women sentenced to execution for political reasons published in the governmental newspapers, insisted that aside from their illegal political activities, they committed illicit affairs or 'actions against morals and chastity'.

For instance, Ettelaat Newspaper of December 22, 1981 published a news titled, "17 Royalist and Coup Organizers were Executed."[2] Part of the news says,

Golnaz Naghib Manesh, as per her explicit confession, had illicit sexual affair with an active member of the group; she has an illegitimate 11-month old child.

On October 18, 1981, Ettelaat Newspaper had published another article titled "27 Armed *Muharib* Were Shot to Death in 5 Cities."[3] In this article, while describing the crimes of two female *Mojahedin-e Khalq* members who were executed in Amol and Khorramabad, the newspaper defines team houses and "nests of corruption and prostitution", considering membership in them one of the crimes of those executed.

Demeaning the active role of women and stooping it to the level of someone servicing the needs of men in political organizations disrespected those women and discredited a lot of female

---

[1] Witness Testimony of Tahmineh Pegah, Justice For Iran.
[2] Ettelaat Newspaper, December 22, 1981, No. 16607.
[3] Ettelaat Newspaper, October 18, 1981, No. 16553.

activism in the eyes of Iranian families and society as a whole. In the cultural context of Iran where any relation between men and women is always scrutinized, publicizing such t language can create a serious obstacle for women's political participation in the future. This was a very conscious and intentional effect of news stories that accused women political activists of sexual promiscuity in team house, thereby asserting that female political activists spread corruption and prostitution. Such reports in the major mass media strengthened the image propagated by the regime, that politically active women lacked initiative and autonomy or a political identity.

Touching the Woman's Body during Torture

Lashing or whipping with cables was one of the most prevalent forms of torture of political prisoners in the 1980s. This method was so common that to a large extent, when the political prisoners speak of 'torture' they mean being lashed.

In this method of torture, a prisoner is usually laid on a bed with her hands and feet tied and she is lashed with a cable on the soles of her feet and in some cases on other parts of her body. Due to the intense and, as prisoners say, 'indescribable' pain of this type of torture, the prisoner usually struggles to release herself or her body inadvertently jumps up and down. To prevent the moving of the prisoner's body, usually one of the interrogators would sit on the female prisoners' waist. Meanwhile, many witnesses describe that to prevent hearing the screams of the prisoner while she was being lashed, usually a kerchief or a piece of foam or similar item was stuffed in the prisoners' mouth. In such cases the female prisoner fully felt the body of the male tortures on top of her and her feeling of shame and anger intensified her pain of torture. Other than in a few exceptional cases, there were never any women present while the female prisoners were being tortured.

According to prison authorities in the 1980s, lashing, or *ta'zir*, was a permissible sentence and punishment as per *shari'a*, by opinion of the religious magistrate. This likely contributed to the fact that despite receiving 3620 complaints of torture in 1981, the official investigating committee dismissed complaints of lashing completely.[1] In fact, amongst the criticisms that Hoja-tolislam Khalkhali leveled against President Bani Sadr in order to demonstrate Bani Sadr's lack of competence was that Bani Sadr considers *ta'zir* performed by the Islamic Revolutionary Courts as a form of torture.[2] Clearly, the regime supported lashing. That the committee stated all 3620 complaints were completely un-founded belies the superficial nature of the 'investigation' to be-gin with.

In recounting her experience, Mojdeh Arasi says,

> They took me to the basement of [Ward 209 of Evin]. They said that I have to lie on the wooden bed. I had only a skirt and socks on, under my *cha-dor*. I said, "What does this mean? Just like this? They said that they would cover me with a blanket. I had no opinion about this and couldn't imagine what would happen when I am lying down and a blanket is covering me. They laid me face down on the bed and tied my hands with wires. When they were lashing me the wires that were tied very tight hurt me more than the lashing... I don't know what happened but I jumped around half a meter to one meter. Nothing could cover me then, blanket, skirt, nothing. If I was wearing anything other than pants, it wouldn't help. Then I felt like they were calling each other and showing me to one another while they beat me. I accepted to lie on the bed because I thought he'll throw a blanket on me and it'll be fine. I really had no idea what would happen. From the way they laughed and called one another and then became silent I realized that they were looking at me... I was jumping involuntarily. Then one of them came and sat on me. He sat backward on my waist. He opened his feet and sat, like he was sitting on a bike. He held my mouth too from the back be-cause I was screaming... a religious man is sitting on your back, holding your mouth while they are

---

[1] Plan of Bani Sadr's Lack of Competence in Majlis June 20, 1981; Kahlkhali: He Calls Ta'zir in the Revolutionary Courts Torture!, Islamic Revolution Website, available at:
http://www.ical.ir/index.php?option=com_mashrooh&view=session&id=187&page=3051&Itemid=38
[2] Ibid.

lashing you. After the torture ended on the first night, I couldn't even get up, I couldn't walk. I couldn't even hold myself up. Then that same person was telling me to fix my *chador* and observe my *hijab*! He was sitting on my back two minutes ago and now he was saying that I should cover myself. Then he gave me a pen [so that he didn't have to touch my hand].[1]

In fact, while transferring prisoners who were blindfolded the rule of not touching a stranger was fully observed. Yet when it came to interrogation and torture, the rule was disregarded and broken.

Nasrin Parvaz has a similar experience of her torture at Evin:

> The first interrogator, who was beating me, while my hands were tied, would sit on me so that he was in the curve of my back. I was laid down. My hands were tied. He was beating me and when he got tired he would give the lash to someone else and come and sit on me in a way that his waist would fall in the curve of my back. Or as I was lying down, he would stand next to me and stick to my body, put his hand on my back and smoke his cigarettes.[2]

Tahmineh Pegah speaks of her experience in November of 1982 at Joint Committee detention centre:

> I remember once after torture I could not even hold my head up. The torturer himself took me to the wall and told me to jump on my feet so that the swelling calms a bit and I would be prepared for the next beating. This was an opportunity provided for the torturer to be alone with me. I remember that he would stick his body to mine while I stood next to the wall. My back was to the wall and I was facing the torturer. He was telling me to jump but I had no energy. I could not hold my head up. I was confused but felt that he was sticking his body to

[1] Witness Testimony of Mojdeh Arasi, Justice For Iran.
[2] Witness Testimony of Nasrin Parvaz, Justice For Iran.

mine. His excuse was that other prisoners who pass by should not see me. Either way I was blindfolded and that was not necessary. I thought of this later on.[1]

Sitting on the waist or buttocks of the female prisoner was a method employed in 1983 at the Joint Committee detention centre.[2]

While some prisoners believe that the pain of having the interrogator touch them was not worse than the lashing, Shokat Mohammadi who had similar experiences at Evin says,

> After the torture one of the *pasdars* came and sat on my feet. He was feeling my body. I felt like my feet were flaming ovens. Very easily, one of them came and sat a little lower on my thighs. He was talking to the other one. This was very ordinary to them. I however felt terrible. I had rather that they torture me but not sit on my thighs. Even if they torture me again. This really bothered me a lot. It was different. For me it was very special. I was willing to be beaten but not touched. It was very disgusting to me and much harder than torture.[3]

Mojdeh Arasi speaks of the compounded torment women feel while being lashed as:

> The fact that you have to pay attention to so many things, don't give any information, don't tell on anyone, don't act political, and yet protect your body and sexuality as a woman, that we had to be more afraid and worried when facing them. This was really difficult.[4]

Physical contact between interrogators and female prisoners while torturing them was not exclusive to Tehran prisons. Sanam Ahmadi speaks of her experience from Seyyed Ali Khan detention centre of Isfahan that was under the command of *Sepah*. She

---

[1] Witness Testimony of Tahmineh Pegah, Justice For Iran.
[2] Witness Testimony of Mitra Tahami, Justice For Iran.
[3] Witness Testimony of Shokat Mohammadi, Justice For Iran.
[4] Witness Testimony of Mojdeh Arasi, Justice For Iran.

recounts a case of group torture where a female *pasdar* was involved as well:

> I was sitting when a man came and pulled both my legs as if I was a sheep. My butt hit something and I felt like he is tying me down tightly as when they take a sheep somewhere. He hit me to the ground and even my tailbone hurt. I asked what he was doing. He told me to shut up and not make a noise. I asked again what they were doing. He said, "nothing, we want to caress you a bit." Then he said, "see these, touch them. This has business with you." He was laughing as if this was a joke. He gave it to me and I realized that it was something like a cable. He asked which one I like and wanted to be caressed with. He was holding two things. I didn't even want to touch it but he kept putting my hand on it and telling me to touch it. I realized one was thicker than the other one. I was laying face up. When he hit me the first time I was shocked. The pain is more intense when you are angry too. I always worked out and was in shape. I would struggle so hard until one of the *pasdars* kicked me in the chest and I spread across the floor. He put his foot on my breast and was pressing and moving it around. He was massaging my breast with his boots. My breast with his military boots! It was years since I got my period but my breast were always very sensitive and he was pressing on them with his feet. I couldn't do anything. My hands were tied too. I couldn't move but could fully understand that he was enjoying this. He put his feet on my breast and enjoyed it because he could do that! In fact, he was showing me that when he can put his feet there, he could put it anywhere. It hurt so much that… well it is painful! I struggled hard. I have softer bones and so I was flipping and turning. The *pasdar* had his foot on my chest and turned it and I kept getting on. The *pasdar* insulted me, called me a whore and said, "Look she got me up!" I was pressing so hard that although he was putting all his might on my chest with one foot,

I was trying to get out of the pressure. I was turning and remember that my head hit his other foot. I could hear them laughing and heard a female *pasdar* speaking.

One of them, a female *pasdar* [I realized from the movements of her hands on my face that she was a woman] brought something like a blanket or a cloth or something to put in my mouth because I was screeching and I am sure it was very staggering. I always had a loud voice. She stuffed them in my mouth and then laughed. She was short and I think dark skinned. I don't know how long it took and how long they beat me but it was humorous for them. I don't think that it was real torture. They just wanted to say that they could do that [rape][1] with me as well. Their demeaning behaviour was the worst part. That he put his foot on my breast. And why am I saying this? The reason is, for one, they never asked while torturing me to confess to anything. No such talks. It was as if they brought me to show me that they had the power to torture me and harass me even if I have nothing to say. The one beating me, as if he hadn't beaten enough people, was frustrated and angry and was using vulgar insults. He opened my legs and said that we were all raped in the team houses. I wasn't focusing on their words but on that I was in pain and couldn't scream anymore. It was as if he wanted to enforce his power on me and control me. He was calling me 'mother fucker' and other terms I do not recall. But I remember that they were all sexually vulgar. Eastern men always attack in a sexual manner because I think in this way they get the result they want. He was complaining about my struggling. He opened my legs and I was still on the floor when he kicked me from behind so hard that I lifted in the air. I wasn't very light either, around 64 kilos. I was athletic and all muscles. I sat on my two feet and he

---

[1] In their testimonies, female prisoners use words such as "that thing" or "this thing" or "any malady" to refer to rape.

kicked me between my legs so hard that I was flying and fell from one end to another. I fell on my hand because my hands were cuffed still and I remember that my shoulder dislocated. I bled so much from this blow. Wonder how he did it. How is it physically possible to lift someone off the ground with one kick, I wonder! I don't know what condition I was in that he was able to lift me. To be thrown from one corner to another with one kick from a boot. I don't know how long I was there but I could no longer scream. I couldn't speak any more. Later I realized that I had bled. I was sweating a lot and had not realized the bleeding. It was cool but because the room was closed in I was hot. Also, intensity can cause sweating. I felt like I was so nervous that I came down with a fever. I was there for a bit… and then one of them, a woman came and asked me to get up. I felt like I was shaking from within… I was shivering and yet sweating and had a fever and was bleeding.[1]

At the time of her arrest, Mona Roshan was the only female prisoner of *Sepah* detention centre in Karaj. She narrates how she was tied to a bed while pregnant. A male *pasdar* also sat on her waist. According to her narrative, at least three men were in the room and the torture that included touching of her waist, face and other body parts was committed in front of them and with their collaboration:

The day after I was arrested they took me for torturing. They wouldn't touch me when they took me because I am a stranger to them. They would give me one end of a pencil or a shoe or a kerchief and the *pasdar* held the other end so that our hands would not touch. He took me a long distance; the detention centre was a confiscated house of a wealthy man from Karaj. He took me like that into the yard for a long distance and we entered another place. There were two rooms; the first had table and chairs for interrogation and the second had a stor-

---

[1] Witness Testimony of Sanam Ahmadi, Justice For Iran.

age room. It was the torture chamber. They took me there. I was telling them I was pregnant and they responded to me with insults and demeaning phrases. They started to tie me to the bed, my hands and feet. Then he started lashing me. I was screaming and wiggling around. He sat slanted in the curve of my back and tried to hold my face with his hands because I was screaming and struggling. He couldn't but kept trying to touch my face and I only screamed. He shoved something like a handkerchief in my mouth and continued the lashing. Another two were standing as I recall and were counting and chanting '*Allah u Akbar*', '*Ya Zahra*' and '*Ya Hossein*'. One of them was sitting on me and the other two standing and lashing me. While they were lashing me, the one who sat on me played with my leg and scratched it. When they lash a person too many times the leg becomes numb so he was scratching my leg with his pen to circulate the blood and take away the numbness so I feel the lashing. They lashed me 70 or so times. I felt like I was passing out and couldn't breathe well because of the handkerchief in my mouth. I was struggling and he was sitting on me trying to grab my hands. Then one of them noted that I was no longer making any noise and that they should let me go. And they did. He took out the handkerchief. I was really passing out because I couldn't even breathe anymore. He let me go and untied me. I sat there and they didn't even offer me water or anything.

A short time passed and then they said that I should stand and walk. I couldn't walk and felt like my feet had swollen and gotten very large. One of them came and held my hand without a kerchief or anything else. I thought then that they suddenly didn't care about not touching a stranger woman! In the interrogation chamber none of these mattered. I think it was all talk because they observed it in one place and didn't care about it in another. He grabbed my hand and was pulling me to make me walk. I was walking like a person walking on nails or broken glass. Every time I put my foot down, I felt like I was stepping on needles and broken glass each time. I was screaming and making a lot of noise but he kept forcing me to walk. Then they took me to the cell... insults and belittling was a daily routine. Especially because I was pregnant. He said that I didn't think of my baby, and if I had such [political] aspirations why did I even get pregnant, and a bunch of other vulgar insults that I really can't recall. But I do remember that as my first interaction in prison, especially since I wasn't familiar with the prison environment, the insults really hurt me a lot... and when he touched my face. Because he could not do it! My eyes were closed but his were not. He could put the handkerchief in my mouth directly. That he tried to touch me, my face, my body, my legs, and that he was sitting on my waist really bothered me.[1]

Shahin Chitsaz had a considerably worse experience, "At least three men were beating me and taking turn in doing so. They insulted me and used words such as 'whore'. One of them would sit on my back. Once when the interrogator was sitting on my buttocks I felt his hard member. It bothered me a lot."[2]

Although it is unclear the degree to which the interrogators took sexual pleasure from touching the prisoners' bodies, the contacts instill a feeling of torment due to being unwantedly touched. In the course of our research, we discovered that sitting on the back of the prisoner was also common practice in the case of male prisoners, in order to keep them immobile while lashing them. But the social atmosphere surrounding the relationship of men and women in Iranian society, as well as the prison authorities' view of women, makes all the difference when the same act is performed on the female prisoners.

As discussed, not only was the prison atmosphere very affected by the sexual separation derived from *shari'a* based principles governing the relations between men and women, but also

---

[1] Witness Testimony of Mona Roshan, Justice For Iran.
[2] Witness Testimony of Shahin Chitsaz, Justice For Iran.

the women belonged to a society in which not a lot of physical contact existed between men and women outside of the framework of family and in some cases close friends. In fact, such contacts were frowned upon. Also, in the predominant Iranian culture, any form of contact between any unrelated man and woman is considered a sexual violation. In such a culture, even if sitting on the body of the woman was necessary for the torture, for young women experiencing it, due to their mental pretext as well as the sexualized atmosphere in the prisons, the act was nothing but sexual harassment.

Battering Female Genital Areas

Striking the genital organs is an expression we have used to describe a series of tortures female prisoners describe as 'kicking between the legs' or 'kicking the buttock' or 'kicking to the backside'.

In the process of researching this report, we encountered various witness testimonies regarding the striking of women's genital areas at several Iranian prisons, particularly in Isfahan and also Evin prison of Tehran.[1] However, it appears that more research needs to be done to assess how widespread the use of such a violent method of torture was- one that at times caused tearing in the womb, heavy bleeding, and even the death of foetuses in the womb- and whether or not it was common in prisons of different cities.

Results of our research shows that at least at Ghezel Hesar prison, where a large number of female prisoners were being kept, striking the genital area was indeed a common method of torture and punishment. In September of 1981, a few months after the start of widespread arrests of political activists across Iran, since most small cities did not have a women's ward, the female prisoners of those cities were moved to Ghezel Hesar prison on the outskirts of Karaj, near Tehran. Most of those women had been tried and sentenced to imprisonment in their respective cities and had been transferred to Ghezel Hesar from the *Sepah* and *Komiteh* detention centres of those cities.

---

[1] Witness Testimony of Sanam Ahmadi, Justice For Iran; Witness Testimony of Soudabeh Ardavan, Justice For Iran.

Although no detailed statistics exist on the number of women who were imprisoned in Ghezel Hesar between 1981 and 1985, based on the descriptions provided by our interviewees it can be estimated that an average of over 500 women were held in various wards of Ghezel Hesar.

Haji Davoud Rahmani, who between summer of 1981 and July 1984 was head of Ghezel Hesar Prison by order of Asadollah Lajevardi, had absolute power in torturing political prisoners in that prison. He employed many different methods of torture, some of which were unique in their form and extensive execution.[1]

Haji Davoud Rahmani

Haji Davoud was described by the female prisoners to be a heavy set man with large hands And feet. Female prisoners say that he personally, as well as in collaboration with other male employees of Ghezel Hesar prison, repeatedly struck blows to the genital areas of female prisoners, while also using other forms of torture and verbal harassment.

Farzaneh Zolfi, a 16-year old student, was transferred from a detention centre in Masjed Soleiman to Ghezel Hesar in mid-August 1981, with a three-year imprisonment sentence for supporting the Communist Union of Iran. She says:

> It was September 1981. We small city girls were just taken there. We were around 300 to 400 people. There was a long corridor that separated the wards from one another. It was so long that they travelled it with a bicycle. They took us there and said that we had to crawl that length on our chests... there were old mothers with heart problem amongst us. There was also a nine year-old girl names Fatemeh. But they said no one is exempt. They said that we had to crawl the whole length of the way and then return. While we were crawling and had no energy left, seven or eight *pasdars* constantly kicked us between

---

[1] See this link for more information regarding serious violations of human rights inflicted upon the female political prisoners by Haj Davoud Rahmani:
http://justiceforiran.org/human-rights-violators-individuals-databank/hajdavud/?lang=en

our legs with their boots. I bled and others did too. There were not enough sanitary pads for everyone. Fatemeh got her first period there… as I speak of it now I feel the pain in my body… imagine, over 300 women crawling on the floor of a corridor with *chadors* and blindfolds and they kicked the ones who were left behind and told them to hurry up and move ahead. They constantly kicked us between our legs with their boots and called us shrews or other such insults. It was the first time I was hearing such insults! Haj Ahmad, deputy of Haji Davoud, was one of the people who yelled insults. We had to move so fast to reach the beginning of the line because if we were left behind they would hit us again. The mother I spoke of and many other girls had pain in their chests.[1]

Farzaneh Zolfi also recalls Mina Toudeh Rousta, one of the girls who was beaten a lot during the crawls and was executed a few days later:

The day after, they made us stand and forced insomnia on us. Forcing insomnia was a regular thing they did and was really effective. The girls all had psychological episodes… Haji Davoud would get stuck on some of the girls. That day he came and started bothering Mina Toudeh Rousta and another person. Imagine, a group of us were on this side of the ward and another group on the other side, standing next to the cells. Haji Davoud called Mina Toudeh Rousta and brought her to the middle and started kicking her backside and buttocks. Mina Toudeh Rousta had bulging buttocks even from under the manteau [because we were inside the ward] and she was not wearing a *chador*. The next day they said that she should collect her stuff and leave. Later we heard she was executed while she only had an imprisonment sentence for one year… the other girl that Haji Davoud kicked a lot on the buttocks that day had a beautiful face and body and

---

[1] Witness Testimony of Farzaneh Zolfi, Justice For Iran.

was amongst the girls who, due to their beauty, were subject to extra violent abuse by Haji Davoud.[1]

Mina Toudeh Rousta, a *Mojahedin-e Khalq* supporter and a teacher in one of the villages of Karaj, was 21 at the time of her arrest. Farzaneh Zolfi describes her as a calm and timid girl. According to information available at the Boroumand Foundation website, she was executed by a firing squad in Karaj on September 3, 1981. No information is available about her trial and the charges against her.

Forcing prisoners to crawl and striking blows to their genital organs was not limited to the aforementioned incident. Niloufar Shirzadi was a student supporter of *Peykar* and was sent from Evin to Ghezel Hesar for the remainder of her 2.5 years sentence. She says:

> If there was an attempt on the life of anyone outside the prison, we knew they would come for us the night of it. The girls would pack their [crotch] with all the scarves and extra fabrics they had. We knew that [Haji Davoud] would take us to crawl and then hit us from behind. He would hit us here [in the crotch area]. We would crawl the length of the unit all the way to *zir-e hasht* and yet still get beaten. They hit us with chains, gun muzzles, sticks, and cables as well as kicking us. Some of the *pasdars* would even put their feet on our feet to stop us from moving and then beat us, saying that we were lagging behind. A group of the girls who were physically incapable of keeping up with the rest were beaten more so than others… I was personally hit a few times from behind… then in order to not get beaten you had to move faster than your friend who was crawling next to you and yet you knew that she would get beaten once you got ahead of her… this incident [of beating the genital organ] was so intertwined with other tortures, so tied to one another that we could not even pull them apart, mostly due to the pain it inflicted and the scary amount of

[1] Witness Testimony of Farzaneh Zolfi, Justice For Iran.

stress we were under. All we could do was to try as
hard as we could to bear it and not break… we were
never given the chance [to properly analyze the mat-
ter].[1]

*Drawing of Souda-
beh Ardavan based
on a sketch she drew
on one of the 'endless
nights' and redrew it
outside of prison.*

Another common form of punishment at Ghezel Hesar
Prison was being forced to stand and stay awake facing the wall
while wearing a *chador* and blindfolds. Soudabeh Ardavan who
was arrested for supporting the *Fadaian-e Khalq* (Minority) was
moved to Ghezel Hesar from Evin prison in 1981 for her two-
year sentence. They later added three more years to her sentence,
and an additional 2 years and 6 months for refusing to give an
interview. She is also an artist who drew prison life while she was
kept with other women. She speaks of the 'endless nights' at
Ghezel Hesar prison, where female prisoners were beaten and
forced to stay awake:

> 'Endless nights' was an expression Haji [Davoud
> Rahmani] himself used. The story goes that Soheila

---

[1] Witness Testimony of Niloufar Shirzadi, Justice For Iran.

Hajizadeh, a *tavvab* in charge of ward 8, was holding the confiscated crafts and personal items of female prisoners in her room. So the girls [prisoners] had taken them back. Haji came and asked, "Who did this?" and naturally no one said anything. So Haji took everyone to the long corridor that connected the wards to each other and made us stand with our *chadors* and blindfolds facing the wall. Along with a few other *pasdars*, he started beating us. They would beat us with whatever they could get their hands on. Haji said that these nights are endless. They kept insulting and beating us until they would leave around 3-4 am when they were out of breath from beating us. We would spread right there on the cold floor of the corridor out of pain and exhaustion. This punishment continued for ten nights until the prison wardens got tired of it![1]

Sometimes, prisoners were not allowed to approach the wall in order to rest a little.[2] Monireh Baradaran says:

It was 1983 and they punished us a lot. On many nights, they would take us and stand us up. At times it would extend into days. They would make some of the girls stand for 2-3 days. We know how hard it was; your back ached and you got very tired and wanted to lean against the wall or put your head on the wall. It was so severe that our tiredness would be relieved even if we would put one finger to the wall. Then if you would approach the wall even a little- the guards who were wearing sneakers so as to prevent you from hearing their footsteps- would suddenly kick you… However, Haji [Davoud Rahmani] wore military boots and would enter walking from the beginning of the corridor and making fun of the prisoners. Then he would suddenly kick someone. Haji's kicks were famous. He would kick you between the legs from behind and you would lift in the air and fall to the ground. This happened

---

[1] Witness Testimony of Soudabeh Ardavan, Justice For Iran.
[2] Prison Memoirs, Soudabeh Ardavan, P. 46.

to me. Some of the girls would bleed afterwards but I don't recall bleeding.[1]

Parvaneh Alizadeh theorizes that the reason behind the physical tortures and verbal abuses commonly administered to women at Ghezel Hesar prison was that Haji Davoud Rahmani and other prison guards were thugs who considered women to be only suitable for 'sex' and could not accept that women could be their own persons, so they used those methods to belittle them.[2]

However, Farzaneh Zolfi says,

> It is clear to me why they would hit us between the legs. I think that because they are religious, the Islamic Republic has an ideological view of this matter as well. They viewed us as captives and allowed themselves to act towards us in any manner they wished. In essence they considered themselves our owners. According to the *Koran*, it is permissible to rape a war captive… Many times the interrogators who acted violently towards the girls would say, "They are our captives. They are women and we are permitted to rape them."[3]

To sum up: Based on the results of this research, in contrast to what one might expect of an Islamic regime, it can be said that the majority of female political prisoners experienced at least one form of sexual harassment. What this means is that, if we were to rely on the definitions resulting from the decisions of the International Criminal Court, certain forms of sexual torture were inflicted on female political prisoners in a widespread manner. Amongst these was verbal abuse inflicted with the intention of demeaning female political prisoners to the level of a sexual object, and denying her political identity. Many of the women interviewed considered the pain caused by insults to far exceed that of lashing, a serious form of physical torture, as the former questioned their identity as a human being.

---

[1] Witness Testimony of Monireh Baradaran, Justice For Iran.
[2] Indirectly quoting from the Witness Testimony of Parvaneh Alizadeh, Justice For Iran.
[3] Wintess Testimony of Farzaneh Zolfi, Justice For Iran.

However the sexual tortures inside prisons were not limited to verbal insults. Many female political prisoners were placed in conditions where they feared being raped. Some were even threatened with rape. Fear of rape was especially more prominent in prisons where all the personnel, including the wardens, were male. Furthermore, the women's bodies were assaulted in a variety of different ways. Although the Iranian regime's principles of *shari'a* ban any contact between female and male bodies, except in familial or spousal relations, female political prisoners reported that inside interrogation and torture chambers, the torturers and interrogators sat on different parts of the their bodies, particularly their buttocks and waists, while lashing them. These reports were common in prisons across the country.

However, for the first time, this report has uncovered an extraordinarily violent method of torture prevalent at Ghezel Hesar prison, one of the largest and most populated prisons of the 1980s. Haji Davoud Rahmani, head of Gehzel Hesar prison, and other male prison authorities, forcefully kicked female political prisoners between their legs while forcing them to crawl on the floor, or stand facing the wall. The violent kicks caused heavy bleeding in many of the female prisoners. Some of the female prisoners had never before spoken of this form of torture, only recounting it during our interviews. Three decades later, the severe trauma caused by this torture is still present in those who suffered through it.

VI- Pregnancy, Birth and Motherhood in Prison

VI- Pregnancy, Birth and Motherhood in Prison

Gender-based Discrimination

In addition to the diverse and brutal forms of gender-based violence we have explored above, female political prisoners were also subject to a host of other quotidian discriminatory behaviours, simply because they were female. Just as outside the prison walls, women's dress code was a stringent site of control in the prisons and female prisoners were uniformly forced to wear the *chador*. Though a male prison uniform existed, this was hardly enforced, apart from a few exceptional cases. Also, male prisoners who smoked were given a cigarette quota after the completion of their interrogation, investigation and trial. This same quota was not extended to female prisoners, merely due to the fact that prison officials considered smoking to be obscene for women. This situation mildly improved in prisons of Tehran after the visitation of a government committee and the complaints of the female prisoners.

However, the most deplorable case of such forms of discrimination occurred when women would have their monthly menstruation cycle. Being in a male-dominated environment, when many of them would notice the signs of bleeding while in interrogation or torture chambers, or cells guarded by men, they naturally had no choice but to ask the male interrogators or guards for sanitary pads. In response, they faced a whole host of belittling insults spewed at them by the guards, often accompanied by a total or partial deprivation of necessary sanitary products. Monireh Baradaran remembers a young girl who was too embarrassed to ask for a sanitary pad from the male prison guards, and instead had torn her clothes and used a piece of them each time.[1] Sara L. remembers a cell in Tabriz Prison where the female prisoners were held captive by the head of the prison who had no knowledge of feminine matters and refused

---

[1] Witness Testimony of Monireh Baradaran, Justice For Iran.

to give them sanitary pads. According to her, the floor of this cell, as well as the clothing of the prisoners held there, were covered with dried and fresh bloodstains.[1] In other prisons as well, sanitary pads were handed to female prisoners sporadically and much less frequently than needed, and were accompanied with insults and demeaning remarks.[2] Farkhondeh Ashna speaks of a girl who sat next to her in the hallways that led to Evin's Prosecution Office. She was around 14-15 years old and had her period. Farkhondeh who was wearing a blindfold says, "When the interrogator got her up for interrogation, he said loudly, "Ah! She is bleeding like always!" and threw her on the ground. The girls did not make a peep."[3]

Another case of gender-based violence experienced by female prisoners was the torture and harassment of women for what the prison authorities considered 'homosexual behaviour'. Monireh Baradaran speaks of a young girl named Mitra who was lashed in 1981 for having amorous relations with her ward mate Parvin. After severe punishment, the two were separated.[4] Mitra Haghighat Lager says, "In winter 1983, when I entered Adel Abad prison in Shiraz everyone was talking about in incident a few months ago. They said that every night, they would roll two girls who had been reported on by the *tavvabs* to have relations with one another from the stairs. Then they would beat and belittle them. Not only were the two girls, but the whole ward was constantly suffering by the officials."[5]

As the above examples indicate, the lines between discrimination and violence can easily blur, as many consider being deprived basic sanitation and hygiene necessities, as well as facing constant degrading remarks and actions during menstruation, as a form of psychological and physical abuse. Moreover, it is undeniable that the severity of the abuse, violence and trauma suffered by pregnant women or those who delivered their babies inside the prisons or were imprisoned alongside their children in the 1980s is perfectly compatible with the international definitions of torture. For this reason, we dedicate the following section to tortures suffered by women merely due to being mothers.

---

[1] Witness Testimony of Sara L., Justice For Iran.
[2] Witness Testimony of Soraya Zangbari, Justice For Iran.
[3] Witness Testimony of Farkhondeh Ashna, Justice For Iran.
[4] Witness testimony of Monireh Baradaran, Justice For Iran.
[5] Witness testimony of Mitra Haghighat Lager, Justice For Iran.

Motherhood in Prison

The Convention against Torture describes torture to be any action done by officials or their affiliates that causes extreme physical and psychological pain. Comparing this definition with the testimonies of women who were either pregnant, had delivered a child, or had a child with them in prison, we can easily see that experiencing 'motherhood' in prison during the 1980s was torture in and of itself.

Since the prisoners of the 1980s were very young, it followed that a large number of the imprisoned women, mostly newlyweds, were either pregnant or accompanied by a young child at the time of their detention. Many of them were arrested along with their child because either the baby was not yet weaned or there were no family members around at the time of arrest to trust the child to. They suffered the first days of detention and interrogations, arguably the worst time of their ordeal, alongside their young children.

From amongst our interviewees, fourteen were either pregnant- and had delivered their baby during detention or suffered a miscarriage- or were arrested alongside their young children (see Appendix III). Different forms of torture suffered, either partially or fully, by the aforementioned individuals were: miscarriage due to physical torture, delivery in extremely hard conditions and deprivation of basic medical treatments and facilities, severe deprivation of the necessary needs of a young child (such as formula, diapers or even cloth diapers), threats of taking the baby and placing it in an orphanage, and suffering due to lashing and tortures in front of their young children. In ward 4 of Ghezel Hesar alone, between May and November of 1982, 19 children- from infants to three year-old toddlers- were imprisoned alongside their mothers.[1] In this manner, a large number of female prisoners were subject to forms of torture for the simple fact of being or becoming a mother- tortures that their male counterparts have never experienced in prison. Although the above does not constitute sexual harassment or torture, because this form of torture is undoubtedly gender-based and was implemented on a large scale inside prisons, we dedicated a portion

---

[1] Witness Testimony of Soheila Bahadori, Justice For Iran.

of this report to discussing it. Particularly since those who endured it repeatedly said that the pain of lashing was far easier to endure than that of the long-term psychological traumas that both mothers and their children suffered, which remain in their psyche, even to this day.

Miscarriage due to physical torture: Female prisoners reported numerous cases of miscarriage amongst their fellow ward mates due to physical torture. At least two of our witnesses suffered miscarriage due to severity of physical torture. Sara Raha'ee, who was arrested on her two year-old son's birthday and barely pregnant with her second child, miscarried when she started bleeding as a result of being lashed and it was confirmed by a doctor who examined her later that she had in fact miscarried a child. She says, "I even told the interrogator that I was late [in getting my period] but it didn't have any effect on the tortures administered."

When Kianoosh Etemadi, a leftist group (*Sahand*) supporter refused to assist in recognizing leftist activists, her interrogator-who introduced himself as Hamid and was in charge of her case file at the Joint Committee- beat her as punishment, and she suffered a miscarriage:

> That godless man kicked me so many times between my legs that I felt something happening right there and then. I felt it! I said to him that I have to go to the bathroom. He was pretending like nothing happened and kicked me into the room. It wasn't an interrogation room but just a regular one. He had gone mad! I don't know how to explain it but he had become wild. Finally he left the room as I was screaming and shouting, but he didn't let me go to the bathroom. He just up and left! There was no one there to help me. Someone else came and I told him that I have to go to the bathroom and said that I think I suffered a miscarriage. They just sat me there. My clothes had gotten all bloody. Finally they brought someone in [to help me].[1]

---

[1] Witness Testimony of Kianoosh Etemadi, Justice For Iran.

Even when the tortures did not cause a miscarriage, the pregnant female prisoners were constantly concerned about miscarrying or suffering damage that would irreparably harm their foetus. Mona Roshan says, "I continually feared that I would deliver a dead baby. They barely fed us anything."[1]

Pregnancy and delivery under harsh conditions and deprivation of medical treatment: Numerous testimonies demonstrate that women who were arrested in the early 1980s were deprived even of the most basic medical care facilities. Arrested in 1981 in the small city of Gachsaran while in the final months of her pregnancy, Manijeh says:

> They were difficult times because I had serious cravings. They placed us in a tiny 2 meter by 3 meter room they called a 'container', in the yard of the *Sepah* intelligence office where SAVAK used to be located. There were 18 of us in that room and we couldn't all lie down to sleep. Some had to curl their feet one way and some another. Another girl and I were pregnant and the container was extremely hot.[2]

Shayesteh Vatandoust, who was imprisoned between 1981 and winter of 1986, was rearrested shortly after her nuptials while pregnant in summer of 1986, six months after her release. She was beaten so severely during her interrogations that she says, "Until the last months, I felt like my baby was between my thighs. I couldn't walk or stand straight for too long."[3]

Shayesteh's testimony, along with others like it, demonstrates that, contrary to popular belief, pregnancy did not result in lesser torture or abusive experiences. Instead, pregnant women faced a slew of special sexual insults and vulgar terminologies. Arrested alongside her husband in Karaj, Mona Roshan says:

> I told them that I was pregnant and they responded with insults and demeaning terminology. Then they tied me to the bed and started lashing me. I was screaming and shaking non-stop. Suddenly, he laid

---

[1] Witness Testimony of Mona Roshan, Justice For Iran.
[2] Witness Testimony of Ruhangiz, Justice For Iran.
[3] Witness Testimony of Shayesteh Vatandoust, Justice For Iran.

his side on my waist. They were repeatedly insulting and demeaning me saying things like I wasn't thinking of my baby and that if I had such [political] plans then I shouldn't have gotten pregnant. Terribly vulgar insults that I can't remember now…[1]

Tuba Kamangar spent the majority of her pregnancy, her delivery, and its follow up at a detention centre near Nashur village of Kamiaran while under constant threat of rape.[2] She describes her delivery as:

My condition in prison continued until nine months. My baby was born. When my baby was born they didn't provide me with anything in the room. I had contractions and pains for three days. I couldn't even get up and when I would get up to go to the bathroom I would pass out. I knew I couldn't deliver the baby either. They didn't even bring a midwife for me.

I don't even know how my baby was born. I was unconscious for two full days and was bleeding heavily. They brought my older sister and [my mother-in-law]. My sister said that when they arrived, I was bloody all over and my own clothes were under me. She said that I had nothing else and 4-5 men were standing around the room saying that nothing must happen and no one must attack. They said that this was what it was like when they arrived. I was unconscious for three days until my baby was born. The next day my sister screamed and cried and begged for me to be taken to the hospital, until finally 4 guards took me to the hospital in Sanandaj. They threatened that when I got better they would come after me, and I was guarded every day. They said they would attack the hospital. My placenta had not come out [with the baby] so they had to perform a surgery. After one day in the hospital, I woke up.

---

[1] Witness Testimony of Moha Roshan, Justice For Iran.
[2] Witness Testimony of Tuba Kamangar, Justice For Iran. This statement is available in Appendix I of this report.

My baby was a girl who is now in Kurdistan. After two weeks in the hospital I was able to sit, even just on the hospital bed. After two weeks they returned me to my room in the prison with my baby.[1]

Severe deprivation of facilities needed for care of infants: As stated earlier, many women were arrested along with infants who needed more specific care facilities than older children. The majority of the witnesses stated that upon arrest, they were not given permission to take extra formula or clothing for the child, and were told to only take what materials they would need for a few hours because they would be released soon. Yet their detention and interrogation period lasted months, during which they were deprived the care facilities needed for their young children.

Hunger and lack of necessary food is a recurring motif in the testimonies of these mothers. Sa'ideh Siabi narrates how she gave her own blood to her infant son in order to quench his hunger:

> On the first day, my milk dried up. It was so bad that when my child was suckling my breast blood would gush out. I don't know if it was from stress or torture. My child was hungry for days. Finally I realized that I have no option. When they brought us food, potato or Ghormeh Sabzi- if you can call it that because the food quality was terrible- or baked beans, I would skin them and chew them in my mouth and then place it in my baby's mouth. My four-month-old baby was being fed with legumes and heavy foods. After a while, the amount of food they gave us was so little that my child cried of hunger. There were times when because I had not given any information, they reduced the amount of food and it wasn't even enough for me to eat. When I saw that my baby was so hungry, I would chew on my fingers and let them bleed and have him suck it. They barely gave one serving of food each day. I did this because my son was so hungry; otherwise I had

---

[1] Witness Testimony of Tuba Kamangar, Justice For Iran.

no choice when he was so hungry and crying and restless. I had no choice! I was in a solitary cell! When I think about that time, I can never forgive myself. Even to this day I cannot look straight into my son's eyes. I always feel that I steal my glance from my son.[1]

Soraya Zangbari speaks of her conditions; for six months, she wasn't given hot water to mix the formula or diapers to change her 45-day-old baby:

I couldn't produce enough milk and my baby was hungry. She was crying non-stop. More importantly, the whole time we were in that cell, her digestive tract was not working properly. A week would pass and nothing would come out. She would pick her feet into her stomach and scream. I would walk in the cell for hours while she screamed and grabbed my body. When I would check her diapers, they were bloody because she was trying to squeeze things out. Once when she had the digestive block, she cried for hours and hours. Finally the guard came and said, "Give me the baby." I did so and the guard left. The whole exchange took a few seconds. I was so tired and helpless that I gave my baby to the guard who then shut the door and left. It took a second for me to realize it! "Good Heavens! I gave my baby away with my own hands!" I was dumbfounded! I really felt like I had turned into stone and that it was over. Until they brought the baby back. I could hear her crying and it was getting closer to me. When I got the baby I opened her diapers and was looking for a needle mark or something. For a long time I was looking. I had thought that maybe they gave her a shot to kill her because no sound was supposed to come out of the cell. I was waiting for days for something to happen to her because I really thought that they gave her a shot to kill her.

[1] Witness Testimony of Sa'ideh Siabi, Justice For Iran.

...there was a doctor but it served no purpose. There was Doctor Shams who herself was a prisoner. A very good doctor! I repeated that I needed to take my baby to a doctor until they finally took me to see her. At first they gave me the formula that my family had brought but no hot water. I kept banging on the door asking for hot water and they said that I had to give them a container to put the hot water in. This is while when a person is placed in a solitary cell, they search her to make sure she has nothing with her. I told them that I didn't have a container and they said, "That's your problem," shut the door and left. My baby was screaming. After I finished the first can of formula, for a long time I would use it to get hot water. The water would turn yellow because the container rusted. I was so nervous every time I fed my baby wondering what the rust would do to her. But I had no choice. My baby was hungry and I had to feed her.

I had no cloth diapers for my baby. There was a piece of cloth hanging under the sink in the room, probably to clean the place with. I had one regular cloth and half a bag of diapers I brought from home. I kept asking for diapers but they didn't have any and since I hadn't been given visitation rights yet, none had been sent for me from home either. So I used what I had. I would use the cloth diaper and then my headscarf. During the day I used the cloth and scarf. At night I would wash and dry the scarf and use it as a sheet for her because the military blankets were so rough. Then in the morning, my headscarf would change role again and become diaper. I had washed her diapers so many times and squeezed them so hard that my hands were blistered. I would fan them in my hand to dry them quickly and change my baby fast and wash the headscarf so I could put it on when they called me for interrogation. The other cloth was too small and couldn't be used as a scarf. I only used the cloth diaper and my scarf. One time when I woke up in the morning I washed the cloth diaper, but as soon as I opened the scarf to change her I noticed that she had peed and there was a large wet circle in the middle. At that time the guard opened the door and called me for interrogation. I didn't have time to wash the scarf so I put it on like that and went for interrogation.[1]

Sara Raha'ee speaks of her initial interrogations along with her two year-old son while she was held at ward 209 of Evin prison:

My son had severe diarrhea. I would hold him above the toilet in our cell at 209 and he would discharge water. Two Kurdish girls from *Komala* were with me in the cell. They told me to put a piece of paper under the door and have the wardens come.[2] I placed a piece of paper under the door. At that time, there was a *tavvab* girl who was responsible for the cell and giving tea and such things. I think they executed her later. I told her that my baby was really sick and if possible she should tell my interrogator to take my baby to the doctor. She said she'd tell them. She told them and I took my son to Sheikholislam Zadeh.[3] He said that my son had colon inflammation and had to drink water, edible physiological serum and compote. I don't know what religious holiday it was- Ali's martyrdom[4] or such- but the interrogators were gone for 3-4 days. They returned me to the ward and I gave my prescription to Soheila [Haydarzadeh], the *tavvab*, and she said she'd give it to my interrogator. A day passed. My baby's eyes had dried up and he was really ill. I didn't know what to do. I had nothing. No extra

---

[1] Witness Testimony of Soraya Zangbari, Justice For Iran.
[2] At ward 209, the inmates were not allowed to bang on the doors to call the warden. They had to instead place a piece of paper under the door so that the warden would see it and come to them. This process usually took a long time.
[3] Dr. Shoja'eddin Sheikholislam Zadeh was Hoveida's Minister of Health. He was imprisoned along with Hoveida and a few others of his statesmen during Jamshid Amuzegar's tenure in order to calm the revolutionaries. Although released on February 11, 1979, he was rearrested, tried and sentenced to a few years of imprisonment. He usually saw sick inmates and those injured under torture at Evin's clinic.
[4] Imam Ali, the first Imam of the Shi'ite Muslims.

underwear or cloth diapers. Only what we were wearing. I placed the paper again and asked what happened [to the prescription]. "At least give me a glass of hot water or tea to give my baby." The doctor has said for me not to breastfeed but I was doing that and it had made the situation worse. She left and came back 2-3 hours later and threw in two boxes of biscuits from the little window in the door of the cell. I didn't know what was happening anymore and yelled all the insults I knew at her. "You think my baby is a dog? If you have problems with me you can deal with me. I am a mother! Why would you throw the biscuits from the window at me?" She didn't even bother to open the door. She could have open it and handed me the biscuits like a human! I had gone mad.

My voice had trailed off and reached the interrogators. The interrogator came and told me to put on my *chador* and go with him. I picked up the baby and went with him. Where do they take me? To a room that was smeared all over with faeces and blood, piled on the floor and filled with flies. The blood on the wall was as if someone had rubbed bloody hands there. It was clearly a place for punishment and was not a normal cell as those have a washbasin and a toilet. I had a sick baby in my arms. We were there for 4-5 hours. I had wrapped us with a *chador* and since thankfully, there was a water faucet there, I would cool of my baby's hands and body every so many minutes. Wherever you could put your feet there were piles of faeces and blood. Even the wall was smeared with filth. I put the baby on my shoulders and pulled the *chador* over him. I was getting tired as I held the baby the whole time we were there. There was nowhere to put the baby. I told him to put his heads on my head and pulled the *chador* on him. He did that. They called us after 4-5 hours. He told me to apologize to Soheila [Haydarzadeh]. I said I would never do that because I asked her for water, which is what the doctor prescribed.

He said she was not at fault [for not filling the pre-scription]. I said, "Maybe so, but she didn't have to throw the biscuits at me." He said that I had to apologize and I refused and said that I didn't do anything wrong. They took me to the cell and my cell mates told me that the guards had asked them about what had happened, to which they responded that [Soheila Haydarzadeh] threw the biscuits from the window and didn't open the door. Around 10-20 minutes later Soheila Haydarzadeh came and apologized to me. I said nothing. 2-3 days later they brought me tea and hot ware and a bowl of yogurt.[1]

Soraya Zangbari says, "Once my baby had a fever and de-veloped convulsions. This was so painful for me that for years, the mere thought of it would bring me convulsions too!" She says:

When he turned three months old I asked to take him to the doctor for scheduled immunization. They took me and he got his shots. I told the doctor that I had heard when the baby is vaccinated he might have a fever and convulsion and that I didn't know what to do. I was really scared. He said that he would give me medicine, and if the baby devel-oped a fever I should give him the medicine. I came back to the ward and told the guard that the doctor was supposed to give me medicine but he said that it had not arrived yet and that they'd give it to me once it came. I was dropped in the cell. I waited and waited but no medicine arrived. My baby slowly started becoming restless. I knocked on the door and as usual they came shouting, kicking and screaming, telling me the medicine had not arrived. My son was more restless. When I touched his body it was very hot and he slowly started crying. I kept knocking on the door and they kept shouting and kicking at me. Meanwhile my son was crying louder and louder and his body was getting hotter. He was crying and his cheeks were flushed. There was no

---

[1] Witness Testimony of Sara Raha'ee, Justice For Iran.

use. I was walking in the cell and every so often I would knock on the door. They wouldn't even bother to come. Suddenly I realized that he was very hot. I took his clothes off but there was no use. He was crying for hours and was very flushed. I sat on the floor and put the baby on my knees. I took off his clothes and diaper and was staring at him. He was crying and so was I. Suddenly one side of his face was convulsing. Then the other side. Then the whole body! I didn't know what to do so I put him down and splashed him with water. I had nothing! I don't know how long I did this but eventually when I touched his body, it was cold. After a while, someone opened the door and upon seeing me decided to forgo the beating and kicking. He gave me half an aspirin and left. His hands were so filthy that I didn't give the medicine to my son. Later I went to see Doctor Shams and told her about what had happened. She said that I dodged a serious danger because when a child has such high fever it is very dangerous to reduce it so quickly. It was very dangerous.[1]

Soraya's son lived with her in the general ward until the age of five.

Banoo Saberi was imprisoned along with her 2 ½ year-old daughter and three-month-old son for two months at a cell inside the Joint Committee. She says:

I barely had any time to use the bathroom and had to wash the cloth diapers quickly too. I didn't even have any diapers. When I was arrested, I had on a dress under my manteau, a yellow dress with brown edging that my mother had sewed for me. I tore the sleeves and used them as diapers for my son. I would take the kids to the bathroom, ask Bahareh [my daughter] to keep my son occupied so that I could quickly wash the diapers. I would tell Bahareh to pee quickly because otherwise she couldn't come

---

[1] Witness Testimony of Soraya Zangbari, Justice For Iran.

back. Then I would wash and hold my son. Sometimes I wouldn't get to do anything myself. I didn't
even have soap or detergent.[1]

Banoo Saberi was under a lot of pressure due to her infant's
illness:

> When they arrested us it was only a day after my
> son was circumcised. I had to clean him with white
> alcohol. But of course there are no facilities to do
> such things in prison so his scars got infected. My
> baby would cry and wail and I couldn't do anything
> to quiet him down. His genitalia was swollen and in-
> fected. They kept knocking on my door asking me
> to shut my baby up. One day I had my Bijan on the
> floor and had opened his diapers. I was really upset
> and as soon as I touched his genitalia puss spilled
> out. I was really upset. His diapers were opened and
> he was crying. The entire genital area was red and
> infected. Suddenly I heard someone say, "Put your
> blindfolds on." I did and as soon as he walked in,
> before he could finish saying, "This kid needs to…"
> he saw my baby on the floor and said, "What is
> this?" I said, "This child has been circumcised, I
> keep telling you! He needs to be taken care of." He
> said, "Well, your baby is paying for his parents." For
> the first time, I cried and tears flew from under my
> blindfolds. I said, "Well then empty the cell next
> door and drag my parents in there too so they can
> pay for me." The next day they took him and got
> his doctor's information too. That night, they took
> me to a hospital in Iranshahr that they said be-
> longed to *Sepah*.[2]

About food shortage for her and her children, Banoo says,
"Bahar was so hungry. When we went to interrogation she
would lick her hand and drag it on the tables because there were
food crumbs from what the interrogators had eaten. Then she'd
eat that."[3]

---

[1] Witness Testimony of Banoo Saberi, Justice For Iran.
[2] Ibid.
[3] Ibid.

Threatening mothers with taking their children away: One of the most prevalent threats during the interrogation of women who were arrested with their young child was that the child would be taken from them and either given to an orphanage or families who were 'fit' to raise them. In at least two cases (Karun prison of Ahvaz and Bandar Anzali Prison), prisoners testified that instead of handing them to their parents' families, the children of executed *Mojahedin-e Khalq* supporters, were given to "*hizbullahi*" families who could not have a child.[1]

Soraya Zangbari says:

> Repeatedly, they told me that they would take my baby and that I was not fit to be a mother. This was a great fear of mine. Every morning when I woke up, I would hug my baby and think about how many more days I would get to keep him. Every time they called me for interrogation, I would speak to him and tell him that I was unsure whether they would let me keep him when I returned... I saw people who were tortured and dragged themselves on the ground and wondered how I would be able to carry my baby if I would get to that point. I deduced that they must at some point come and take him away. This was one of my biggest fears. Also, they would suddenly and without warning hit me upside the head. I would get shocked and always worried that I would drop the child, so in order to hold on to him I'd claw at him and he'd scream. This happened all the time.[2]

A few days after her caesarean operation, Mehri Elghaspour was arrested along with her infant daughter. In the first 3-4 days while she was kept at Sahra *Komiteh* of Ahvaz, she was deprived from seeing her baby. She says:

> The interrogation came and said, "We'll give your daughter to a *hizbullahi* family so that they can raise her to become a good *hizbullahi* girl." This wounded

---

[1] Witness Testimony of Mehri Elghaspour, Justice For Iran; Witness Testimony of Shayesteh Vatandoust, Justice For Iran.
[2] Witness Testimony of Soraya Zangbari, Justice For Iran.

me much worse than the lashings. Imagine, you are a person already tortured [by the caesarean], you are bleeding, you had an IV in your arm, and are confused with your head spinning and a thousand thoughts circulating in it about what to say and do, and what not to say and do, and you also have a baby and are constantly thinking what might happen to her. What if they don't feed her? What if they give her to a *hizbullahi* family? All of this was in my head… during those four days at Sahra *Komiteh*, I didn't see the baby at all. I was constantly asking about her and wondering if she was eating. They would say, "Don't worry. The kid is with a *hizbullahi* family now. They must be feeding her." The sorrow of this nearly killed me and still bothers me. Sometimes I wonder what if that had happened. My daughter's childhood always bothers me.[1]

Similar testimonies demonstrate how interrogators in different prisons treated pregnant women and young mothers. They were also told they were 'corrupt women' who did not deserve to be mothers and were continuously threatened that their baby would be taken from them. Mehri Elghaspour's testimony regarding this issue is very eye opening:

I asked them to bring my baby so I could breastfeed her. They said, "A child whose very inception was by a forbidden act does not need to feed. How do we know that this child is your husband's? You guys don't believe in such things! You lived in a team house." I thought they wouldn't feed the girl until she [dies] and that pain nearly killed me. It still bothers me. What bothered me more than anything else was not the lashings but what happened to my daughter in those days.[2]

Shortly after, due to the spread of scabies in Karun prison of Ahvaz, Mehri gave her daughter Marziyeh to her mother outside of prison. Because Mehri's mother was incapable of taking care of a baby, the responsibility was handed over to Mehri's

---

[1] Witness Testimony of Mehri Elghaspour, Justice For Iran.
[2] Witness Testimony of Mehri Elghaspour, Justice For Iran.

sister, an ardent supporter of the Islamic Republic. For this reason, Mehri was visited by her daughter only a handful of times
during her 8 years of imprisonment. Her young daughter Marziyeh was not told that Mehri, who was in prison, was in fact her
mother. Instead, Marziyeh knew Mehri as 'communist auntie'.
After her release, through restless work and a lengthy process,
Mehri was able to regain custody of her daughter.

Sa'ideh Siabi and her 4 month-old baby experienced similar
situations at Tabriz Prison:

> One of their tortures was that they told me that I
> was a faithless mother and a Muslim mother must
> [raise] the child. "This baby belongs to God and Is-
> lam. You don't deserve him. We will take him from
> you and give him to foster care. You should not be
> subject to this blessing handed by God." Then they
> sent a female *pasdar*- we could see female *pasdars*- I
> kicked her in her stomach and she left. The male
> *pasdar* came. I was squeezing the child in my arms.
> He first tried to open my arms by force. When he
> couldn't do that he pulled my son from his shoul-
> ders. He pulled the child to get him out of my arms
> and I resisted the maximum that I could. At that
> moment I heard a sound of cracking from my son's
> spine and thought that my baby is being cut in half
> so subconsciously, my arms opened and he pulled
> my son out of my arms. My son still has that pain.
> His sciatic nerve always pains him and the verte-
> brate [he damaged]. I knew where it was because I
> felt its exact location. He later would touch that
> place and was in pain. When I came to Canada I
> took him to a doctor. He was 16-17 years old by
> then. Later on his back pain was worse and he took
> a lot of ibuprofen and now… in fact I have to take
> him to a dentist tomorrow because his teeth and
> bones have lost their density.[1]

Although upkeep of young children was very difficult in
prison, separating from them had its own pain for mothers, a

---

[1] Witness Testimony of Sa'ideh Siabi, Justice For Iran.

pain that lingers to this day. Mona Roshan whose baby was
handed to her mother-in-law immediately after her delivery says:

> There were no agreements made with me. They
> didn't allow me to make a decision whether to keep
> my baby or hand him to my mother-in-law. After
> all, I was a mother and was just experiencing the
> motherly feelings. My breasts were producing milk
> and I wanted to feel those emotions by holding my
> baby in my arms and breastfeeding him. They took
> that away from me too. In fact they allowed her visi-
> tation for this purpose because for 7-8 months after
> my arrest I wasn't allowed any visitation. The female
> *pasdar* who was the only person I was allowed to
> speak with said, "We have no room for babies and
> the brothers have decided that you hand your baby
> to your family." That night I had a high fever and
> shivers. The nurses said that it was lactation fever
> and if I didn't deal with my breasts they would de-
> velop an abscess. They administered a shot to dry
> up my milk and tied up my breasts to prevent the
> milk from collecting there and getting infected. In
> that manner I was in the hospital for 3-4 days with a
> fever and shivers until I got better. I was hospital-
> ized for 8 days and then they returned me to the
> prison.[1]

Four months after her arrest, the authorities decided that
Sara Raha'ee's son had to be sent out of the prison to remain
with her husband's family. She describes her feelings:

> The day he was leaving the ward I tried not to cry
> and send him out a man. I will never forget. He was
> two. I gave him his sack of clothes and he was drag-
> ging it on the floor. Then I told him, "Darling, be
> strong. When you go out of here, remember me. I
> want you to turn out to be a good man." He said,
> "Ok, Maman (mother)! I'll always be a good man."
> Then he left. He was bald at that time. Aside from
> the one visitation I had with him around four weeks

---

[1] Witness Testimony of Mona Roshan, Justice For Iran.

after this incident, I didn't see him for a year and four months. During that time I was in solitary and they wouldn't grant me visitation. When I later saw him his hair had grown long. That whole time in the solitary cell I imagined him bald so when I saw him with the long hair, that they had cut in a pageboy fashion, I said, "Darling your hair has grown so long!" he said, "Mommy, my hair has been long for a long time!"[1]

The pain of being lashed and tortured in the presence of the young child: In many narratives and stories, when the female prisoner was being tortured her young child was either in the room with them or somewhere nearby. The feeling that her child was witnessing her torment has created an unimaginable and unexplainable anguish for these women. Sara Raha'ee explains her torture:

> A fat woman arrived to take my baby. I pulled and she pulled. I screamed and the baby screamed... eventually I let go. Imagine, while I was being *ta'zir* [lashed]... this is so hard for me to recount... my child was there. Sometimes I ask him questions to see if he remembers anything and feel so relaxed when he doesn't. When he was crying and they were lashing me it was truly painful for me. If I was alone it would have been different. But in front of the baby... Later in life I always felt like I couldn't make up for it... either way, I was resisting and screaming and they were dragging me. They couldn't drop me on my face and so tied me face up. They lashed me on my breasts. Later when I came to the cell my breasts were bleeding. I couldn't breastfeed my baby and so I stopped breastfeeding and started giving him the food we were given.[2]

Sa'ideh Siabi's four month-old son was also present throughout her tortures and even her rapes:

---

[1] Witness Testimony of Sara Raha'ee, Justice For Iran.
[2] Witness Testimony of Sara Raha'ee, Justice For Iran.

I was placed in conditions under which I was raped in the worst possible manner. I could not scream. I could not avenge myself. I could not make a move and show my hatred. Eyes blindfolded and mouth shut and my baby in the corner of the torture chamber! Later I researched a lot on this topic. This is why I say that although my child was a baby, he witnessed it all. I don't know why but this is a feeling that I continue to have until today.[1]

To sum up: While generally being a woman in the Iranian prison system brings with it a set of gender-specific limitations, in the 1980s, the testimonies of our interviewees demonstrate the extensive and brutal forms of outright violations and torture that female political prisoners were subjected to, simply for being females. As discussed, the majority of female prisoners of the 1980s were teenagers and young women. As would be expected, a notable number of them were pregnant at the time of their detention, or had their young children with them. Being pregnant or having children brought with it specific and increased forms of abuse in torture, some of which led to the miscarriage of the foetus, others resulting in prolonged illnesses of the children, and also psychological trauma for both mother and child, often for years to come. Thus experiencing motherhood in prison undoubtedly one of the most painful experiences for a large number of female political prisoners. From food deprivation that led to perpetual hunger of the young children, to the deprivation of basic needs of infants such as diapers and clothing and lack of medical care, to physical torture that prevented women from breastfeeding or being able to care for their children, to the trauma of being beaten and even raped in front of their children, motherhood inside Iranian prisons during the 1980s was a horrific experience that has thus far not been examined as a form of gender-specific torture. Indeed, the everlasting agony instilled in female political prisoners by these experiences itself nothing short of torture.

---

[1] Witness Testimony of Sa'ideh Siabi, Justice For Iran.

Conclusion:

A First Step to Address Sexual Torture in Iran

This project has been set up to examine the extent to which women political prisoners have been subjected to sexual torture in Iran since the establishment of the Islamic Republic in 1979. In spite of the various challenges that this project faced, the results of the study have far surpassed initial expectations. The preliminary phase of research indicates that female political prisoners have been subjected to sexual torture in Iranian prisons, particularly during the 1980s. It is in this light that JFI chose to focus the first phase of research on this period. The primary research questions included: *In what manner and to what extent were sexual torture and rape practiced against female political prisoners? Were rape and sexual abuse widespread? Were there systematic acts of rape and sexual violation?* The next set of questions was focused on who the perpetrators and executors were and what official positions, do any among them occupy today? A third set of concerns included examining the reasons behind the long period of silence by interviewees, other victims, and those aware of the abuses. The researchers were concerned with the reasons why victims had not gone public about these atrocities as they were taking place or, at the very least, at some point over the past 30 years since their occurrence. In order to answer these questions JFI explored the political and social context of Iran in the 1980s, particularly with respect to women in the public sphere.

Hundreds of thousands of Iranian women participated in the 1979 revolution demanding democracy; however, as women lost many of their rights under the Islamic Republic, growing disillusionment led many of them to join political opposition organizations. The fast-paced political changes of the first decade of the revolution dramatically changed their lives. This time period saw the imprisonment of thousands of girls and young women who were tortured and/or executed. For those who were not imprisoned, they lost close friends and relatives to torture and execution, and were often forced to abandon their political activism. Yet others escaped Iran out of desperation.

Women were subjected to rape, sexual abuse and execution, despite the government's claim that morality, and in particular sexual morality, was the cornerstone of the regime. The data collected through interviewing and documenting first-hand witness accounts of large and diverse groups of ex-prisoners in and out of Iran indicates that certain forms of torture and sexual harassment against female political prisoners in the 1980s were systematic and often widespread. Perhaps the most notorious action of the regime during the 1980s was the rapes of hundreds of young virgin girls the night before their execution in the name of religion. The data has made it clear that the rape of virgin girls prior to their execution was a systematic policy carried out in Iranian prisons during the 1980s. The rapes were justified under the religious term of *siqih*, (temporary marriage) which was a deliberate misinterpretation of Ayatollah Montazeri's edict that girls should not be executed. Although Ayatollah Montazeri had convinced Ayatollah Khomeini that girls (young women) should not be executed in compliance with religious doctrine, the judicial and security officials wilfully interpreted the order as a mandate to kill, as long as the girls lost their virginity prior to their execution. The prolonged nature of this type of torture implicates the entire regime, not just those who committed these crimes, as it is now clear that higher officials were aware of what was occurring in the prisons and that they tacitly approved these practices by remaining silent.

Report findings also demonstrate that marrying off the female political prisoners to various members of Revolutionary Guards or other supporter of the regime was a recurring issue in the

1980s. Many of the prisoners either experienced it themselves or witnessed their ward-mates coerced into marriage. Personal vendettas, a desire to control the female prisoner after her release, and dominance were all factors that led to the use of marriage as a tool for torture in prisons. Based on the detailed interviews with former female political prisoners, pressuring the prisoner to accept marriage was often done by placing marriage as a condition for release or as a guaranteed exemption from torture and, in particular, execution. Many of the female political prisoners resisted the severe and unbearable pressures and did not agree to enter into marriage in prison while many others did. However, even those prisoners who 'agreed' to marry could not be classified as having entered a 'consensual' relationship because the conditions necessary to form real 'consent' were absent inside the prisons. These marriages are thus classified as *forced* marriages and any sexual relation resulting from them a form of sexual torture in accordance with the principles of international law. Those who perpetrated these rapes continuously enjoyed impunity as a result of the absolute denial by Iranian officials that there was any wrongdoing in the prisons of the Islamic Republic of Iran.

The analysis of interviews as it is presented in this report has made it clear that the majority of female political prisoners in the Islamic Republic's prisons experienced at least one form of sexual harassment. Different forms of sexual torture were inflicted on female political prisoners, but all occurred in a widespread manner. Amongst these was verbal abuse intended to demean the female political prisoners to the level of being a sexual object. Aside from mere verbal insults, many female political prisoners were threatened with rape and forced to live in constant fear. The fear of rape was particularly prominent in prisons where all the personnel, including the wardens, were male. The women's bodies were also assaulted in other violent ways. Female political prisoners reported that inside interrogation and torture chambers, the prison officials would sit on different parts of their bodies, particularly their buttocks and waists, while lashing them.

Furthermore, this report has also uncovered an extraordinarily violent method of torture prevalent at Ghezel Hesar prison, one of the largest and most populated prisons of the 1980s. Male prison authorities, including the head of the prison, forcefully kicked female political prisoners between their legs while forcing them to crawl on the floor, or stand facing a wall. The violent kicks caused heavy bleeding in many of the female prisoners. Many of our interviewees had never before disclosed this method of torture, even though everyone interviewed who had suffered through it revealed continuous and irreparable harm from this form of abuse.

Given that many of the detained women were young, a notable number of them were pregnant or had their young children with them at the time of their arrest. Pregnancy and the presence of small children in detention augmented the physical, psychological and gender-specific abuse endured by women prisoners. Increased forms of torture led to miscarriage of the foetus or the inability to breastfeed, and abuses such as deprivation of food, diapers, milk formula, clothing, and medical care, prolonged the illnesses of children in the wards. Physical torture, such as being beaten, lashed, and raped in front of their children, also created psychological trauma for both mother and child. Motherhood in prison was undoubtedly one of the most painful experiences for a large number of women political prisoners, however these horrific occurrences had not been examined, prior to this report, as a form of gender-specific torture.

It is the hope of JFI that this report and its relevant documentation will elucidate the pervasive nature of gender-specific torture in Iranian prisons and instigate opportunities for a more systematic analysis of sexual torture, as well as a wider platform for public discussion on the way in which victims of sexual torture and sexual abuse are treated in Iran. This research demonstrates that torture rooted in sexuality left the deepest and most painful effects on the prisoners who experienced it. Its in-depth interviews convey that the most painful part of the sexual torture experience is having to deal with the silent suffering of a forbidden pain. The victims' long silence was primarily caused by the normative Iranian culture that, until recently, blamed the victim of sexual abuse and sexual torture and by implication their families, rather than the perpetrator.

This research is a first step towards examining the use of rape and other sexual abuses in the prisons of Iran under the Islamic Republic. JFI hopes this research can break the long and dark silence of Iranian society, a silence that has failed the nation in protecting and providing support for countless young women, whose only crime was that of political expression and participation in public sphere, one that the regime intended to monopolize for their supporters and loyalists. Public dialogue on the reasons behind the silence and societal soul-searching is a required first step for Iranians today in order to develop a cultural coding that removes shame from the victims of sexual violence and transfers it to the perpetrators. The development of a general consensus on the forms of retributive justice and public identification of the perpetrators is another step that is crucial in order to ensure the condemnation and deterrence of such behaviour in the future. This public discourse may also go a long way to help initiate a healing process for the victims and the families and friends who suffered the loss of their loved ones. Hence, a third crucial step is reparative justice with a focus on the victims of these crimes.

At the national level, a process of creating an atmosphere that provides victims with the possibility to speak about their experiences, particularly through the formation of support groups and access to psychological services without the fear of social repercussions or the breach of cultural taboos. Furthermore, the development of a long-sought democracy in Iran depends on whether the nation fulfils its commitment to freedom of expression, protection of human rights for all and development of a pluralistic political culture through law and national instruments. A recognition of the women who, because of their political participation and vision of a more inclusive role for women in the public sphere, have suffered excruciating repercussions, would have to start with documenting the truth of what went on and continues to go on behind the walls of Iranian prisons.

At the international level, JFI calls upon the United Nations, international organizations and EU member states to support its proposal for the appointment of a special or joint envoy focussed on sexual torture in Iranian prisons *with a particular focus to* fully investigate the use of *rape of virgins as a torture mechanism in Iranian prisons.* The proposed envoy may be mandated to carry out a full fact-finding mission both in and out of Iran *in order to bring to account those responsible for the use of this mechanism against Iranian prisoners.*

It is the hope of JFI that the launch of this first of three reports, will serve as a stepping-stone in achieving the wider goals of freedom of information, freedom of expression, an end to torture, and ultimately, justice for all those who suffered in the past and those who continue to suffer such abuse in the Iranian prison system of today. We also hope other stakeholders will initiate and conduct research in areas not yet documented or outside the scope of this project. These reports are fundamental to Iranian history and, as disheartening as they may be, are the ingredients for social change, end to torture, acceptance of freedom of expression, and the protection of human rights for future generations.

Appendices

Appendix I: Witness Testimonies

Witness Testimony of Marina Moradi Bakht (Nemat)

Name and Surname: Marina Moradi Bakht (Nemat)
Date and Place of Birth: 1965, Tehran
Date of Arrest: January 1981
Accusation: Collaboration with Leftist Groups
Date of Release: Middle of 1984
Current Situation: Married with one child residing in Canada. She published her memoirs in English entitled "Prisoner of Tehran". Her memoirs were criticized and brought under suspicion by some of the witnesses we spoke to for this report.[1]

I was 16 years old when I was arrested. Although many of my friends, classmates and schoolmates were arrested, I always told myself, "What can they do to me even if they arrest me? I am nobody, I have done nothing!" This is despite the fact that I had spoken against the government a lot at school, had participated in most demonstrations and stuck my nose in things that were not my concern. But I was not really active in the way others were.

It was around 9:30-10 pm. I was in the shower when they rang the doorbell. When my mother called for me, because normally no one visited our house at 9:30-10 pm, I immediately realized that it had to involve my arrest. When I opened the bathroom door, two *pasdars*, both armed, were standing there. When I saw them I felt like I was in a dream. It was a feeling like I was having an out of body experience. I think this was because I was shocked. I lost all ability to think logically and felt nothing. My parents were crying and I was looking at them bewildered, wondering why!

---

[1] See Imaginary Evin in "Prisoner of Tehran," Monireh Baradaran, simple truth website, available at http://monireh-baradaran.blogspot.com/2007/07/blog-post_1809.html; and Prisoner of Tehran, devaluing prison memoirs, Iraj Mesdaghi, Neither Alive Nor Dead, available at http://www.irajmesdaghi.com/page1.php?id=113.

Then they took me to Evin but it took a while before I was interrogated. I sat in the hallway for a while. I don't remember how long it took. I had a chance to think about the things that had happened. One thing that always bothered me in the beginning was why did they want me?

When I was arrested they told me to wear a *chador*. I said, "I don't have a *chador* because I am Christian." It was very interesting for them. They said, "What? You are Christian?... Ok, that is fine, wear a head scarf and follow us." At Evin Prison I was the only girl sitting there in the hallway who didn't have a *chador*. I didn't see anyone else without a *chador*. It was like I had a bull's eye on my forehead. I was thinking to myself, "Many of the people here must be leftists! How is it that they all have *chadors* and I am the only one who doesn't?!"

The hallways were very silent. We were sitting and waiting for the interrogation. There was a girl sitting next to me who was crying and it really upset me. I turned to her and asked, "Why are you crying?" she said, "I am afraid! They will kill us." I said, "No, they won't. You shouldn't cry like this and make so much noise." She eventually calmed down.

Then they called me for the interrogation. I don't remember if there were any sounds around me. It was very quiet. The interrogation was very polite, even strangely so. [My interrogator was named Ali.] As soon as he started asking me questions, from the very beginning, my problem was that I had on blindfolds and couldn't see him. So what really bothered me was not the questions he was asking. His questions and manner of speech were very polite and calm. It was like I was sitting in a café and speaking to a person. What bothered me was that I couldn't see him; didn't know whether he was sitting, standing, or what. Didn't know who he was, what he looked like. This bothered me a lot. Then he started to read to me from the *Koran*. It must have been 3-4 am.

I was tortured once. Hamed lashed me. Ali didn't directly lash the soles of my feet but he was standing there. I couldn't understand how a person with any level of humanity in him could stand and watch a 16 year old girl be lashed on the soles of her feet and then tell her, "I love you; you should marry me!"

After Hamed lashed me, he left the room. Ali came and untied my hands and feet, held my hand and told me to sit down. I said, "I want to go to the bathroom." I couldn't get up so he helped me get up. I took a few steps and before I left the room he let go of me and told me I have to put on my blindfolds. He placed the blindfolds on my head and gave me something to hold on to. I don't know if it was a pen or a piece of wood or what. He gave me one end of it and led me the rest of the way with what he had given me to hold. When I was in the bathroom, I felt sick and passed out. When I came to, I was in the same room and Ali was sitting next to me. This was not the only time but there were many other times when he would hold my arms up or get close to me. Every person has a private sphere and reacts to another person entering it. Many times when I was alone with Ali, before the marriage situation came about, he would enter my private sphere and I would react and pull myself back. However, he never acted this way when we were in the hallways or going places and others were around us. He would always keep his distance during those moments.

After the interrogations, they took us out one night to a place in Evin. I don't know where it was. They took our blindfolds off. There were a group of *pasdars* standing there with guns. Then Ali came and pulled me out of the line of people, placed me in his car and returned me to the building where the interrogations were done. There he told me that I had received an execution order but he reduced it. He said that he believed me and had turned my sentence into life imprisonment. So he sent me inside the ward. I was new to Evin and had no idea how the court system worked. There were no specific laws or systems in Evin either. Still, although he had said all of those things to me, the entire 5-6 months that I was in Evin, I kept thinking of how I had done nothing. What basis did they have for giving me an execution order and then a life sentence? I thought to myself that it was all nonsense. This was my hope. I spoke to the girls in the ward and many of them didn't even have a sentence. Many said that there were no checks and balances and that even if what [Ali had said] was true, they may change their minds later. In fact my hope was that even if they had said to me that I have an execution sentence, or life imprisonment sentence, or whatever, since there are no checks and balances, it could change.

Therefore, when they called me for an interrogation five months later, the possibility that they want to execute me didn't even enter my mind.

After they interrogated me, they sent me upstairs to ward 246 and, as I recall, to room 6. I was there for 5-6 months and they never called me for an interrogation. The whole time I was in the ward I had no knowledge of anything other than what the girls said when they would leave and return. I would ask them what was going on and how things were. Many people were in an utterly uncertain situation. Also, when they called you for an interrogation it was unclear what they would then do to you!

Finally, they called me one day and took me in for an interrogation. If I remember correctly, it was in the afternoon. They announced a few names and my name was among them. They put blindfolds on me and took me to the interrogation building. I sat on the ground of a hallway, close to a door, as before. Then, they called my name and I guessed that the voice was Ali's but I wasn't sure. There was a room right next to me and I entered it. I recall that he closed the door. I sat. There were no torture devices in the room. I noticed that he was limping. Then he sat and said, "I haven't seen you in a while. I have been gone for a while. How are you?" I said, "I am fine thank you. How are you?" he said that he was fine. "I had gone to the war front for a while to fight but I was shot at and as you can see I am limping." I said that I had noticed he was limping. He said that he had returned to his job at Evin.

Then he paused and started talking again. He said, "Listen! Pay attention because I want to tell you something important, so pay attention to what I am trying to say." I told myself, "Fine!" He said, "Look, I have thought a lot about this issue and have lost a lot of sleep over it. While I was at war I thought a lot about it and now I am sure that I want to do this and want you to think about it. I want and have decided to take you as my wife."

For a moment I thought he was joking but then immediately realized that no one joked at Evin Prison. The matter was not a joke. He really was saying that he wanted me to marry him! Since I was a 17-year-old girl at the time, and after 5-6 months at Evin still did not understand these issues well, I said to him, "But how can that be? How can this happen? I don't love you." He said, "It has nothing to do with love. I am saying that I want you to marry me. If you create trouble or reject me, you parents and boyfriend Andre will be arrested." I was stunned that he knew the name of my boyfriend because as far as I could recall I had never mentioned his name. Unless someone else had mentioned his name or they had gotten the information from somewhere else. Anyway, he said that if I caused trouble he would arrest my parents and my boyfriend Andre. I was baffled as to what to say. In fact, I think my mouth was hanging open. Then he said, "You have three days to think about this and to tell me if your answer is yes or no. But remember what the consequences are if you say no." Then he got up and said, "Let's go." I was still shocked and frozen when he told me to go. As I recall, I was standing in place staring at him. He put the blindfolds on me. I repeated again, "But I don't love you. I am from a Christian family; these things don't go together!" he said, "Yes, I know all of this and have thought about it. I like you and think that this is a proper, good and appropriate decision. That is all. You have three days to think about the matter. Go and think and don't forget the consequences." Then he guided me out of the room.

Three days later they called my name again: "Marina Moradi, come for your interrogation." They took me again to the same place, even the same room. I don't recall anymore. Ali was there. He said, "Did you think about what I said? What is your answer?" I said, "I have thought about it and my answer is that I will marry you. There is no problem. I'll do whatever you ask of me but don't bother my parents and boyfriend. I'll do what you want from me and won't argue with you, no problems." He said, "I promise you that I will be a good husband for you and protect you" and said a bunch of other things that I wasn't really listening to. That was it. He sent me to the ward and told me that he will come after me in a few days.

I was arrested in January 1982. This situation happened in the summer of 1982, probably around June of 1982. There was a ceremony at Ali's parents' house. It was very short, maybe 15 minutes. I don't really remember because I was very nervous. Prior to this event I had never been to a Muslim wedding and had gone only to one Christian wedding, which was that of my brother.

There were no chairs or tables in the room at his parents' house. There was a white tablecloth on the ground, some sweets, a *Koran*, candles and a bunch of other similar things. Then they brought me in the room. Before going there they gave me white manteau, white pants, white socks and a white *chador* and other things to wear. I wore them and put the *chador* on and they told me to sit somewhere. Finally, there was me, Ali, his parents, his sisters and her husband and the religious magistrate. Everyone was standing, but Ali and I were sitting. The magistrate sat; they told me his name but I absolutely have no recollection of it because it was not a well-known name or someone that I would later recall. He said a few words. Then he spoke to me, he said, "Miss Marina Moradi, are you willing to take this man as your husband?" and I said yes the first time he asked. I had no idea that you are not supposed to respond the first time. Apparently they all were very surprised but, it did not matter anyway. I said yes and they gave me something to sign and I signed it without reading it. I don't even know what it was. They put a paper in front of me and said sign here and I signed; that was it, over!

The first time we had marital relations was in the house he had bought that I was staying at. I was a 17-year-old girl and such talks had never taken place in our house so I had no idea what the situation [sexual relations] was like. The first time we had sexual relations in that house, I screamed the whole time. Then he placed his hand on my mouth and said, "Don't scream or you'll see much worse. Be quiet. If you don't resist, if you don't create problems, you won't hurt as much. So don't scream." So I slowly learned to not scream or resist and to not cause a raucous because maybe it would really be better for me. Although I resisted the first few times, I later realized that resistance was truly futile. After that, he returned me to prison to ward 209. There I knew I had neighbours in the other cells and if I wanted to scream, what effect would it have on them? So I decided to close my mouth and let him do his business so that I could be left alone. No matter how long it took, ten minutes, fifteen or twenty minutes or even half an hour, it would eventually end and be over with. Either he would fall asleep or he would leave. So I slowly learned to bear it. Each time it was extremely painful. There never was a time when I wasn't in pain. I bore it and then learned that he was correct, the less noise I made, the less trouble there was for me.

We were at Ali's house for a few days and then he returned me to Evin. I requested to be sent to 209. I couldn't bear the girls in the ward asking me where I was or guess from my face that there was something I didn't want to talk about. So I said that I wanted to go to the 209 solitary cells directly. He agreed and said that if I wanted to go to 209, I would go to 209. Then they placed me in a cell. Before then, during my interrogation period, I was kept at 209. At that time, I was there for a night or two. The cell I used to be in was much worse than the cell they placed me in this time. The other cell I was in at 209 was cold and I would shake all night long. They had only given me one blanket. As far as I remember. There also wasn't a toilet in the cell. This time, they put me in a cell that was very small. If I were a bit taller, if I stood in the middle of the cell and open my arms out they would hit the walls. But it was clean. There was a carpet on the floor that wasn't terrible. They gave me 3-4 blankets. Ali even brought me a pillow. Aside from the pillows and blankets, there was a toilet and a sink in the cell. There was no bed or anything. Everything was on the ground. Whenever Ali would come, he usually brought food with him. He had told me not to drink the tea they served in prison and that he would bring me good tea himself. The tea served in prison smelled bad; they put camphor in it. He brought me the tea that they drank, which was just normal tea. He would come; whenever he could he would show up. Sometimes he would come at 10 am, sometimes at 3 pm, sometimes at 10 pm and sometimes he would even come at 2 am. It really was not predictable when he would show up. Whenever Ali would come, he would sit down and give me the food he had brought and have me eat it or drink the tea he had brought. Then he would take his clothes off and it was obvious what he expected of me. I usually slept the rest of the time. In general, when I get depressed, I sleep a lot. I have the ability to sleep 24 hours or 48 or even 72 hours and only wake up to go to the bathroom and then go back to sleep again. I can sleep without food or ever a drink of water! And I was asleep most of the time during those days.

Then they took me to 246. They started calling me again. Usually, not always, they would call me at night, but sometimes it was in the afternoon or morning. While I was in 246 it was usually at night but not too late, like around 8 pm. Most of the time, I was alone. There were times when they would call me along with others but then afterwards they would call me alone: Marina Moradi, come for your interrogation. I would go, put blindfolds on, and if I were alone, someone would come and take me. There were times when Ali was there and he would come and take me. At times I was taken with a group to the interrogation building. Then, Ali would come and call my name and tell me, "Get up! Let's go." I would follow him and we would go to 209. 2-3 or 4 times a week, they would call me at 10 pm and return me at 6 am. In fact, the times when he was supposed to go home and sleep there, prior to going, he was in the cell [with me]. I had to spend all night with Ali in the cell and each time, the physical pain was unbearable. If I had to choose between being lashed and that situation, I would pick lashing although it is much more painful. When someone lashes you, you maintain your dignity; you are a political prisoner! But when you are in a cell with your interrogator and then such matters take place, there is nothing left! The psychological pain aside, the physical pain was terrible for me too! Ali noticed and was constantly telling me to not be upset and that I was in pain because I resisted. "Don't resist and you won't be in pain." But I couldn't help it. He never came to me without any expectations.

The whole time I was in the prison under these conditions, I believed that no one was aware of it. Maybe I was protecting myself and was being defensive because I didn't want anyone to find out, so I started believing that no one knew about it. This was because it is very difficult for a person to look straight in the eyes of her friends and say, I am my interrogator's wife. How can it be! It is terrible! I poured my heart out to only one person during those days. I spoke to one person about this, which was more like a confessional for me. She was a young mother from Gilan who was brought to my cell in 209 for 2-3 days. She was a very nice woman, very calm, very kind and very good-spirited. She had a baby too. One night Ali came to our door and called me and took me away. When I returned in the morning, she asked me, "Where were you last night?" I said, "Interrogation." She said, "Marina, don't lie. Where were you last night?" then I told her the story and said that I was his wife. She said, "By God! How is this possible? He threw his own wife in prison?" I said, "No! I wasn't always his wife," and then told her the whole story. The poor soul was very shocked in the beginning. She couldn't comprehend how this was possible at all. Then when she saw how upset I was and that I was crying heavily, she said, "Why are you upset? This is not your fault! You are not to blame here! You are the victim of this man. Why are you torturing yourself like this?" Then she asked me if I told anyone. I said that I hadn't and anyway, what was I going to tell them! She said, "You are looking at yourself like you are to blame when you are not at fault." I said, "All this aside, if they take you to the ward, don't tell anyone!" She asked why she shouldn't do that. I made her swear to God that she would not tell. She said, "Fine, I promise." Later they took her. When I went inside the ward, I realized that no one knew so she had stuck to her promise.

In the ward, I was so consumed with my internal thoughts and defences that I never paid any attention to what people were doing. I was caught up in my own problems and tried to control the situation to the extent possible. I slept a great deal of the day. I could sleep during the noise of the goings and comings for 7 hours or so. Sometimes the girls would try and wake me up, for food or whatever else, and they had trouble in getting me up. They really had to shake me to be able to get me up. After that situation, I had psychological problems and could not pay attention to my surroundings.

Another thing that is significant in my opinion is that after I was released from prison, I lost all ability to enjoy sexual relations with my own husband, whom I love and married by choice. I mean that basically I don't have the ability to enjoy sexual relations. This feeling does not exist for me. My husband is a man who I married when I was released from prison[1] and I was and still am truly in love with him. So I really love him but [sexual] relations have become a kind of duty for me.

Torture can take different forms. Can forcing insomnia on someone for a week be torture or not? If you throw a 16 year old girl in a cell and then bring a religious magistrate who declares that you are now married and can do your business and then you rape her, is this torture or not? What is the goal of torture? Is the goal of torture extracting information or destroying a person? I don't know what Ali's goal was. Whatever it was, what he was doing to me was in my opinion torture. It still affects me. Those

---

[1] According to Marina, interrogator Ali was killed in a street fight some time after their marriage.

who were tortured, those who were lashed, many of them were my friends. I was tortured too. I was lashed too. But if one of those people were taken inside a room, and a religious magistrate came and read the marriage verses, and then that girl was raped, could she still look at [torture] in the same way? Taking pleasure from a condemned person is the sickest joke a person can think of!

Witness Testimony of Azar Al-e-Kanaan

Name and Surname: *Azar Al-e-Kanaan*
Age when Arrested: *21*
Date of Arrest: *Beginning of fall of 1981*
Verdict of the Revolutionary Court: *Two and half years' imprisonment*
Date of Release: *March 1986*
Charge: *Support of Rah-e Kargar*

When I was arrested, my daughter was exactly eleven months old. I was supposed to go to Saqqez to see someone. I left early in the morning so that I would return by the evening, because back then, after four pm the roads were closed. One of my sisters and my daughter Nina accompanied me. I had a carrier. Since my daughter had heart problems and her aortic valve was not functioning, every once in a while I took her to Tehran or Tabriz for a check-up. That day, my excuse was that I was going to Saqqez and from there to Tabriz.

They stopped the car in Divandarreh. The guard that checked the car asked: Where are you going? I said, "I am going to Tabriz, I am taking my daughter to the doctor." He said, "What is your name?" I gave him a fake name. He looked at me a bit and said, "Aren't you Azar? And this is your daughter Nina? And this is Nastaran or Delbar," who were my sisters who usually accompanied me. It was as if I had an electric shock. I was shocked. I couldn't move my tongue. I was lucky I had pomegranates in my purse. I excused myself to peel it for my daughter, before they searched me. While they were searching my bag, along with the pomegranate that I supposedly peeled for my child, I swallowed the letters I had with me.

They took us to a building that was a military base. They brought a female guard. My eyes were blindfolded. She said to bring all of my clothes. When they arrested me, I was wearing a manteau and pants. I used to go out chic and fashionable. The manteau and pants that I wore back then may have seemed very flashy/trendy to some, but it showed my personality.

They searched through everything. Even in Nina's diapers, and emptied the bottle. While I was naked, I realized they brought someone and asked, "Is this her?" that person said, "yes." They asked me to quickly wear my clothes get my things together. They had separated my sister from me in Divandarreh, and took me and Nina with a car back to the Sanandaj *Sepah* office.

The real interrogation began there. The interrogator introduced himself as Sadeghi. He was Fars; in fact, we didn't even have any Kurdish interrogators. He had a perfect Tehrani accent. You couldn't tell if he was Isfahani or Turk. Then they took my wedding ring and all the gold I was wearing, and said "we have had our last words with you, are you going to talk or not?" I said "I have nothing to say. I was taking my daughter to the doctor in Tabriz. This is the name of her doctor. I have an appointment. You can call and check to make sure." I was thinking to myself that if they call, I didn't have an appointment or anything. But in the heat of the moment, you say whatever that comes to mind.

Sadeghi and the other ones insulted me a lot. Since I was caught, they kept cursing and saying words that meant I was a corrupt woman. They used a Persian word used for a prostitute; they said "lakkate." I told him "why are you insulting me? You don't know me at all."

For example, they said "where is your dishonored husband? If you were important to him, he wouldn't let you be here with us." They said words with the intention of crushing you, or words that meant: cover yourself corrupt woman, whore. I screamed, "You have tied my hands, and my feet, my *hijab* fell, what can I do? Why do you look?"

As soon as we entered, they took my daughter away and took me to a room where Sadeghi interrogated me. But I could hear Nina moaning asking for her mom. When he said his last words to me, as he called it, he said "lay her down and beat her as much as you can." I said "What have I done that you want to beat me for it?"

They took me from a room that was his office to a hallway where there was a toilet and a bed for torture. After that, we entered a room that looked like an L, which was the interrogation room. There were three or four interrogation rooms that were separated from the torture rooms with curtains. They laid me down there and started lashing the soles of my feet and my back. There, they were also beating another young man. Someone was also sitting there, and they had covered him up. They laid me down and started beating. They wanted to know who I wanted to meet in Saqqez, and I denied everything. The one who became my main interrogator was called Hashemi. He approached me as he was holding my daughter. She was crying constantly, saying "No mommy! No mommy!" A while passed and I couldn't forget her calling for her mom. Of course, she was only eleven months old, and didn't understand that they were beating me and I was screaming. The interrogator said "See, your daughter is crying, say it!" I said "I don't have anything to say." And Nina kept saying "No mommy! No mommy!" Then I think that they lashed me for so long that I vomited and then they moved me to a cell. When I woke up I was in a cell and my daughter was with me. I was bleeding heavily from the lashings.

At that moment I kept thinking to myself "What happened to us? Why did I get pregnant when my situation was like this? Why did I put my baby in this condition?" As I was thinking these thoughts, I dragged myself to the toilet. The toilet was inside the cell. I vomited, and then I think I passed out again. When I regained consciousness, I saw the interrogators were talking, but they had taken Nina. Later, when I was released, my sister said that when I had passed out, they took Nina to her. Later, every time I was interrogated, they took my child out to my sister, but I didn't know this and was so worried about where she was being taken.

From that moment on, I developed a uterine bleeding problem, and even later, when they took me from Sanandaj Prison to Tehran's Joint Committee, and then to Ward 209 of Evin Prison, I was still bleeding. When I was tortured at the Joint Committee, my bleeding got worse. I couldn't even walk. They didn't give me sanitary pads, so I was bleeding [all over my clothes]. After a while of being in the hallways of 209, I spent some time in the clinic. Nina was with me all along, for the 3 years and 3 or 4 months after the arrest. I was in Ward 209 when they finally agreed to let Nina go. When I requested baby formula, because the food available had camphor and I couldn't give it to a child, the interrogators said that tomorrow your daughter will turn out like you, and we have to deal with your daughter also. I had diaper-trained her. I remember when we went for interrogations, and she wasn't wearing a diaper. The clothes I had in my bag for her when they arrested me were two Kurdish pants and two T-shirts. She looked so pretty, like a Vietnamese child. She was round and white with bangs. I had to make her wear those clothes, because we didn't have anything else. When we went for interrogations, many of the guards who worked there called her to take her and buy her cheese puffs and candy. I wanted them to take her to give her something to eat, but in the back of my head I was worried, hoping they wouldn't do something to her. But she was very smart, she ran back and the guard said "Ma'am, she has to go potty. Take her to the bathroom." I took her to the bathroom, and said "go potty" and she said "I don't have to go potty." I felt that she lied to them. She got the snack and said she had to pee to return to me quickly. She didn't eat what they bought her either. A couple of people where hanging in the corridor, with tied hands. She opened her bag of cheese puffs and said to them, "Have some cheese puff uncle." She talked with a sweet Kurdish accent.

After a few months, I agreed to let my daughter go out. She had a heart condition. Sometimes when we were in the cell she had shortness of breath. There was not enough air. Her lips got blue. She vomited twice, and they took her to the clinic. The doctor ordered that the child should leave the prison. They contacted my parents and my brothers and gave her to them without allowing me visitation to see them. They thought I was executed, and that is why they gave her to them. Rumor spread in Sanandaj that I was executed, and my husband [who was a runaway] heard the news of my execution. They prepared a biography of my activities in a [party affiliated] magazine, [and were about to publish it] when one of the girls was released and told them that I was alive and they shouldn't publish anything.

In the spring of 1981, they returned me to Sanandaj. I spent some time in the *Sepah* Prison of Sanandaj, and some time in Revolutionary Court of Sanandaj at a general ward.

At 12 midnight they came for me. I was in the cell. They said: "Come with all your things and your kid." I said, "I don't have a kid." They said, "Where is your kid?" I said, "I let her go out. Didn't you let her go out?" They said, "In the letter we have, you should come with your child." I said, "It has been a while since they've returned my daughter to my family." I was worried that based on what they said, they hadn't returned my child to my family. In the car, the guard kept asking questions, "Where is your kid?" and I kept asking, "What did you do to my kid?" He said, "We came from Sanandaj; we don't know anything. They had ordered us to go bring the mother and daughter." I was terrified not knowing to whom they had given my daughter. As soon as we got to Sanandaj, they took me in for an interrogation. I said, "What did you do to my child? My daughter has a heart condition; the doctor ordered that she be removed [from prison]. They said they gave her to my family. Who did you give my kid to?" I said "It's been about 2 years since I have been arrested, why don't you give me visitation?" I was worried [and wanted to know] if they had given my daughter to my family at all or not. Finally, they gave me visitation and my parents came. My first question was about my daughter, and I was relieved.

I was released in March of 1986, and was arrested again on September 20, 1986.

The second time, I was arrested was because I helped a lady leave Iran with the facilities that I had. My phone conversations with my husband were being tapped. The last time I talked to him over the phone was September 20, which was our wedding anniversary. I told my husband, "Telephone three." I meant that the phone was being tapped, but I was not sure to what extent it was being tapped. My father's house didn't have a phone and I was staying at my uncle's house and living there. I was supposed to return on September 20. I was going to my dad's house to go shopping, buy shoes and something else and then get out of Kurdistan. I had just returned from my uncle's house to our house that they knocked on the door. I was wearing a skirt and a shirt, with no *hijab*. They came into our house, carrying weapons and Kalashnikovs. I was knitting. Nina started crying. I was consoling her, so that she would stop crying. One of them said, "Yes, she is a guerrilla baby! Don't cry guerrilla baby!" I said,

"Do you have an arrest warrant for me?" He said, "This is from the Revolutionary Court, the Revolutionary Guards" and hit the magazine of his gun. So the second time I was arrested, it was related to a phone call, and helping some people leave Sanandaj. They also arrested my nephew. This time Nina stayed with my mom and sister.

They took me to the same building they had taken me the first time. This time, my interrogator was Behrouz. He was a Turkish boy. He spoke Persian when he was angry; it was obvious he was not Fars. His Persian was mixed with Turkish. When they came to arrest me, he was the one who use the bolt handle of his gun when I asked if they had a warrant. He was also the one who told my daughter that she was a guerrilla girl so she shouldn't cry! He was wearing a neck scarf, like the thugs from mechanic shops.

I spent the entire day of my arrest behind a curtain on the other side of which they were torturing people. I was sitting on a chair, and the interrogator was sitting with his legs parallel and touching mine. I kept pulling my leg back, and he kept coming forward, and asking nonsensical questions. He asked if I was a smoker and if I wanted a smoke. "Do you want me to give you a cigarette?" I said that I didn't and don't like smoking. On the one hand they beat someone, on the other hand they treated them this way. Imagine, you are somewhere with your eyes blindfolded and have no control over anything. A man is sitting in front of you and his breathing, his jokes, his proximity to you, his talking, were not normal. It was disgusting. On the other side, in the hallway, they were lashing someone and this guy was pretty much flirting with me. I felt him touching me, touching my legs. I was disgusted by his hands. I knew these weren't normal touches like when I touch your legs. His breathing, his tone of voice, I felt there was something strange about it.

The day after the arrest, September 21, they put me in a car and took me from Sanandaj to Orumiyeh to meet with a religious magistrate so he would order me to be lashed. I don't know his name because they took me without a word, without either of us talking. They took me in a room and returned me the next day. When they returned me to Sanandaj, I asked the interrogator, "How many lashes did he write?" He had written

75 lashes. I said, "Your magistrate either doesn't know how to count, or has never been hit with a cable! Otherwise, your religious magistrate knows that if I am whipped five times you would have to keep taking me to the doctor for ten years! Did he write this for a donkey, or a human being? A human should not be lashed with a cable!" He said, "I know neither lashing nor words affect you, but I'll do something that you can't keep your neck up when walking in the streets." I said, "Like what would you do?"

I was under a lot more pressure in the interrogations during my second arrest, much more than the first time. Even though I was familiar with prisons, the way he treated me was to break me down. He said, "You were walking in the streets with your head held high; I will break your neck and bring you down." I did not even think he was going to rape me. I said, "you want to bring the neighbour?! The neighbours know I was not involved in any activity with them."

When I was threatened, we were in the hallway. Of course, we were always alone. Where we were was quiet. He made the same disgusting gestures again. I could not do anything, but tried to pull away. For example, I wrapped myself in my *chador*. He said, "Why do you cover yourself so much?" In those conditions, you subconsciously cover yourself. It's not in your control. I was never religious, and never will be. But the other person who was supposedly my interrogator, made gestures and actions that made me constantly pull my leg back, but there was no space. There was a wall and the chair. I kept pulling myself back and he kept coming closer. I could hear him breathing. In fact, it was in my face:

- So, what did you do to so and so?

- I have no idea. I have no clue what you are talking about!

He wanted to know through whom I had helped that lady leave [the country]. I said, "I don't know. I have no idea." I admitted to talking to my husband over the phone. I said, "He is my husband. I talk to him. I don't deny it." He had listened to my private conversations with my husband and said these things.

They knew I didn't give in under lashes. It had become certain to them that they couldn't make me talk. He kept saying, "I will do something to you that out of shame you will not keep your head up in front of others."

This type of investigation had emotionally crushed me. Truly, it was much harder than the first time. During torture, they pulled my hands, and my legs, they would move them here and there. They sat on my back. Their gestures were disgusting but this second time it was completely different. He kept saying, "We will do something to break your neck." I kept thinking to myself, "What are they going to do? Who are they going to arrest? What will they do to make me keep my head down from shame?" I was wondering what it could be.

Until, the last night he talked to me, he said, "I'll give you 24 hours to think. If you talk, then good. If not, it is up to you, so to speak. Whatever happens is your fault." I remember we were in the hallway that night. It was the hallway for men's cells. I mean, when you exited the interrogation room, first there were their offices, then there was the men's ward. There were hallways with men's cells on the right, and a wall on the left. There was a radiator that they tied my hands to, and I laid there.

Often, Behrouz would come for interrogations at night when other interrogators were not there. That night I thought that it would be like any interrogation. He said, "I can't stand it. Either you speak or whatever happens, you are at fault." I really thought, as he had done before, that he was approaching me and getting close to me to scare me. I really didn't think that he was going to do anything. When he pushed my *chador* to the side … my hands were tied and I kept pulling myself towards the radiator. My hands were tied, I could not do anything. He started unbuttoning; I thought he was trying to scare me. I could not believe that he was going to do something. When he was done with the buttons, I kept saying "what are you doing?" I could tell from his every movement that he wanted to do something. He touched my body. I raised my voice. He took off the kerchief he had around his neck and stuffed it in my mouth… the struggles, they are futile, but one has to struggle. I am sure people in the cells there could hear the sounds of my struggle and my handcuffs hitting the radiator. I am sure they knew what was happening. He undid the buttons and took off my Kurdish pants. I really struggled as much as I could but my hands were short and the fruit hanging high. He was stronger than I was. When there was no turning back, what could I have done? He put my pants back on and buttoned me up.

Maybe some people see this as torture. But I consider this to be beyond torture. After a while I could no longer feel the pain of lashing. But this will forever be with me. Its pain lingers. No matter what I do, I can't forget it. What kind of torture is this that I can't forget? It has been years and I have not been able to solve this problem. When he was raping me, the problem was not that he was enjoying my body; it was that he was demeaning me. The other problem was that my hands and feet were tied and I could not do anything. When he lashed me, he threw me from one side to another, whatever he did, I felt good. When I said "no" under the lashing it made me feel powerful, but here the fact that I could not defend myself, made me not be able to digest it, and resolve this for myself. Under the lashes, it is so easy, with pulling away and screaming, you could, but in this situation, you could not scream. You could not move your hands. The guy was holding your legs. Your body was in his hands. He was humiliating me with his gestures and everything he did. But under the lashes you feel powerful. There, I was completely crushed. I was not myself for a while. That was when I felt that the only thing that could save me from this issue was suicide. After the rape, I attempted suicide twice in prison.

The first time I cut my wrist. I saw it bleeding. It got infected and that was it. They sent me to my cell after the rape. The second time I attempted suicide with sleeping pills, the same pills they gave us and left them at the cell door. I got a few from someone else and I picked some in the hallway. Either way, I was seriously determined to kill myself. I don't know how many pills I took. I took them around 6 or 7pm. The next day, when they brought breakfast at six in the morning, they realized that I had taken pills and took me to the hospital.

After the rape, I never saw Behrouz again. My second interrogator was called Qasem. He didn't know why I had attempted suicide. After I came back from the hospital, I told him, "If I have the chance, I will kill myself again. This time you saved me, what are you going to do next time? The interrogator gave my dad visitation and said that I should talk to my dad. "Tell him what you don't tell us." Everyone knew me in the hospital. They contacted our house quickly and reported that I had attempted suicide. My parents knew. My dad came and asked, "Why has my daughter attempted suicide. Tell me the reason." He said, "We don't know why she has attempted suicide. Ask her yourself." To be honest, I still don't know if Qasem knew that Behrouz had raped me or not. Or if he knew, whether he imagined that I would tell my dad or not. Because when I went to meet with my dad, I looked like a crazy person. When my dad described it to me later, he said, "When I came to see you, I thought you had gone insane. Puffy eyes, bloated face." In the span of a week, I had cut my veins and took pills. It was 2 or 3 weeks after my arrest.

My dad asked, "Why did you attempt suicide?" I told Qasem, "You really want me to tell my dad why I attempted suicide?" He said, "Yes." I told my dad. My dad was crying and saying, "You have a child, why did you do it?" I said, "Dad, you want to know why I attempted suicide? It was because they raped me. My dad only said, "I don't have anything else to say. I will go and raise your daughter, and will wait for you until you get out. Until then…" He then got up and left. When I was released he never asked me about it. Never. Every time he came to visit me, he cried. I will never forget my dad's tears. Every time he came, I felt that he was a father telling himself, "This is my daughter and I could not do anything to help her."

My dad left and Qasem was shocked. When he took me back to the cell, he talked to me. He said, "Are you sure?" I said, "Yes I am sure. How can a person not be sure? Go ask Behrouz! Why don't you ask Behrouz?" He talked to me, but didn't go into details, and didn't follow up with it either.

But I am sure that the interrogators were there that night. Other people were there too. Behrouz could not do anything alone. Other people had to know. But Qasem was acting as if he didn't know. But I am sure Behrouz wouldn't do this on his own. Since he had repeated that he would break my neck and not let me walk in the streets [proud].

My dad did not tell my family. My mom never talked to me about it. Later, when I gave an interview and talked about it, my younger sister said, "Now I know why after the visit, dad was a different person. He didn't talk to anyone, and only said, "Raise her kid until she comes out of prison. After that, dad was not the same dad." She was right. Anytime he came to visit me, he came in crying and left crying. Every time he came, I thought that he was thinking this is the last time he would see me. Maybe the reason was that they thought because I was raped they would execute me. When they released me I could not believe they were letting me go. Especially since I was being held in the discipline ward in the basement of Sanandaj Court's prison.

They took me to court. They had called my dad and asked for a house deed. He brought a deed. They said, "We don't accept this deed. Bring two other deeds." My brother-in-law brought a deed, and my brother brought his house deed. Then the assistant prosecutor gave me a list to sign. I said, "I am not signing this." He said, "Your dad is waiting." My dad also said to sign. I said, "Dad, do you know what they want me to sign? It says if the neighbour's son does something, I have to report it. If anyone does something I have to report it. If you accept, I'll sign it." I said, "I'm not signing this, if you want to you can let me go, if not then don't let me go. In fact, I don't want you to release me." I told my dad, "I am fine here. I am comfortable. What is the problem? Go home and take your deeds with you." When they released me, he said, "I could not believe you would say those things to the assistant prosecutor." I said, "Of course I would say those things."

I never mentioned it to the people in prison, because I understood their psyche. To be honest, I did not dare. I felt if I said it, they would think I wanted to [have sex with him] too. Actually the atmosphere among the political people was not healthy enough to mention this issue.

Witness Testimony of Sa'ideh Siabi

Name and Surname: *Sa'ideh Siabi*
Date and Place of Birth: *July 11, 1960, Ardebil, Iran*
Date of Arrest: *December 22, 1982*
Accusation: *Collaboration with Toufan Marxist-Leninist Organization*
Date of Release: *March 1985*

I was born in Ardebil. It can be said that my family was po-litical. I became familiar with politics through my older brother. My father also played a large role in explaining political issues to me. I was very curious. My inquisitive spirit would not allow me to sit calm and still in one place for too long. I was born in an underprivileged family and have fully tasted poverty and prosti-tution.

In 1980, because a large branch of *Toufan* had been estab-lished in Tabriz- prior to that although Ardebil had a branch, Tabriz did not- my husband and I relocated there to start our activities. We were both arrested on December 22, 1982. We had an *ezdevaj-e sazmani* (organizational arranged marriage). In Tabriz, we established a committee for the party. After a few months, I got pregnant and my child was born and was 3.5-4 months old when we were arrested.

We were arrested in our house in Tabriz. My husband's name was Towfigh Adib.[1] It was 4 am and I had woken up to breastfeed my child when I noticed we were surrounded. It was 5 am when they took us to Tabriz's *Sepah* office. We were ex-posed by one of the Organization's members. They took my son and me to a solitary cell. First it was a very small cell that only had room for standing. It was previously a stall and was made of metal and was very cold. Azerbaijan's cold winters are famous, particularly in Tabriz and Ardebil. Interrogation and tortured

---

[1] For more information about the life and death of Towfigh Adib, look at "Remembering Comrade Towfigh Adib, Symbol of Resistance Who Joined the Eternal History of the Revolutionary Toilers of Iran," *Toufan*, available at:
http://toufan.org/Maghalat%20jadid/Tofigh%20Adib.htm.

started right there. Later, they took me to a normal cell that belonged to the *Sepah*; it was all in the same building. First, we went there and after a few basic questions about my name and surname, which had all been told to them before, they took us inside *Sepah*'s prison and there was a cell there. This cell was one meter by one and half or two meters. I was with my son.

When they separated me from my husband, he turned to me and said, "If I have done you any wrong so far, I hope that you forgive me." This was very hard for me to hear so I said, "No, they have said that that they only have a question! We will go back." He said, "No! Please be more clever and smarter than this! We have a lot of work ahead of us. Be careful!" I paid more attention and realized that there will be no return. So I defended my stance fiercely. So far as it related to another person, I denied and said that I didn't know them but where it was about me and my ideology, I insisted and stood my ground. I didn't say anything that was not necessary to say but about matters that needed to be said I made decisions wisely and strongly and answered strongly. This caused them to torture me more. Tortures were back to back and they would not even allow a moment or breather. They realized from the first moment that I am not someone to give in so easily.

Insults were very frequent and started from the first moment and with my name. My name is Sa'ideh. As soon as I introduced myself- which was unnecessary because they knew me- he said, you are not Sa'ideh but *saliteh*- shrew." It was the first time that I heard that term. I said, "Yes, I am saliteh which is a derivative of the term *tasalot*- dominance; I have dominance over everything within my surroundings. Thank you for giving me such a name." The interrogators and *pasdars* realized that I was not joking around! The smallest insult they called me by was prostitute and whore in Azeri Turkish.

In Azeri, when they curse they say- excuse my expression- "I fuck it." They would repeat this word comfortably hundreds of thousands times. They would say it about my whole body, my parents, my creed, religion, beliefs, my personality and even the smallest part of my body. The torture began there. In the first stage they told me that apparently I wanted to be beaten. They used vulgar terminology; "we will teach you, make a human out of you. You will finally see the results of your activities." I have never heard anyone use the term 'whore-like' but it is an expression in Azeri. This meant that the person in discussion is no longer a human and was used as a rag for all men because she was found in a team house.

All of our household items, including cameras and things like that, which were very expensive at the time, were taken by them and later confiscated when we were at the Police Prison. They said that we were faithless and owning such items is *haram* (unlawful), so they confiscated them. It was *haram*, but they used all those items in the prison mosque!!

Before going to prison, I had educated myself and read the book "Djamila Boupacha" [by Simon de Beauvoir] about matters relating [to rape in prison] I could make certain guesses. However, such matters had been archived by my mind and I had thought that because they were Muslims and were behaving in accordance to Islam, [rape] would not happen here. I never even imagined! I never imagined it; only believed it possible for other countries. I was personally ready to be beaten. I recall that I used to always tell my brothers to beat me and fight with me in a way that would prepare me for torture under pressure. That way I'd be strong. I practiced this at home myself but I didn't think that sexual torture could occur. The torture began first by beatings. They beat with cables and whips and particularly on the soles of the feet and the waist. It was surprising that at all their procedural levels, they respected religious teachings. Before men would come to administer the beatings, female *pasdars* would arrive and strip us naked and then cover us with a sheet, tie our hands and feet and then wrap our hair- this was very important because men could not see our hair.

They tied the scarf in a manner that would not cover the back of the neck. They lashed from the top vertebra in the neck to the bottom most one. They would not beat any lower than that. They would beat us until the sheet was buried into our skin. Our bodies would be cut open and the sheet would be embedded inside the cuts. When they beat the soles of the feet, they would tie the feet up and beat the soles. They would count: "today only thirty lashes; sixty lashes. It is your *hadd* (limit)." After they performed the *hadd* they would immediately bring us down and force us to walk. They said that we had to walk. Naturally, since our feet had swelled to the size of pillows and were black and bloody, it was impossible to walk but they would step on our feet with their boots. Later I realized that they did it so that blood didn't clot under the skin of the soles of the feet. They would step with their boots on our feet and our feet would go numb. My baby was with me throughout the entire torture sessions. He was 4 months old at the time. He was very impatient and crying and begging continuously. I only remember once when they gave him to the cell next door. Otherwise, he was with me through it all.

They raped me in two rounds; one was in my cell and another in the torture chamber.

In the round of rape that was in the torture chamber the number of perpetrators were more than two. The first time I was having my period. The female *pasdar* asked me if I was having my period and I said "yes, I am" because I thought she is going to give me a pad. After they tortured me in the chamber, they raped me. I passed out. When I came to I realized that I was bleeding but thought that it was the period blood but then noticed I was raped because my backside was hurting. I noticed that I was raped anally because I was having my period. I will never forget those moments.

When they tortured us, they would tie us face down. We would lie facing the ground because they would beat our back and the soles of our feet. But when the plan was different, they would lie us down on our waist. Once the torture was over but he pain was still too much, they would start the raping. I would not pass out completely; it was an unusual feeling that I can't describe. Frustration took over because I could not do anything. The frustration was so strong, particularly because I had so much hatred towards them, that at times I thought my brain purposefully shut itself off for a moment. There were moments when everything would shut off. When I pushed and forced myself later, I would remember. I don't think that this behaviour is normal. It seems rare.

Without a doubt, there was more than one person who would torture me. When one would get tired he would hand the cable to another one and would tell him, "*Ajrakum Indallah*- your reward is with God." The new guy would tell the tired one that his reward is with God. [Reward] from the blows you inflict. I heard that well. The other one would curse and this one would continue.

Because my eyes were blindfolded I couldn't give you any names. One of the big shot torturers whom everyone knew was a man named Abulfazl. He was one of the famous people in Tabriz Prison who delivered the *coup de grâce* [to those executed] and tortured people. I don't know what his real name was but he was known as Abulfazl.

In a vulgar manner, they would tell me, "Pity for such a beautiful body, such a tight … (excuse me!) Why don't we have the permission to benefit from them?" Although [the rape] was conducted in silence, they said these things when they were alone with me, I think. Or maybe others were there too. At some point everything became personal and the feeling that there were others in the room always weighed on me. I am positive, a hundred percent sure, that there was more than one person.

Sometimes I felt that it took hours, even years. It appeared so long to me. I would struggle with myself to not make any sounds because I was thinking of my baby who was crying there. There was much pain in my body, on my back, the soles of my feet. My back had been tortured recently and it was impossible to sleep on it; I would pass out from the pain! Hours seemed like weeks to me. It was so painful that the time seemed endless.

When they would leave, a woman would come and open the coverings. She pulled the sheet from our bodies that were torn underneath the sheet and the flesh and body had become one with the sheet. They would pull clothes over us and throw us in the cell.

After the first time, when I came to, I felt the pain all over my body. I hated myself. I hated myself more than ever. I hated my body parts. I was crying in my own solitude and hoping for death. It was always hard on me because my son was there. I always think that my son remembers them. I don't know why I feel that way. One day when my son was older, in 4th or 5th grade, he came home and was upset and crying and throwing things around. He said, "What is this situation you have placed us in? I am destitute." I asked what the problem was. He said with tears, "I was fighting with one of the boys and he turned to me and said, "Go and collect your mother from under the *pasdars*!" this was very painful for him and he could not understand it due to his age. The way he explained it, he had seen himself as helpless. Because he had not been able to defend himself, the situation had really bothered him. I had shown no reaction to what happened to me in prison after I was released until I came to Canada and exposed everything. Prior to that, no one knew and for that reason, I think that he had realized some of the stuff that had happened.

Another matter that was very painful for me was that my husband was in the men's section of the prison. The issue had not been resolved for me when I was in prison at that moment but I can talk about it right now. My husband had written a letter and spoke of me as being as pure as the ocean. Although I knew that and knew that he was sure of my purity. He kept repeating it every opportunity he got, but I was sure that he could hear my voice when I was being tortured. The torture chamber was so that I could hear his voice too. However, although I had pain in the beginning, I controlled myself and made no sounds later on.

At times, I am reminded of when I was making sounds, even when it was muffled. Even that bothered me; I tried not to make any sounds. When I think about it, I realize that I was willing to be tortured a hundred times more but not hear the sound of my husband being tortured. The sound of him being tortured, towards the end, turned into something similar to howling because he was in so much pain.

Once, one of the *pasdars* entered my cell with prior planning. He had emptied the cells adjacent to my cell. I didn't know what his plan was. Apparently he was one of the people who had raped me before. [I didn't know] because they took us to the torture chambers blindfolded... when they interrogated us we were blindfolded. Apparently he had seen me there and liked me, according to him. After he raped me in my cell, he promised to bring my baby some milk, diapers and other supplies. I never saw him after that and he didn't do anything for me either. From the manner of his attitude and his actions, I think he was one of the rapists in the [torture chamber]. If I saw that person right now, I would certainly recognise him because I didn't have blindfolds on in the cell.

He had emptied all the cells. The way I counted, it appears to me that there were six cells. They were empty that night and I was alone. Each night they changed the guards on the rooftop, whether they were *pasdars* or guards. This time it was different. He came and opened the opening and looked at me. I got scared and got myself together. He had the key and everything. The night watch was supposed to be a man and he wasn't there. Every two nights, there was a male guard. Two nights there were female guards and one night there was a male guard. That night, there was a middle-aged man and it was clear that he knew noth-ing of prison and being a warden and only did the work because of the *shari'a* edicts. It seemed he was trying to do everything in an Islamic manner but he didn't. [The rapist] opened the door and came inside. First he told me that he was coming in. I said that he couldn't and that I would scream but then he said that I could scream but there was no one there to hear me and that he had already planned everything.

From his manner of speech, while he was raping me, from his manner of raping, I could tell that he had been present each time [I was raped]. He was certainly amongst the interrogators. I could tell from his voice and mannerisms that he was present each time. He talked about my body while doing the deed, using obscene terminology. For example, he said, "That stupid man, how come he didn't recognize your value? He doesn't deserve you. They are asshole people who didn't value you. It is a pity!" and such things. He used certain terminology in an obscene fash-ion, "Similar things have happened to you time and time again in team houses so it is not a big deal. This is my turn. This is my share. You are only a rag, a whore."

All these problems aside, I also had to be on alert because they asked tactical questions and repeated questions in different ways, and the problems with having a baby and no supplies on the other, pain of torture for myself and having my husband tor-tured, personal problems of how I felt after I was raped, how I could walk with injured feet, hoping my child would fall asleep and that I could walk a few steps [were all things I dealt with].

I grew up in a very conservative atmosphere. I had no boy-friends and no knowledge of sexual matters. The first time I had sexual relations with my own husband whom I loved very much, was scary for the both of us. The issue of sex was unimaginable for me. I didn't know anything. I was completely a virgin! This was how I was under those conditions with my personality. I was so serious and tough with the boys that I knew. People I used to go hiking with, that those who later told me that they had loved me never dared express it to me. This spirit was very normal amongst the girls in the 80's.

Later, when I went to the police prison, the taboo that still exists amongst prisoners reigned supreme. When I asked other prisoners if they did to them what they had done to me they would all shake their heads. Then I would say, "They are such animals! What does this mean? It's like Iraj Mirza's poem; they do everything with you but under the cover of *hijab*." Then they would show the same reaction. I have so far never seen people talk about it in that manner; they empathized with me. For this reason, I think that they were most likely in the same boat.

I always wanted to escape this fact and not think about it. But I finally broke the taboo within myself and realized that I have to pay attention because the problem would not solve itself by me trying to forget it. In fact, it would get much worse. Thankfully, I got to this realization. I told myself that I have to break the taboo, find myself once again and recognize how things were and what they were like. I was using all my brain-power for this and when I told others in the cell and ward, they would mostly respond with silence.

This was painful for me that many people did not believe me or asked me not to talk about it. It particularly became much more painful later. It was because they considered the problem to be very vulgar and ugly. Of course, it is very vulgar and ugly. I was placed in conditions under which I was raped in the worst possible manner. I could not scream. I could not avenge myself. I could not make a move and show my hatred. Eyes blindfolded and mouth shut and my baby in the corner of the torture chamber! Later, I researched a lot on this topic. This is why I say that although my child was a baby, he witnessed it all. I don't know why but this is a feeling that I continue to have until today.

When they realized that their actions did not break my spirit, they started torturing and harassing me through my son.

One of their torture methods was telling me that I was a faithless mother and that a Muslim mother had to [raise] the child. "This baby belongs to god and Islam. You don't deserve it. We will take him from you and give him to foster care. You should not be subject to this blessing handed by god." Then they sent a female *pasdar*- we could see female *pasdars*- I kicked her in her stomach and she left. The male *pasdar* came. I was squeezing the child in my arms. He first tried to open my arms by force. When he couldn't do that he pulled my son by his shoulders. He pulled the child to get him out of my arms and I resisted as much as I could. At that moment I heard a sound of cracking from my son's spine and thought that my baby is being cut in half so subconsciously, my arms opened and he pulled my son out of my arms.

After the first day or better said, on that first day, my milk dried up. It was so bad that when my child suckled my breast, blood would gush out. I don't know if it was from stress or torture. My child was hungry for days. Finally I realized that I had no option. When they brought us food, potato or Ghormeh Sabzi- if you can call it that because the quality of the food was terrible- or backed beans, I would skin them, chew them, and then place them in my baby's mouth. My four month-old baby was being fed with legumes and heavy foods. After a while, the amount of food they gave us was so little that my child cried of hunger. There were times when because I had not given them any information, they reduced the amount of food and it wasn't even enough for me to eat. When I saw that my baby was so hungry, I would chew on my fingers, let them bleed and have him suck it. When I think about that time, I can never forgive myself. Even to this day I cannot look straight at my son's eyes. I always feel that I steal my eyes from my son's. But I had no other recourse. When he cried and was frustrated from hunger, what other option was I presented with?

Three days before Nowruz of the following year they executed my husband. It was 1984. He was subjected to torture for the entire period of one year and three months he was detained for. On Nowruz when his mother and sister went to visit him, they told them to stay for a while and did not accept the fruits they had brought. The family thought that maybe since it was Nowruz, they wanted to grant them visitation in person but then they were handed the will [my husband had written]. I came to know of my husband's execution 2.5 months later. I was later released around a year after his execution, in March 1985.

Witness Testimony of Banoo Saberi

Name and Surname: *Banoo Saberi*
Born in: *Isfahan*
Charge: *Collaboration with Tudeh Party of Iran*
Date of Arrest: *August 1987*
Date of Release: *February 1988*
Current Residence: *Six years after her husband was executed in the prison massacre of 1988, she left Iran along with her two sons and has since been living in the USA.*

Our family was politically active. My mother was a person who was never afraid and never prevented us from being activists. Another reason [that made me become active in politics] was that one time when I came home, I noticed that small booklets were placed behind the door. I brought them inside and showed them to my father. He said that they belonged to the *Tudeh* party. They allowed us to read the booklet but then they burned them. Every once in a while I would see the publications. I didn't tell my father about them anymore but even when I did, he would no longer burn them because he had made a place for us to put them so we could read them again. After a while, my mother came and told me that a lady wanted to speak to me. I went to the door and saw that a lady was there. She said to me, "I am contacting you on behalf of the *Navid* Group.[1]" This story goes back to before the revolution.

Once or twice I went to Tehran to get Navid. It was an underground group in Isfahan. I had gotten in touch with them around the time of the Revolution. They worked within the framework of the Democratic Women's Coalition. From that time on, I started my work with the *Tudeh* Party in Isfahan. I was twenty at that time, had graduated from university and had been working as a teacher in the village of Ghanaviyeh, a subsidiary of Mobarakeh (in Isfahan province).

---

[1] *Navid* Group was one of the largest affiliate groups to the *Tudeh* Party of Iran that was formed in the 1970's. The group published a self-titled publication between 1975 and 1977. The archive of this publication is available at:
http://www.rahetudeh.com/rahetude/Navid/Navid.html.

The Revolution happened. I was in Ghahnaviyeh when the protests of the teachers and the demonstrations started. We took part in the demonstrations and the protests and organized the teachers' demonstrations. I remember that it was the beginning of the Revolution and I was teaching thirteen primary education classes in the villages in addition to doing my own work. On the *Tudeh* Party establishment's side, I was responsible for the city divisions. I also was responsible for advertising for the women's coalition and for the division in one of the party's areas.

Our house was targeted. I was constantly arrested [while selling publications and doing activities]. We were famous in the neighbourhood. This was how the Islamist forces became found out about us. One day they broke our car windows. The next day, they slashed our tires. This was how they showed their opposition to us.

I had my comings and goings until one Monday, it happened. It was April 10, 1982. At the time, veiling and other such things had not become prominent.

I don't recall when *hijab* became mandatory in schools and in the workplace but I think it was not until 1983 when it became a law. I only kept my *hijab* in my place of work and if I was going to a government office such as a ministry and other government centres where they would not allow you entry without a *hijab*. All other times, when I was going to a friend's house or such, I would try and go without a *hijab*. I remember that I was wearing a dark grey circle skirt and a pink button up shirt. I used to have very long hair down to my hips that I had recently cut short. I was returning home. It was dusk and was getting darker. There were dark grey clouds in the sky that made it even darker. Our ally was long and our house was well inside the ally. I passed a three road and before I got to the next intersection where there was a playground, headlights of a car shone on me from behind. Before the car got to me, it came to a screeching halt that filled me with a sense of insecurity. I shook off the fear and didn't allow myself to get scared. I continued to walk when they called my name. They said, "Stop!" when I stopped, one of them said to me, "we are from the *Komiteh*, you have to come with us." I asked them what their business was with me. This was around the same time they announced that if someone wanted to arrest you, you should ask them to show you their ID cards. He said that we should go into the light. Because the war was going on at that time, the lights would turn off after a certain hour; the only light around us was that of a store. He said, "Let's go there and I'll show you." Before I could move, I felt a pain in my neck and then they threw me in the back of the car. Two people were sitting there and one person in the front. One of them put his feet around where my neck was and the other put his feet on my legs. I could see their faces as well as the driver's face in the dim light. I couldn't see them clearly, but I could certainly recognize them. Later on, I even thought that I saw one of them, the one in the front, somewhere.

Then, I noticed that the route they were taking would in no way lead to a *Komiteh*. We lived off of Apadana 1. From there, they turned onto Apadana 2. Back then, the whole street had not been built yet and was kind of barren at the end. It was then that I realized they were not going to *Komiteh*. I had guessed certain things from their actions- one of them pushed his boots under my skirt- but I didn't want to believe it. I tried not to think of it.

...

It got fully dark outside. Where we went, the ground was really hard. When they harassed me I tried to dig the earth but all I got was a few pebbles. They took turn doing their business. Initially I screamed and yelled a bit but when I did that they insulted me more. They said things like "you guys share women anyway. Isn't this what you want?" This was why I didn't say anything later on. I counted; I pressed my teeth waiting for them to be finished. I closed my eyes and continued to count. I remember that I was stuck on the number nine. I don't know why I couldn't move past it. I would count to nine and start over. I still have the same habit. For example when I go to the bathroom I count the tiles; when I walk on the balcony I count my steps. Whenever I walk up or down the stairs I count the steps I take. I usually count my steps whenever I go for a walk. When I catch myself, I stop. I think this counting has remained with me from that time. I start counting especially whenever I encounter a problem.

One thing that comforted me was that I was certain they would not keep me alive after they were finished with me. So I was waiting for them to be done and then kill me.

Before this incident I was a loud and happy person. I liked dancing and giggling and wearing stylish clothes. I never faced violence at home. We had a regular family. I had not encountered violence until that moment. This incident was the first such a thing I encountered in life and it affected me deeply. I don't recall laughing whole-heartedly after that incident. I don't remember it at all. Maybe I would laugh but it didn't mean happiness. I was greatly humiliated. This feeling of degradation bothered me a lot and continues to scare me, even today.

Aside from the degradation, I felt a lot of pain. It wasn't just them. I felt that they shoved whatever they could get their hands on inside me…

There were two houses in front of our house. They dropped me in front of a large door that they had for entering cars into the yard. They left. First I didn't realise where I was, but after a bit of time, my eyes got used to the darkness and my head stopped spinning. I pulled myself up and sat in a corner. There, I regain some of my consciousness. I don't know how long it took and what happened in the meantime. I felt a great deal of pain in my belly and was bent over for a long time. Aside from feeling dumbfounded, the pain was also ringing in my head and wouldn't allow me to get myself together properly and think of something else. All I remember is that when I entered the house, everyone was sleeping. All the lights were out. When I opened the door to enter the hallway, I heard my mother say, "Honey, where have you been?" I said that I was at a friend's house and that that person's father brought me home. My mother said that I should have stayed there and not come home. I went to the bathroom and started washing myself with a loofah and a pumice stone. My tears started falling. I don't recall crying until that moment. There, under the shower, I started crying. The next morning, I saw black stains on my cheeks and chin and noticed that the collar of the shirt I was wearing was torn. I don't know if my mother realized what had happened to me from the stains and my emotional state but if she did, she never said anything to me.

I no longer felt safe. Whatever I saw in my way or whenever something happened, I thought it was related to me. For this reason, I spoke to the party and told them that I didn't want to do political work anymore. [My establishment officer called on me[1]] and talked to me and I cried nonstop. I told him. He said that we couldn't let this go so easily. He said that a criminal matter had taken place and that we should file a complaint. At the time I couldn't think straight and thought that this matter had to take place. He was older than me and I respected him. So when he said it I didn't object to it. I agreed because I was confused. While we were talking, he dealt a blow to me as well. He asked me if I was pregnant. It was the first time that I had thought about that matter. You can't imagine how I felt. Suddenly, I realized that I couldn't remember when I got my period. I didn't want to tell anyone, my mother or anybody else. In truth I didn't know how to tell her. I couldn't see her break and crumble. So I got an appointment with a doctor on Shamsabadi Street. When the doctor tried to examine me, I held myself so tight that the doctor was not able to do anything. The doctor told me to go home and told the secretary to return my money. The examination didn't happen. While I laid on the examination bed, I bit my hand so frequently and so hard that when I was told to leave my hand was black with bruises.

I would start crying uncontrollably. For example, if I was combing my hair in front of the mirror, suddenly my tears would start flowing. I had changed. I attempted suicide a few times too.

One of those times was when I thought I could be pregnant. But then I got my period and realized that I was not. Sometimes I wanted to stab myself in the stomach with a knife. This happened frequently. Every time, something stopped me from doing it. I wondered what my mother would do, or my sisters… there were other thoughts too. On the other hand, something was calling me to stab myself.

So my party officer had said what he had to me but later he mentioned nothing of the follow up or complaint. He said that they would go and speak to the *Komiteh* people themselves. He said that he had spoken to Zavarreh-ee and told him what had happened. They had said that it was not the first time that some-

---

[1] This individual who shall remain anonymous currently resides in Europe.

thing like that had happened in Isfahan and they had three such cases. Apparently one of them was a girl supporter of *Rah-e Kargar* and another had gone mad. This is what I recall from my conversation with my officer. They had offered some solutions too. Like they had said that I should go to the *Komiteh* and look at photos of the members of the *Komiteh* and identify the ones who did that to me, but then rebutted this by saying that they couldn't expose all their members to me for identification. They finally said that I should file a complaint at the police office and they would follow up.

At the same time Abbas[1] proposed to me. I said that I didn't want to marry anyone. He said that if it was due to the incident, he didn't care. This really hurt my feelings because I thought that other than my officer, no one knew about the incident. How come he knew? Later I found out that [my officer had told my brother-in-law] and my brother-in-law had told Abbas. He said to me that Abbas told him about his impending proposal and he said to Abbas that if he wanted me he needed to know that such a thing had happened to me. He said that he told Abbas because he wanted to know what his reaction would be but Abbas had said that he really loved me and he now respected me even more because he thought that this matter was akin to being lashed.

I told Abbas that he had to have a lot of patience with me. In truth, for a long time, sexual relations were like a nightmare for me and they never became normal. To me, Abbas was always a friend, a comrade, a doctor and everything else combined. He really helped me later in life. [When we had a baby,] I took care of the baby very well. I changed her and did other duties and put cute clothes on her. But I never enjoyed the laughter and playing of my daughter the way I should have. I was always introverted and never felt happy from the depth of my heart.

When we got married, the second group of the party's leadership[2] was arrested and we became homeless. We went to Bandar Abbas and then came to Tehran and lived in hiding. From 1983 to 1986 we lived in hiding. On July 31, 1986, someone

---

[1] Abbasali Monshi Roudsari, member of the *Fadaian-e Khalq* Organizaiton (Majority) was arrested in 1986 and killed during the mass prison execution of the political prisoners in the summer of 1988. For more information about him, see
http://www.iranrights.org/farsi/memorial-case--5224.php.
[2] This would be the *Tudeh* Party's leaders.

knocked on our door. I looked from the window and saw the shoulders of a group of men. I asked Abbas who they could be and he said that he didn't know. Abbas opened the door to see who they were and saw that they were inside the yard and in the hallway. There was 2-3 of them. They came and arrested Abbas and took me and the children with them. My daughter was 2 years and 5 months old and my son had just entered his fourth month of life.

When they arrested me I was with two children. My husband was taken, but my entire fear was that the incident would repeat itself for me. Later, they did not encounter me as a political activist for a long time. I never said that I was political and Abbas used to say that his wife- me- had mental problems and didn't do political work.

On September 27, they arrested my brother-in-law. They showed him to me inside the Joint Committee. My interrogator told me to collect my stuff. When I did and came inside the stairs they kept me there waiting for another person so arrive and I saw that Abbas had collected his things too. He was holding a blanket. Towards the end of October, they took Abbas and me to Isfahan.

After they arrested my brother-in-law, they took my children and gave them to my mother. The kids were with me for around 2.5 months. In the beginning I didn't have milk for my son. My milk had dried up and there was a food shortage. My son was just three months old. They didn't allow me to take a bottle for him either. They told me that I was to be released and that they only had a few questions. Without any milk, my son's circumcision scab infected and he had bloody diarrhea; I had a lot of problems.

When they took the kids, I was a bit relieved. When they took me to Isfahan the interrogators told me that they knew I had been violated. That was the word they used- *ta'adi*, violate. They said that I should write down what had happened. Then they took Abbas and me and kept us in a sort of a hallway that was closed in by blankets at the entrance.

First, they threatened me a lot as if to bombard me. One would be replaced with the other. Before one would leave the other would come and ask if I was involved with this person or that person. I kept denying everything. They would come back again and say that so and so had written that I was involved with them. They were trying to tell me that I was a prostitute. Then they placed me with Abbas. When they placed me with Abbas, I told him that they had said such things to me. I cried and Abbas said to me that they had told him the same things. He said that they had put 120 confessions about me in front of him and said that they had been made about me. They had told Abbas to tell me to write about my issues and they would release me. I said that I would not do that. Abbas asked why I wouldn't. I said that I didn't see the logic in making my life a point of arbitration. "An injustice has been done to me and now they want me to write such things?" Further, they had told Abbas the issues and had not considered me worthy to tell me directly. They had told Abbas that I should recant the complaint that I had filed and then they would release me. Abbas asked them what guarantee they would give about releasing me and they had said that they would not give any. They had said that I should not discuss the issue of rape in the court and take it off of my case file. But I was not taken to court at all for me to even bring it up. I was released in February of 1986 during the investigative stages but Abbas was kept until 1988 when he was executed.

Later on, they pressured me a lot about this issue, asking me who I was with sexually and what I did; who my lovers were and how I satisfied myself since my husband was gone. I always said that this was something that happened to me and they were trying to make me seem like the guilty party! They were always trying to say that I was a slut and had relations with different people.

In 1992, they started summoning me again. Each time there was a different excuse. Or they wanted me to do something for them, which I refused. They threatened to take my kids from me by creating a case file that suggested that I did not possess proper moral quality. They summoned me on a daily basis.

In 1994, they summoned me again to the intelligence office. They asked me to bring my son and I did. Then I realized I could no longer handle it. Three days after that I left the country.

Witness Testimony of Tuba Kamangar

Name and Surname: *Tuba Kamangar*
Date and Place of Birth: *Kurdistan*
Date of Arrest: *June 1981*
Accusation: *Collaboration with Komala*
Date of Release: *August 1982*

I was arrested in 1981 in one of the villages of Kamiaran. [First] I was at home but because my brothers were *peshmergas* (armed Kurdish fighters), our house was set on fire by the Islamic Republic. Along with my mother we accompanied the *Komala* Party and went from one village to another with the *peshmergas*. We were with them. At that time I was 17. I married one of our *peshmerga* comrades. It was more of a forced marriage by the party. The first week after my marriage, the battle between the Kurdish Democratic Party and the *Komala* began. Without the knowledge of *Komala*, I returned to the village where I was arrested. Two of regime's mercenaries were arrested by *Peykar* and handed to *Komala*. At that time *Peykar* was small and was comprised only of a number of people who would accompany *Komala* into the villages. After two weeks of being in these villages- it was the beginning of my pregnancy too because I got pregnant within a week of my wedding- around 3 am they came [for me]. They had reports that I was in this village so they came and arrested me. My husband escaped.

They had reports that I was in the village, in Ta'eeneh. They knew my family because they had set fire to our house. Two of my brothers were *Komala peshmerga* and had been martyred. They came at 3 am and surrounded the house. They had given them my identification and how I looked and what kind of body I had because there were 4-5 other women in the house I was at.

Those who had come for my arrest were all men. They were *pasdars* there as well as *jash*. They were from Nashour village. From amongst those who had come, I only knew one. He used to be a *peshmerga* for *Komala* but had then surrendered himself and become armed and accompanied the [regime forces]. I forget his name but I knew him. There were many others amongst them who knew my family.

Acquaintances who knew my family by first and last name came into the room. They took me out of my bed. I didn't show any reaction because it was very normal for me that they were arresting me. I knew it. The first moment when they took me out of my bed they showed a flash light in my face and immediately recognized me.

They brought me to another room. They said, "We only have business with you. We will take you and you will be released this afternoon."

My mother was not with me at that moment. She was in hiding. They kept me in that house until 4 am and then took me with them. More than 200 men were there. Wherever you looked, at every corner of the house, there were 4-5 men standing.

If they thought my husband was in the house, because he was armed, they most certainly would have set fire to the whole village and arrested him. But he wasn't there; he had escaped.

At 4 am they took me with them. By then the village people had woken up and realized that they had arrested me. They got really upset. They all came to the end of the village to beg them not to take me. I was very young, about 17 [or 18] years old. They didn't allow anyone to come with me. They took me and around 8 am we got to the village of Nashour.

They had brought a lot of cars to the end of the road. At that time, in most of Kurdistan villages, and particularly in the Kamiaran area, there were many bases. There was at least one base every fifty meters. They brought all the women and children of the village so they could see me. All the people had come and were looking at me. Those who were armed left me alone. We were in a large courtyard with high walls. The man who was their leader [head of the prison] had two wives. They all left and it took until 12 noon. They threatened a lot. My crime was that I was with *Komala* and my family was with *Komala* as well. In fact we were doing secret work in the villages and collaborating with the city branch of the organization. On the first day, they threatened me. They said, "You are a new arrestee. You will be here with us! Either you will marry one of us, or you will be executed." I said that it would be better to be executed than … he said, "You either have to marry one of us or be executed." Right there, I said that I was pregnant. It had been three weeks since I should have gotten my monthly cycle. I said that I was pregnant and got a bit scared.

At that time, they were under a lot of *Komala* pressure [to release me]. They all left and placed four guards to watch me. One of the wives of the head of the prison- who had two- came to me. She cried a lot and said that she was very upset they had arrested me. She had a girl with her and said, "You are the age of my daughter but don't worry, believe me that I will not let anything happened to you, even if it costs me my life. Don't be afraid." I said nothing, not even a word.

I stayed in the courtyard on that day. I said in the corner of the yard because all the rooms were filled. They were either releasing someone or transferring that person to SAVAK's former prison in Sanandaj. They emptied a small room for me with nothing in it. It was summer time. I stayed there. Truth be told, they didn't physically torture me but mentally, they tortured me a lot. Whoever entered my room was a bastard. Each room of the building had someone in it. They had built little windows for them too; basically they had built a prison. All of those arrested were either family members or sisters of *peshmergas*. Whenever each guard would come in, he would make a sexually suggestive threat. For example, "we want to be with you tonight", "tonight we want to sleep with you", "we like you, you are so young, such a waste!"

There were three guards who were very good humans. They really helped me psychologically. The other, however, would come inside and discuss sexual issues, discuss sleeping with me; they would say, "We want to sleep with you. You are a young woman and having sex with you would be very pleasurable."

They would say such things when they were alone. One person would come to the front of my window. The room had a small window. I was always at a corner of the room. He would open the window and say such things. Another person was guarding the door. I always had two guards, one in front of the window in the yard and another in front of the door. The prison was on a main road. They pretended like the person who was at the door had not heard anything, but others, who were in the prison while I was, who were mostly parents of *peshmergas,* would hear. Because I was always inside the room and they always spoke to me in that manner from in front of the window, the fact that they were bothering me and harassing me psychologically like this had been talked about all over Kamiaran and even Sanandaj. This was pressuring me a lot. Those who were nice to me, the biggest help they gave to me was informing me of *Komala*'s situation. Later they brought announcements of *Komala* for me. They said, "if they do anything to you, physically, we will certainly set fire to this village. We will not allow a *Komala peshmerga* to be insulted in this manner." This situation lasted six months. When *Komala* would attack and damage the villages, this would increase the times they would touch my breasts and other such things. But they could not rape me. They knew that the 3-4 people [there] were in touch with *Komala* and were worried that they would inform the party if they went further.

Every day, *Komala* would threaten them that if a hair was missing from my (Tuba) head, they would all be massacred. They feared that if they got closer to me, the threat would be carried out.

When they did these things, I only screamed. As I said, they took others in prison to the stables too. This was not like other places, like SAVAK prison in Sanandaj, where there were different floors and where they could take me to the basement. So when *Komala* attacked, they took us to the stables in the village. They would push me in the darkness, throw me, touch me and tried to get closer to me in the darkness. I would scream and then they would keep their distance.

The only thing I ate or drank during first six months was buttermilk (*dough*), without any accompaniment! The health condition was so bad. When winter started, I had nothing in the cement-built room. There was a foam mattress with nothing on it. There was a light too. My legs would swell each night. I could not sleep at all because I was afraid. They had the lock and key and everything. My stomach was slowly growing. After six months, they sent me to SAVAK prison in Sanandaj.

There were three other women in prison aside from me. Mostly they were wives of the *peshmergas*. They had different sentences, for example, they would be released after a month and so forth. Their condition was better than mine because when they were arrested they were together, all three in the same room. I was alone.

I don't think they were threatened as much. As I said, the three of them were in the same room together. Usually attacks were less likely to occur when prisoners are in twos or threes. Even the men who were arrested were placed in separate rooms; each in a room alone. But these three women were together. I was alone in one room.

My entire pregnancy was spent in this manner. After six months, no matter what they did, I was not willing to give up in any way and said nothing about the party or the work they did. Mohsen Rezaei [the *Sepah* commander), who now runs for the Iranian presidency, was visiting Kurdistan prisons during those days. He came. They spoke to Mohsen and said that I was in prison for six months. That my crime was that I was *Komala* as was my family, that it had been six months and I was not willing to say anything or marry any one of them although they threatened me a few times. After six months, they took me to SAVAK prison in Sanandaj. There, I was kept in a solitary cell for a week. Within that week, Mohsen Rezaei came three times and started the trial process for me. They brought one of the *jash* (traitor) from the village in which I was imprisoned to translate. On the first day, they didn't even blindfold me. The second day, I was in the cell and they said, you have been imprisoned for six months and your crime is that you are a *Komala* member. Rezai said a lot of nonsense about *Komala*, yelled insults and said, "Be assured that we will bring them all to you, one after another, and you will be executed along with them, one after another." I said, "Fine! It's not important! You can execute me; I have no problem."

I was six months pregnant. When they took me downstairs on the second day, they blindfolded me. I know that we went down a lot. We were at the Sanandaj SAVAK office. Each floor we climbed down I could hear the screams of girls from the corners of the prison. The whole six months I was in the village prison and felt like I would be killed any day, but I hadn't been bothered as much as I was during that week. Each floor we went down, he would say, "All these people who are screaming are your comrades, *Komala* members. They are being tortured and raped." Mohsen said this.

I didn't know how to speak Farsi then and so they had brought someone [to translate]. I was blindfolded. Someone was holding my hand. Mohsen Rezaei was with us. He said, "We will do this if you don't talk." I said nothing; he was the one who used the term 'rape'. He said, "These people who are screaming are your like-minded supports and comrades, *Komala* members." I said nothing. Then they took me inside a room and I sat on a chair. They said it was 9 am. They questioned me until 8 pm. They didn't even give me water to drink. They said, "You will remain here." Mohsen said, "You can't be any stronger than the others. You can hear all the noise they are making and you know what it is. Just know that we will do much worse to you."

He said, we will do one thing. Maybe we will allow you to remain alive until your child is born. If we can, [we will wait] until then. If not, so be it. It is not important." I said, "It is not important. [I'll be like] all other humans who wasted away." In truth I had no fear and the only thing that happened and really bothered me was that I couldn't cross into the lower level without hearing the screams and yells.

Unfortunately they wouldn't allow anyone to visit or see me. Because they knew that we all know one another. There was no one there. During that one week at Sanandaj prison, I was alone inside a small cell with a toilet and a bed. No one was there. The last day of that week, Mohsen Rezaei came and said, "we are returning you to the village prison where you were kept but I have spoken to the head of that prison and said that you are to be executed either before your baby can be delivered or after the delivery. There is another simple solution too; you can marry one of our Muslim brothers." I said nothing.

Then they returned me to the prison in the Nashour village. I remained there. It was winter and very cold. I could not sleep because I was afraid that they would rape me if I fell asleep.

The guards were the same ones as before. They lived in that village. It was their job. They would conduct operations, attack

Komala, and leave; but guards were there 24 hours a day. They would leave and other guards would replace them. I came back to the village and the head of the prison of that village came and said, "Mr. Rezaei spoke to you and gave you his last words. His thoughts are the same as mine. Either you marry one of us or you will be executed." I said nothing. I went inside the room. They locked the door and I sat down. I remained there until I was about seven months pregnant. They continuously harassed and propositioned me. They would knock on my window asking, "Would you sleep with us tonight or tomorrow night? Ok fine, if you don't feel like doing it tonight you can do it tomorrow night. Promise us that you will sleep with us." Very rudely they would say, "We have nowhere else to take you so you have to do it right here. We have to be together in this room. If you are OK with it, it won't be a problem. We will be able to do it." There was a lot of psychological pressure on me that continued throughout the seven months I was there. Then, I sent a message to *Komala* about my physical and psychological conditions. My physical condition was such that I would fall if I tried to stand up. I would pass out. I had no nutrients and was also pregnant. They sent message to *Komala* and *Komala* was planning on having me discharged by exchanging me. At the time, *Komala* sent them a message to take me to Sanandaj and hand me over to my husband's family through a third party. At that time, two of the religious zealots who were important for the regime were captured by the *Peykar* guys and handed over to *Komala*. In fact, my arrest was based on the fact that they wanted to keep me hostage to have the [*Komala*] hand the two over in exchange for me. They released me and I escaped but *Komala* did not release their guys. So, they arrested all of my family who were in the city. *Komala* took me to my mother's house and I went and handed myself over for the sake of my mother and brothers and sister.

Four people were taken and arrested. They attached my brother to a car. It was very hard for me at the time. They pulled him on the ground for a hundred meters. I went and handed myself in and said that I was willing to die but not willing to have my brother and sister stay a second in the place where I was kept when I was their age. I handed myself in and my sister and two brothers were released.

This whole situation took three days; I handed myself over and they released all of my family members except my mother. My mother was with me and they kept her for a week and told her that she had to marry them. They pressured my mother too. My poor mother was going crazy. It was hard for me too but we were not in the same room during the week she was in prison. I was in one room and she was in another.

The whole Kamiaran area protested when my mother was arrested. All the mothers of *peshmergas* in Sanandaj came there and said they were willing to give all they had to have her released. My mother was released within a week and I was left there. I stayed in prison for nine months. My baby was born. When my baby was born they didn't provide me with anything in the room. I had contractions and pains for three days. I couldn't even get up and when I would get up to go to the bathroom I would pass out but couldn't deliver the baby. They didn't even bring a midwife for me.

I don't even know how my baby was born. I was unconscious for two full days and was bleeding heavily. They brought my older sister and Dalir's mother. My sister said that when they arrived, I was bloody all over and my own clothes were under me and I had nothing else and 4-5 men were standing around the room to make sure that nothing happens and no one attacks. They told me that this was the situation when they arrived. I was unconscious for three days until my baby was born the next day. That day, my sister screamed and cried and begged for me to go to the hospital until they finally took me to the hospital in Sanandaj with four guard cars. They threatened that when I got better they would come after me and I was guarded every day. They said they would attack the hospital. My placenta had not come out [with the baby] so they had to perform surgery. After one day in the hospital, I woke up.

My baby was a girl. After two weeks in the hospital, I was able to sit, even on the hospital bed. After that, the city branch came to take me with them but when they came to the hospital and saw how many guards there were, two at the entrance every day, [they didn't]. After two weeks, they brought me back to my room in the prison with my baby.

My mother then told them that her life was not worth more than mine and that whatever they wanted to do to us, whether they intended to execute us both in Sanandaj prison, we would be together and that she would come with me. She did this because after a month, I was still so weak that I could not stand. My mother accompanied me, but I couldn't stand or really move because I had bled so much. I am not sure why I didn't die! They returned me to the same room in the prison along with my mother.

My mother was there for a week. *Komala* found out about my condition and seriously threatened to set fire to the villages if they did not let me go. Two months after my delivery, they knew I was in a seriously bad condition. They were very afraid of the *Komala* with four guarantees and two houses, they released me.

When my baby was born, one of the officials who always said [sexually charged] things to me, came to my window and started laughing out loud. I looked at him. He asked me how come I was not asking him why he was laughing. I said that I didn't care if he laughed or cried. He would never laugh and always came in angry so to scare me. He said, "I have propositioned your mother. I told her and promised her that either she marries me and you both are released, or she will be in the same condition as you. We also told her that if you don't marry one of us, you will certainly be executed. I said nothing; I couldn't even talk to them and frankly had nothing to say to them. Then a week later, they released my mother on bail. At the time of her arrest, my mother was 45 years old. It was 1981; she is now 75 years old.

They propositioned my mother a few times but she was never afraid and said whatever she could think of to them. They would proposition me in front of my mother. After my delivery! They would say, "It doesn't matter if the baby dies or stays alive, we are careful now to make sure nothing happens to you. It is great because you can now marry this guy or that guy or the other. Or you will be executed!" my mother wasn't afraid of anything because she had also lost two of her sons at that time. She said, "You have set fire to my house, killed my children! I fear nothing! I am here now and if I have just one drop of blood to spare, it belongs to Tuba. I will not let you treat Tuba in this manner. Either we are both executed or both released."

My sister was living with one of our friends at the time. My father passed away when we were little and my mother basically ran the household.

During that time, they gave the baby to my mother and told her to take it with her because they had decided that I would either marry someone or be executed. My mother left. She came to visit me every day but until then I hadn't had have any visitors. I hadn't seen even one person. My came every day, showed me the baby and then left. She relayed the news of my physical and psychological condition to every mother in Sanandaj. *Komala* made threats again; they feared *Komala* at the time. After two months, they released me with a guarantee.

I was in hiding, but my mother had to go in every two weeks in my place to give signatures. My mother finally told me that this manner of life was not sustainable. She said that either I had to stand my ground and show my face in the city or that I had to get out of there. "It is better if you leave because it makes it harder for me [when you are here] and it is harder on my other kids." By the order of *Komala*, I came out into the open. I remained in the city until 1984. Each week, I would go to Sanandaj intelligence and give signatures to show them I was still around.

My child was with me for three years. I gave signatures every week. I knew that if they found that I had contacted *Komala*, I would without a doubt be executed.

This created a lot of pressure on me. The police pressured me a lot. I was followed everywhere I went. If there was something wrong going on in the city, or if I was sitting at home with my child. Anyway, I felt that this was the case every day. Like I said, the Kurds that were *jash* [followed me]. For example, if I would enter my home, which I was renting from a relative, they would tell me, "didn't you see the guy behind you?" I had not. They said that I was being followed 24 hours a day. I realized that I could no longer live that way. I left the city with my daughter in February of 1985 and went to Iraqi Kurdistan. [*Komala*] headquarters were there. I went to [stay] with my *Komala* comrades. I was in Iraq until 1991 and then I escaped to Turkey and was there for six months. I arrived Germany in 1992. At the time the situation in Iraqi Kurdistan was very bad. It was around the time of Halabja, and the Islamic Republic bombed every location we moved to. *Komala* said that those who have children should send them to the cities. "We will be sacrificed and that is fine, but children are innocent." So I sent my daughter to Iran with one of the *peshmerga's* mothers to stay with her paternal uncle. I saw her in 2001 in Turkey. She was 16. She had grown up in Iran and was married. She didn't remember anything but told me, "I don't remember anything but whenever I pass by those villages, I have a bad feeling. I don't even want to see it. It makes me feel strange."

At Sanandaj's central prison and later at the military base and SAVAK prison, there was a guard who always propositioned me and asked me, "Why won't you let us sleep with you?" He said that those who were executed slept with the *pasdar* brothers 3-4 times before execution. To tell you the truth, this really affected me psychologically. Very much so! In fact, I thought about it and was ready for them to rape me; they were not ashamed of anyone! They didn't have an iota of humanity in them. But they couldn't [do anything to me]. Later when I was released and went to stay with my mother, I had nowhere to be and so I lived there. Although I could sleep comfortably while I was there, she told me, "You never sleep! You wake up and walk around and cry. You jump up from bed and sit still." But I had no idea about any of this! It took about three years. I didn't speak to anyone about it then. I told my mother once that they had propositioned me in this way. I also told my brother who came here because both of us were imprisoned and he knew what the prison conditions were like, particularly in 1981, which marked the beginning of the secret branch of *Komala* and was when they arrested many people. My brother said, "It is not important. Even if they raped you ten times, it wouldn't matter. What is important is that you stuck to your beliefs and ideologies and never gave them any information." That is exactly what I did and they didn't rape me, but they tortured me. I still can't, after all these years, sleep comfortably.

At that time in prison, I heard about the raping of the virgin girls. I heard one of the guards say that, as they would say in those times, it is sinful to execute a virgin girl. Before they are executed, one of the *pasdar* brothers has to sleep with them. I was very afraid. I didn't fear execution, but this was an issue for me. In the year and some months that I was in prison, I told them many times that I was willing to be lashed forty times a day but never to be told that I would be raped. They touched my breasts and [the genital area]. This was very important to me. I don't know if it was because of *namous-* my body or what. These things belonged to me!

Lashing was a lot easier for me psychologically. But when they pushed me and grabbed my breasts, whether it was during night while I was asleep or during the day while I was walking, I felt like a wolf had attacked me. A wolf that had no right to attack me! But I couldn't say anything to them. It was hard for me. I don't know why. I even told them, begged them. I think they knew that it was hard for me and that I was not even comfortable to say it. Maybe they could even make it happen one day, rape me; it didn't matter to them. But that they told me that it was very important for me. Like I said, often, *Komala* would attack the villages, place mines in their cars in different parts of Kamiaran. Whenever a villager would shoot a bullet, they would come to me, Forty cars would be dispatched. They would come and inform me immediately that a bunch of them were fighting with *Komala.* Then they would come and psychologically pressure me. It would start from 8 am and continue till 4-5 pm. This strongly devastated me. I couldn't eat anything. I told them, "I want you to lash my hands from morning until night but not say these words or touch me. It psychologically destroys me when you touch me." It was very hard for me. I don't know why. When they would grab my breasts and then push me and throw me against the wall. It was easier on me when they threw me against the wall or even kicked me than when they touched my breasts or any part of my body. This was psychologically hard on me. I couldn't understand it. I couldn't figure out why. I knew that they were bastards and mercenaries. What bothers the most was that you could feel that they were enjoying it sexually.

When they lashed a prisoner, the screaming was enjoyable for them. As much as they raped women then, they rape men now. They enjoyed acts like rape, grabbing breasts, touching the genital area, touching the body. This is torture, psychological torture.

I think their desire or lust to want to rape me is was small part of it. What was important for them was to crush you and belittle you. During that time, 1981-82, they did this to a lot of our comrades. Not necessarily physically, but psychologically tortured. Both in prison and in society. They crushed them. All the torture they endured! In truth they are not human beings. No human being can enjoy harassing another human being. I always felt this way and still do! Even when I think about it now, if I see someone on TV talking about torture and rape, I always change the channel and can't watch it. No matter what channel it is on. I always think, that person [who did it] where was the humanity in him? Where is it now? Because I know how much harassment they subjected people to in those prisons. How many times they put someone on the floor and raped them, tortured them, tried to crush their humanity, the feeling of self, inside them. This was really their main issue.

Once I briefly spoke to *Komala* television. When my family saw the video, they were very upset about why I did not say everything because they knew what happened to me and my mother had been told what they intended to do to their daughter. At night, before I fall asleep, I always remember these things. It is on and off, but very difficult for me. To be honest, I don't want to ever think about it.

Appendix II: Case Studies

Case Study 1: Elaheh Daknama

Elaheh Daknama, 19, was arrested along with 40 other people on June 20, 1981 at a gathering of *Mojahedin-e Khalq* supporters. Marzieh, one of her classmates in high school, says: "Elaheh was a year older than me; both of us were enrolled at Neshat High School. She was one of the *Mojahedin* organizers at school. In June 1981, when I was arrested for the second time, they took me to *Sepah*'s prison and I saw Elaheh there. She had been arrested prior to me along with 40 other girls. *Sepah*'s prison was in Artesh-e Sevvom Street. I was released again 3-4 days while I was there, she was still in *Sepah*'s prison."[1]

Mitra Haghighat Lager who was arrested around the same time in Jahrom says about Elaheh Daknama, "The first time I was arrested was in connection to the demonstrations of June 20, 1981. From Jahrom, they took us to a prison they called Falake-ye Setad or Artesh-e Sevvom in Shiraz. Elaheh was arrested during the mass arrests of 1981… in prison, we didn't speak to one another about personal matters but what I recall is that she was a very happy and energetic girl. We had group exercises with another group of girls; the entire prison worked out a few times a day. She was one of our workout instructors- very happy and strong."[2]

During the winter of 1982 and at the time of her second arrest, Lager was taken to Shiraz for two months. At that time she saw Elaheh Daknama at Adel Abad prison in Shiraz. However,

[1] Witness testimony of Marziyeh Zaboli, Justice For Iran.
[2] Witness testimony of Mehdi Navidi, Justice For Iran.

due to the untrusting atmosphere of the prison as well as the specific circumstances of her case file, Lager did not speak to any inmates at Adel Abad, including Elaheh.

No clear evidence is available regarding the court proceedings by which Elaheh was tried and sentenced to execution. According to the laws practiced at the time, the proceedings of the Revolutionary Court were over in one session and were final and without the possibility of appeal (Procedural Code of the Revolutionary Prosecution Offices and Courts, Ratified June 17, 1979, Revolutionary Council).

Further, it is unclear at what point Elaheh Daknama was transferred from *Sepah*'s Detention Centre to Adel Abad prison, but according to Mitra Haghighat Lager's witness testimony as well as that of Sousan Khoshbou'i, we are certain that Elaheh Daknama was at Adel Abad[1] prison between winter of 1982 and July 1983 and was taken for execution from that prison. Deatinees were generally moved to prison after the completion of their interrogation process. The women's ward of Adel Abad prison was a building with three floors. The circumference of each floor was lined with cells and three people were kept in each cell. The cells were separated from one another by metal rods. There was a long corridor that spanned the inner circumference of the floor. The prisoners on each floor could see other inmates on other floors from between the metal rods on the corridor side of their cells. (see attached photo).

Until her execution, Elaheh Daknama was kept on the third floor of Adel Abad prison along with other prisoners who had remained on their political belief (*sar-e moze*). One of her cellmates says: "She went for execution with a strong spirit. The girls stuck their hands down from between the metal bars of the hallway and she hit their palms from below as a form of saying goodbye."[2]

On July 1, 1983, around 2 years after her arrest, Elaheh Daknama's execution sentence was carried out in Shiraz. At least another 10 young women were executed between June 22 and

[1] A view of one of the floors of women's ward of Adel Abad prison in Shiraz, made available Community Under Siege, Iran Human Rights Documentation Centre, September 2007, P. 30.
[2] The name of witness remains confidential with Justice For Iran.

July 23 of that year.[1] Eight of those ten women were under the age of 25, one of them was only 16 years old.

Aside from Elaheh, her sister Afagh Daknama and two of her brothers were also executed in Shiraz and Tehran for the crime of supporting the MEK between 1981 and 1988.

Mehdi Navidi[2]- whose full name will not be disclosed out of fear for his safety- the closest friend and confident of Seyyed Mohammad Daknama Shirkhar, Elaheh and Afagh's father, states in his testimony that in the last days of his life, Seyyed Mohammad told him a gruesome tale. Elaheh wrote on her clothes that were handed to her family along with her dead body, that she was raped. It appears that at Adel Abad prison, as per the regular procedure observed in other prisons, prior to their execution, the prisoners were given pens and paper to write their wills.

Mehdi Navidi says the following about the matter:

> I was friends with Seyyed Mohammad, who I called Seyyed Aghoo; we were like brothers. Prior to his passing, he was staying with me for 40-50 days be-cause he had had a disagreement with his wife. It was a night in 1991. I noticed that he was very upset and was crying. I woke up from the sound of him crying. I said, "What is wrong?" He said, "I don't have any cigarettes." I said, "Are you crying for cigarettes?" He replied negatively. My house was off of a main street. I went down the stairs and into the street, where every so often a car would pass by. I stopped a car and asked for two cigarettes. Some-how I got the cigarettes and came up, lit one and gave it to him. I saw that tears were flowing down his cheeks. I said, "What is the matter with you? By you and your ancestor, [the prophet], tell me." He said, "I swear to God that I am not upset that they executed my daughters, but I am upset that they raped them." I said, "On your ancestor [the

---

[1] The names extracted from Boroumand Foundation's website are: Mahboubeh Jeddi Gol-berenji, Fatemeh Afrasiabi, ? Panahmand, Roya Hajiani Ghotbabadi, Masoumeh Hassan Zadeh, Maryam Zakeri, Mah Parvin Rabi'i, Zahra Rahmani, and Nastaran Hedayati.
[2] The name and identification of this witness remains confidential at Justice For Iran.

prophet's] soul, are you serious?" He said, "Yes, when we got my daughter's clothes she had written on them, "I was raped; I was raped!" Tears were rolling down his face as he said, "They must have tied her hands and feet and done that to her. I keep thinking about this, that they tied her hands and feet and raped her. Who did this? I don't know who it was or else I would give him what he deserves…" what I am telling you, as God is my witness, I heard from his own mouth. Not a word more not a word less. He died shortly thereafter.[1]

Like many other prisoners who were executed, Elaheh Daknama was transferred from Adel Abad prior to her execution. It is unclear where she was kept between the time she was transferred from prison and when she was executed. Jahangir Islmail Pour, a fellow inmate at Adel Abad says: "The executions did not take place in the prison. They would take those who were going to be executed to 'Chowgn Square', which was located in a large military base named Zerehi Centre."[2]

Hojjatolislam Seyyed Zia Miremadi, Public and Revolutionary Prosecutor of Shiraz, played a significant role in carrying out the execution order for political prisoners in Shiraz both by preparing the indictments of the political prisoners as well as by supervising the handling of the prisons and execution of the sentences. Apparently, the news exposing of the raping of virgin girls prior to execution- which also applied to Elaheh Daknama- was widely disseminated in Shiraz. A month after the execution of the young women in Shiraz, in an interview with Khabar-e Jonoub, Mir Emadi recalls the occurrence of such acts as mere fabrications; "They are spreading rumours that, prior to the execution, girls were married off to boys and then executed… such rumours have no basis in reality."[3]

In November of 1982, Hojjatolislam Seyyed Zia Mir Emadi who was the Revolutionary Prosecutor of Hormozgan, was ap-

---

[1] Witness testimony of Mehdi Navidi, Justice For Iran.
[2] Witness testimony of Jahangir Ismailpour, Justice For Iran.
[3] Press interview of Hojjatolislam Mir Emadi, General and Revolutionary Prosecutor of Shiraz: Rumor of unsanitary conditions of prison and the prisoner conditions - Execution of 300 prisoners and marriage of girls to boys before execution have no basis in reality." No. 889, P. 7, Wednesday August 10, 1983.

pointed, while keeping his previous post on reserve, as the General Prosecutor of Shiraz. In an interview with Khabar-e Jonoub Newspaper, after discussing his actions to crush the *Mojahedin-e Khalq* and the members of Ashraf Dehghani group in Bandar Abbas and surrounding cities, Mir Emadi speaks of the reasons for his appointment to the prosecution office of Shiraz, saying "After I noticed that there was not a lot of work left to do there, I went to Tehran and requested to be transferred to another location where I could be of use and continue my duty… it was suggested that, while keeping my position on reserve, I also become the Revolutionary Prosecutor of Shiraz."[1]

During the trial of 22 Baha'is in 1982 in Shiraz, he asked for the maximum punishment of execution for all of them and therefore, he is one of the officials responsible for the execution of the Baha'is in June of 1983.[2]

According to article 32 of the Procedural Code of the Revolutionary Prosecution Offices and Courts, ratified on June 17, 1979 by the Revolutionary Council, the carrying out of execution verdicts is done with the permission of the General Prosecutor of the country (at the time, Mohammad Mehdi Rabbani Amlashi) and under the supervision of the Revolutionary Prosecutor of the City. Therefore, Hojjatolislam Seyyed Zia Mir Emad played a direct role in the manner in which Elaheh Daknama was executed and the events preceding her execution.

In the latter part of 1983, a few months after a series of executions of female prisoners, including the Baha'i women and Elaheh Daknama and other female prisoners, Mir Emadi was appointed to the post of General Prosecutor of Tehran.[3] He remained at that post at least until December 1988.

---

[1] Khabar-e Jonoub, November 20, 1982, No. 717
[2] Report of Iran Human Rights Documentation Centre, A Community Under Siege: the Ordeal of the Baha'is of Shiraz, available at:
http://www.iranhrdc.org/persian/permalink/3254.html
[3] In his memoirs, Hashemi Rafsanjani writes, "[Mr. Mir Emadi, General] Prosecutor of Tehran came with a group of judges and told me their problems. I spoke to them and promised to provide help." Hope and Concern, Memoirs of Ayatollah Hashemi Rafsanjani of 1985, 2008, P. 255.

Case Study 2: Fazilat Dara'ee

According to the witness statements of all the Kurdish female prisoners we interviewed during our research for this report, the general belief among all female prisoners and their families in various Kurdish cities in the 1980s was that female prisoners were raped before execution. However, they do not remember accurate details about the names of the prisoners or their personal information. Some of the witnesses mentioned names of individuals whose families outside of prison were known to have received pastries as their daughter's *mehriyeh* from a *pasdar*, but since we could not contact the families or primary witnesses for verification, we will not name these executed prisoners.

Kurdish interviewees believe that due to the cultural stigma surrounding the issue of rape, families tried their best to keep it private so their daughters were not shamed.[1]

Tuba Kamangar who was charged by the *Komala* organization to check up on prisoners' families after she was released from prison in 1982, believes that the silence surrounding issue of rape was due to security concerns. She believes: "When I checked up on families in Sanandaj they talked about whether the executed girls were raped. I heard it from their families. These were girls who worked with the underground *Komala*, the majority of whom were executed in Saqqez and Sanandaj. I remember the mothers telling me that when they went to collect their daughters' bodies, they were given a piece of paper that attested to the rape, but none of these people are willing to talk, because they still live in Sanandaj."[2]

Even with all of these obstacles, two of the interviewees gave details about instances of rape before execution in Kurdistan.

---

[1] Witness testimony of Faranak A'eeni, Justice For Iran; Witness testimony of Tuba Kamangar, Justice For Iran; Witness Testimony of Kobra Bane'i, Justice For Iran; Witness testimony of Azar Al-e-Kanaan, Justice For Iran.
[2] Witness testimony of Tuba Kamangar, Justice For Iran.

Fazilat Darabi, 17, from Saqqez, was executed on November 25, 1981, for cooperating with *Komala*. She was among the first groups of women executed in Kurdistan for supporting political groups. Not enough information exists about the exact location of her execution. According to the appendix of the Committee on Human Rights in Iran - Sweden, she was executed by firing squad in Sanandaj. Kobra Bane'i confirmed this fact. However, another witness who was a close acquaintance of Darabi's family remembers that she was executed in Saqqez.

Kobra Bane'i says: "In early 1982, I heard that they took a package of pastries to Fazilat's house saying these are the pastries of your daughter's engagement ceremony."'[1]

In addition to confirming the rape before execution, Mehran[2] who was close to the Darabi family, gave a different account of how the family was informed. "They told the family you should give some pastries or something else, for *shirbaha*- the groom's gift"[3]

She says, "Fazilat supported *Komala* by distributing pamphlets, and nothing more. She was a very beautiful girl. The whole family was beautiful. They said her mother was the most beautiful woman in Saqqez. They were among the wealthy and notable families of the city. To stop her daughter's execution, her mother even went to the office of Montazeri, but they told her there that they couldn't do anything. Even though at that time he represented Khomeini, and he could do it very easily."

They told her that if she repented she wouldn't be executed, but she said: "I haven't done anything to repent. I believe in something and will not change my beliefs. So they executed her by firing squad."[4]

According to the words of this witness, the news of Fazilat Darabi's execution was published in *Komala*'s newsletter which made the people of Saqqez demonstrate and go to Darabi's house.

---

[1] Witness testimony of Kobra Bane'i, Justice For Iran.
[2] The real name and identification of this witness remains confidential with Justice For Iran.
[3] Witness testimony of Mehran, Justice For Iran.
[4] Ibid.

After this event, Darabi's family, along with 23 other families, were exiled from Saqqez to Fouladshahr in Isfahan Province. Mehran, whose family was among the exiled, says,

They took about 23, or 24 families related to *Komala* and the Kurdish Democratic Party, including women, children, infants and adults, to a camp in Fouladshahr, Isfahan. One winter night, at midnight, they came with military forces and ordered them to pack whatever belongings they wanted and forcefully took them to a part of Fouladshahr, Isfahan, that was separated from the city with barbed wire. They told the people there ahead of time that these families were against the Revolution. However, the families made connections with the local people, for example, they attended mourning ceremonies and here and there and mixed with the locals, so people liked them and respected them. Even the stores gave them discounts.[1]

Two and a half years after the exile to Fouladshahr, Isfahan, the aforementioned families could return to Kurdistan.

---

[1] Ibid.

Case Study 3: Leyla Molavi Ardekani

Leyla Molavi Ardekani, a 20 year-old, student at the University of Tehran and supporter of the *Mojahedin-e Khalq* Organization, was arrested in September of 1981 on Enghelab Street in Tehran.

According to information given to the Boroumand Foundation by one of her acquaintances who wishes to remain anonymous, Molavi was kept in the Ferdowsi *Komiteh* office for five days and was then transferred to Evin Prison. She was released on October 13 of that year but subsequently rearrested. An hour and half after her release, armed *pasdars* surrounded her house and the roof of her house while five armed pasdars, accompanied by her interrogator, stormed her house. Molavi was in the shower at the time and was ordered by her interrogator to put her on clothes and accompany the *pasdars*. This was the last time her family saw her alive.[1]

There are discrepancies in Leyla Molavi's official execution date in the existing sources. Boroumand Foundation reported the date of execution to be November 5, 1982 while the *Mojahedin*'s official website notes 1981 as the year of her execution. In their list of 1981 executions, the Committee for the Defense of Human Rights-Sweden announces the date of Leyla Molavi Ardekani's execution to be December 4, 1981.

The family of Nasrin Nekubakht, who was imprisoned at the time for supporting the *Forqan* Group, lived next door to Molavi Ardekani. Nekubakht knew Molavi since childhood. Nekoubakht says the following:

When I was released my mother told me that after Leyla was executed and when her family went to claim her body, they gave the family a sum of money along with the body and said that it is Leyla's *mehriyeh* that they were giving to the family.[2]

[1] The page dedicated to Leyla Molavi Ardekani in Boroumand Foundation Website, available at http://www.iranrights.org/farsi/memorial-case--4008.php
[2] Witness testimony of Nasrin Nekoubakht, Justice For Iran.

Case Study 4: Fariba Ahmadi

Fariba Ahmadi, born in Abadan, was a supporter of the *Mojahedin-e Khalq* Organization. She was spending her prison sentence in Dastgerd, Isfahan, when on August 4, 1988, as a result of the *fatwa* by Ayatollah Khomeini,[1] she was executed along with her sister, Farahnaz Ahmadi, her brother, Mohammad Ahmadi, and over 100 other political prisoners.[2] No detailed information exists about the time and manner of her arrest, and the length of her prison sentence. She was 22 years old at the time of her execution.

All four children of the Ahmadi family were executed for supporting the *Mojahedin-e Khalq* Organisation between 1981 and 1988.

Sanam Ahmadi, a supporter of the *Peykar* Organization who served a prison sentence between 1982 and 1987 and knew the Ahmadi children from prison says, "One day, I saw a funeral announcement that said: to our withered flowers, Fariba, Farahnaz, and Mohammad… and which announced the funeral ceremony. That was when I turned the other way and went straight to Mrs. Ahmadi's house. I saw that it was full of people. The street was full too. They were related to one of my sister's close friends. That friend had told my sister that Mrs. Ahmadi's daughter was raped, and they gave money to Ms. Ahmadi as her *mehriyeh*.

This is why I went to see Mrs. Ahmadi. She was not feeling well, and it is not easy talking to people about these things. I told her, Mrs. Ahmadi, I am so sorry about what happened, I loved them like my own sisters. She said, "I know dear, but they told me my Fariba got married." I told her, "Yes, I have heard. Is it true?" She said, "Yes, a *pasdar* came to our door and gave me a

---

[1] Text of *fatwa* and other information are available in section 2. Women's Political Activities after the Revolution of 1979: a Historical Review.

[2] Mohammad, a prisoner who was at Dastgerd in 1988 says that they executed 90 people by firing squad. Interview with a survivor of the political massacre of 1988, *Fadaian-e Khalq* Guerilla Organization, April 2004, available at:
http://www.didgah.net/maghalehMatnKamel.php?id=24807. Reza Saki, former prisoner also estimates the number of male and female prisoners killed in Dastgerd prison of Isfahan to be between 140 to 150. Mass execution of political prisoners in Isfahan, Bidaran, November 1, 2008, available at http://bidaran.net/spip.php?article180.

couple of coins. There was something else with the coins; they were all in a bag. I said, 'What was it?' He said, 'I just wanted to tell you I married your daughter and this is her *mehriyeh*.' He said for *mehriyeh* I gave your daughter 11 coins of Imam Zaman, and Fatima Zahra *mehriyeh*, and had only said this about Fariba who was the older one."

Mrs. Ahmadi said she insisted so much to convince them to get the money for the bullets so that she could retrieve the body of her three children who were executed in 1988. She took the bodies to Shiraz, and buried them near her other son Khosrow who was executed in 1981.

My sister's friend says Mrs. Ahmadi has gone crazy. She constantly buys henna, incense and candles to take to Shiraz to her children's graves. She tells women "it is my daughters' weddings," and tells men "it's my sons' weddings."[1]

The name Fariba Ahmadi appeared in the list of 1,000 individuals whose execution was published on January 26, 1989 by United Nations Special Representative on the Issue of Human Rights in Iran. This list was developed under the title "Name and profile of the individuals who are said to be executed by the Islamic Republic of Iran on January-December 1988."[2]

---

[1] Witness testimony of Sanam Ahmadi, Justice For Iran.
[2] Information page for Fariba Ahmadi at Boroumand Foundation is available at: http://www.iranrights.org/farsi/memorial-case--2744.php.

Case Study 5: Somayeh Taghvaei[1]

Born in 1972, Somayeh Taghvaei was only nine years old. She was doing her homework when the house she was staying at was stormed by security forces looking for her parents. Somayeh was subsequently arrested. Minutes before her arrest, Somayeh witnessed a struggle between the *pasdars* and two of the members of the *Mojahedin-e Khalq* Organization who were living in the same team house. One of the two men- whom Somayeh considered 'uncles'- were shot in front of her bewildered eyes while the other escaped. It was said that Somayeh was so scared from witnessing the scene that she hid between the kitchen wall and the refrigerator and screamed non-stop.

As soon as she was transferred to Evin, Somayeh was interrogated. She was forced to show the houses of her relatives and acquaintances to the officers. Her interrogations continued until she was released at the age of 14. During the entire five years of her detention, Somayeh was interrogated in various branches of Evin Prison under the supervision of Asadollah Lajevardi, Revolutionary Prosecutor of Tehran and Head of Evin Prison. Meanwhile, the nine-year-old girl witnessed the torture and lashing of other prisoners at the prosecution branches. All the interrogation questions were about Somayeh's parents, Mehdi Taghvaei and Nahid Taheri, who were members of the *-e Khalq* Organization. When Somayeh's parents became aware of the sting operation, they left Iran for France along with their other three

---

[1] Photo and other texts written in this section are in part or entirety taken from the information given by the two witnesses and information published in two memorial journals, one immediately after Somayeh's death and one ten years after it. The identities of the witnesses remain confidential with Justice For Iran. The journals are:
Bulletin No. 10, Second half of Ordibehesht (first half of May) 1998, in memoriam of Somayeh Taghvaei
We have also used the information published in Somayeh's Story, Mostafa Shafafi, London, March 11, 2005, Didgah, available at:
http://www.didgah.net/dastanMatnKamel.php?id=4461

children. Later, they moved to Iraq and to Camp Ashraf. Somayeh was not the only member of the family taken hostage. The security forces also took Hassan Taghvaei, Somayeh's uncle, into custody. Two years after Somayeh's arrest, she came face-to-face with her uncle at Branch 7 of Evin Prison. In a written narration of this meeting, Hassan Taghvaei writes:

Believe me when I say that the weight of the world hanging on my shoulders would have paled in comparison to what I was witnessing. I was completely confused. I stood there staring at her dumbfounded, without the ability to even step an inch forward. My niece held me tightly and kept calling my name. Finally, I knelt and hugged her. My throat was stuffed. I squeezed her, took her scent in and kissed her. I was bewildered as to what she was doing there. She had grown in the two years since I had seen her. Without waiting for me to commence speaking, she started talking while her head was on my shoulders: "Amu Hassan, they arrested me at the Team House. I am staying in the female ward. I do guild work too... her speech and excitement helped me speak again... they had brought Mahdi's daughter to Evin two years ago. They could not find the mother and in order to force the parents to return to Iran and introduce themselves to the prosecution office, they had taken a nine-year-old girl hostage too![1]

Testimonies given by Somayeh's ward mates attest that she was provided with no educational opportunities in prison. She was instead put to work at the women's sewing workshop:

At that age, Somayeh sewed clothes. The sewing machine was as big as her because she was so tiny. She learned to be a seamstress and to sew. This is how she spent her days. Once, when Lajevardi came for a supervisory visit, Somayeh had sewn a button-down shirt. Lajevardi asked her who she had sewn the shirt for and she said it was for her father. Lajevardi said, "So you sewed it for me!" and took the shirt from her.

Initially, she established close relations with some of the female prisoners who either had children or were her mother's age. However, after one of those women to whom Somayeh was very close was taken to be executed, Somayeh didn't eat for three

---

[1] Bulletin No. 10, taken from Tribe of Fire in a Wolf's Trap, Fereydoun Gilani.

days. Somayeh's ward mates decided that in order to prevent further psychological damage to Somayeh's psyche, none of the ward mates would get particularly close to Somayeh. In her last year of detention, the prison officials asked one of the prisoners who herself had a daughter to take responsibility for Somayeh. She asked her family outside of prison to bring clothes for Somayeh and took her to bathe. According to the woman's testimony, during her entire prison term, Somayeh suffered from nightly urination.

She says, "due to psychological and mental pressure she was subjected to, she had nightly urination. The first night, she came to me and said, "Promise not to be upset if I say something." I asked what she wanted to say. She said, "I may wet my clothes at night. What would happen if I am sleeping next to you?" I said it was no problem and that would change her clothes and then take a shower."[1]

It appears that in the first months following her arrest, Somayeh was in much worse conditions. One of the prisoners recounts that Somayeh was given to the supervision of one of the *tavvab*'s named Atiyeh Asbaghi.[2] She used to make Somayeh wear diapers at night. Somayeh had told the aforementioned prisoner that she had pigeons at home and missed them.[3]

Throughout the five years Somayeh was imprisoned, she was never allowed to be a child. The prisoner who had been placed to care for Somayeh describes her days as:

When her work would end in the sewing workshop, she would come to the ward, eat her food, pray and go back to the workshop again. At nights, she used to sit in a corner and talk to me and other girls. Or she would walk to other rooms. Even as a child, whenever the news would come on she would be all ears because maybe she would hear news relevant to her parents. When she walked and spoke, she looked like a miniature doll; she was so beautiful. She had light eyes, long lashes, and a white face. She had an unusual lack of color.[4]

---

[1] The identity of this witness remains confidential with Justice For Iran.

[2] Atiyeh Asbaghi was a member of the student establishment of the *Mojahedin-e Khalq* Organisation. She handed herself over in 1981 and worked in Evin as assistant to interrogators and agents. No information is available from her following her released.

[3] Witness testimony of a prisoner, Justice For Iran

[4] Witness testimony of one of Somayeh's ward mates, Justice For Iran

At times when she slept next to me I placed her head on my bosom. I caressed her and touched her hair. Unfortunately, in those days in the prison, people were so mixed that one could hardly trust the woman sitting next to her. There were those who were executed because of one report alone. Although she was young, Somayeh understood that and tried to keep her silence as much as possible. I seldom remember her joking or laughing. Sometimes I wanted her to play with other kids who were in the ward with their mothers… Even the games were momentary for Somayeh because after them, she would be alone. She sat at the corner of the room and would stare in silence for long stretches of time.[1]

In 1984, the prison authorities called on Somayeh and took her away from the ward. Two weeks later they brought Somayeh back to prison. One of the witnesses says,

When she returned her hands were hennaed. Her nails were hennaed too.[2] She also had a gold bangle. I asked her, "Somayeh Jan, where have you been?" she said, "I was taken to Haj Lajevardi's house." When she returned from that place she was no longer the same Somayeh. She had appeared depressed. Her childish tenderness had vanished. Even her attitude had changed and she had become disgruntled. She was taken from the ward shortly thereafter. I didn't know where she was anymore, but I asked about her from the girls coming from other wards. A few said that they had heard her name called in the branch: Taghvaei.

In 1986, when she was around 14, Somayeh was handed to the custody of her paternal aunt after around five years of imprisonment. After that, Somayeh's paternal uncle accepted to be her guardian and she lived in his household.

In a letter written to her family dated April 16, 1986 and after her release from prison, Somayeh wrote:

"Dear father, if that incident (the conflict and my arrest) had not taken place, I should have been in 8th grade. In order to makeup for the lost time, I am currently studying. If I can, I would like to make

---

[1] From Bulletin No. 10.
[2] Based on Iranian tradition, the hands of a woman about to be married will be hennaed and she will be gifted with gold accessories.

up the missing classes in the three months of summer when the school is closed."

Somayeh started attending school outside of prison. A few years after her release, a woman came to Somayeh's uncle's home and asked for Somayeh's hand in marriage for her son. Somayeh's uncle rejected this, reasoning that Somayeh's parents were not around. Following that incident, Somayeh and her uncle were summoned by the Revolutionary Prosecution Office at Evin Prison where Somayeh was told by one of the prosecution office's officials that if she did not accept the marriage proposal, she would be returned to prison again.

Thus, at the age of 18, Somayeh Taghvaei was married to a man who was a close associate of certain governmental officials and had served in the Iran-Iraq war.[1] The forced marriage resulted in two daughters.

Somayeh was in her early twenties when the doctors noticed of the presence of cancerous tumours in her body. The medical treatment received in Iran was not fully effective. Somayeh's parents left the *Mojahedin-e Khalq* Organisation in 1992 and had since moved to London, UK. Somayeh was sent to London to the care of her parents to pursue further treatment. A year later, on March 15, 1998 and at the age of 25, Somayeh lost her battle with the advanced stage of cancer in a London hospital. She was never given the opportunity to feel secure, safe and calm enough to retell what happened to her in her lost childhood.

---

[1] Our research in finding the name and identification of this man were fruitless.

Appendix III: Details of Interviewees

Names of the prisoners who were interviewed

1. Abbas Daneshvar
2. Akram Mousavi
3. Amir Mirza'ian
4. Anahita*
5. Ashraf Adelzadeh
6. Azar Al-e-Kanaan
7. Banoo Saberi
8. Ebrahim dela*
9. Farah B.*
10. Faramarz Shahbazi*
11. Faranak A'eeni
12. Fariba Sabet
13. Fariba*
14. Farkhondeh Ashna
15. Farzaneh Zolfi*
16. Giti*
17. Golrokh Jahangiri*
18. Hamid Kharrazi
19. Hasan Fakhari
20. Hasan Golzari
21. Hayedeh Ravesh
22. Homa Sadegh*
23. Iraj Mesdaghi
24. Jahangir Esmaeilpour
25. Jila*
26. Kianoosh Etemadi
27. Kobra Bane'i
28. M. Zarkar*
29. Manijeh*
30. Mazar Bokhara'ee
31. Marina Nemat (Moradi Bakht)
32. Maryam*
33. Mehri Elghaspour
34. Mersedeh Gha'edi
35. Mina Entezari
36. Mina Farzi*
37. Minou Homeyli
38. Mitra Haghighat Lager
39. Mitra Razavi
40. Mitra Tahami
41. Mojdeh Arasi*
42. Mona Roshan*
43. Monireh Baradaran
44. Morteza*
45. Naser Khandabi
46. Nasim Maroufi*
47. Nasrin Nekubakht
48. Nasrin Parvaz*
49. Nazli Partovi
50. Nezam*
51. Niloufar Shirzadi
52. Parastou*
53. Parvaneh Alizadeh
54. Parvaneh Aref
55. Rasoul Shokati
56. Sa'ideh Siabi
57. Sara L.*
58. Sara Raha'ee*
59. Sepideh Farsi
60. Shahin Chitsaz
61. Shahla Mihani*
62. Shahla Molavi
63. Shahram Jalali Zadeh
64. Shayesteh Vatandoust
65. Shiva Mahboubi
66. Shokat Mohammadi
67. Siba Nobari (Navak)
68. Simin Behrouzi*
69. Soheila Bahadori
70. Soraya K.*
71. Soraya Zangbari
72. Soudabeh Ardavan
73. Tahereh Dezfouli
74. Tahmineh Pegah*
75. Taraneh*
76. Tuba Kamangar
77. Violet*

* The real name of this prisoner is archived and confidential at Justice For Iran.

Table of Interviewees who experienced pregnancy or motherhood in prison

No.	Name	Prison	Pregnancy	Miscarriage	Birth	With a young child	Explanation
1	Azar Al-e-Kanaan	Sanandaj Prison, Evin				X	Arrested along with her one year-old daughter in fall 1982. They remained in prisons of Sanandaj and Evin for a year and half.
2	Banoo Saberi	Joint Committee				X	The entire family was arrested and she was confined to a cell at the Joint Committee along with her 2 ½ year-old daughter and three month-old son for over two months.
3	Tuba Kamangar	Nashour Detention Centre	X		X		Was pregnant when detained, and delivered her child in her solitary cell while alone and without any medical care or facilities. She lost consciousness and after three days, while she was still covered in blood, her sister was brought to prison to help her and the child.
4	Soraya Zangbari	Evin Prison				X	Arrested on September 1, 1985, and imprisoned with her 53 day-old son. She spent six months in solitary cells at ward 209 with her infant son. Her son was in prison with her for three years, until 1988.
5	Sara Raha'ee	Evin Prison	X	X		X	Arrested on her son's second birthday in July 1983, while unbeknownst to her she was pregnant with another child. Her husband had been arrested three days prior. She had a miscarriage within the first few days of her imprisonment. Her son was with her throughout her prison term.
6	Sara L.	Evin Prison				X	Arrested with her one year-old child, who became ill but was denied medical treatment and facilities, placing extreme pressure on both.
7	Soheila Bahadori	Ghezel Hesar Prison				X	Arrested in 1981 for supporting *Ranjbaran*, and imprisoned along with her 2 month-old son. They remained in Ghezel Hesar until March 1983.
8	Sa'ideh Siabi	Tabriz Prison				X	Arrested along with her husband and four month-old baby. Her husband was executed and she was raped repeatedly in the presence of her infant son. Her child remained with her until her release when he was five years old.
9	Shayesteh Vatandoust	Bandar Anzali Prison	X		X		Arrested during the first weeks of pregnancy. She endured severe torture which took an extra toll on her due to her physical condition. Her daughter was delivered inside the prison, and remained with her until 14 months of age.
10	Fariba Sabet	Evin Prison				X	While her husband was being pursued and forced to flee the country, she was in prison with her 8 month-old daughter. Her daughted remained in prison with her until she was two years old.
11	Kianoosh Etemadi	Joint Committee	X	X			A few weeks into her pregnancy while detained at Joint Committee, she started bleeding as a result of beatings with fists and kicks from her interrogator who went by the pseudonym Hamid. She had a miscarriage.
12	Mona Roshan	*Komiteh* Detention Centre in Karaj	X		X		A month after her arrest in June 1984 she delivered her baby at a hospital in Karaj. After the delivery her child is given to her mother in law at the hospital and she was returned to prison. She was lashed 70 times in the last month of her pregnancy.
13	Manijeh	*Sepah* Detention Centre in Gachsaran	X		X		She was arrested one month before the end of her third trimester and spent her days, until her delivery, in extremely undesirable conditions inside a container with 18 other women
14	Mehri El-ghaspour	Sahra *Komiteh* - Ahvaz				X	Arrested a few days after a caesarean operation along with her days old baby. Her husband had just been killed in fighting with the government.
15	Violet	Evin Prison	X	X			She was arrested at the age of 29 in 1990 for her affiliation with *Rah-e Kargar*. At the time she was one month pregnant and suffered a miscarriage due to severe tortures endured.

Glossary

Asayeshgah: literally sanitarium; a ward in Evin prison

brother: In the vernacular of the government officials in the early years of the revolution, 'brother' was a general term that was used to describe any of male government affiliate or supporter (*hizbullahis*). When used by the prison officials, it usually referred to the guards, *pasdars* or other prison or revolutionary prosecutor's officials.

chador: a long semicircle of fabric, which is wrapped around and is meant to cover the whole female body from head to toe except the face.

chomaghdar: club wielders.

ezdevaj-e sazmani: literally organizational arranged marriag; a marriage that a superior in a political organization arranges for the sake of security or continuity of the member's activities.

Fadaian-e Khalq Guerilla Organization (Minority): a Marxist-Leninist organization that was a section of the *Fadaian-e Khalq* Guerilla Organization, which split off in opposition with the Islamic Republic. The Organization was amongst the first groups to be banned.

Fadaian-e Khalq Organization (Majority): Iranian *Fadaian-e Khalq* Organization (Majority) was a section of the *Fadaian-e Khalq* Guerilla Organization that split off in support of the Islamic Republic and got close to the *Tudeh* Party. Until 1983, this organization tried to support the regime in order to strengthen Khomeini's anti-imperialist position.

faqih: high-ranking cleric who is an expert on *fiqh*. Commonly used synonymously with *mujtahid.*

fatwa: religious edict; opinion exerted by a *mujtahed* or *faqih* on any matter. It is a *Shii* practice that when in doubt, followers of a *mujtahed* ask for his opinion or *fatwa*, which is normally the final say on the matter.

Fadaian-e Khalq Guerilla Organization: a Marxist revolutionary organization which was established in 1971 to oppose the Shah regime's criticism of the communist *Tudeh* party.

fiqh (feqh): Islamic jurisprudence

Forqan Group: an Islamist group which believed in an Islamic government without *velayat-e faqih*. Immediately after the Islamic Republic gained power, the Group started assassinating individuals associated with the regime. The Group was dissolved soon after its central cadre was arrested and executed during the first year following the revolution.

graves, *tabootha:* In 1983, a group of leftist women inmates were taken to an unprecedented punishment ward in Ghezel Hesar Prison. From six o'clock in the morning until eleven o'clock at night prisoners were forced to sit, blindfolded and motionless, in small wooden cubicles, to which they were later referred as *tabootha* (coffins or graves). The head of this prison called it karkhaneh-ye-adamsazi (a human manufacturing factory). Covered in chador, with no movement permitted- the space was so tiny that there was no room to move anyway- while any sound, even coughing or sneezing, was punished by beatings, the inmates felt frozen in an eternal time. The overwhelming silence was broken only by the sounds of beatings and the recantations, religious hymns, or recitations of Qur'an broadcasted from the loudspeakers. Only a small minority of these inmates survived insanity, death by suicide, or falling into the abyss of collaboration as *tavvabs.*

hadd pl. hudood, hodud: literally, 'the limits'. Used mainly in reference to Muslim penal laws, and the evidentiary requirements and maximum punishments as prescribed in the *Koran.*

hadith: reported saying of the Prophet Mohammad.

halal: literally means 'lawful' in Arabic. It usually refers to permissible acts according to the *shari'a* and its antonym is the word *haram* (see definition below)

haram: literally means 'forbidden' and 'prohibited.' This term can refer to things, persons and behaviour.

Hezb-e Khalq-e Musalman: Muslim Nation Party.

hijab : literally means 'cover' in Arabic; a scarf or veil designed to cover the head and neck of a woman; religious covering; modest attire and a headscarf.

hizbullahi: partisan of God; fanatical supporters of Ayatollah Khomeini described themselves as such, conveying the meaning that they do not belong to earthly political parties and only follow God's word through their leader, Khomeini.

Hosseiniyeh: the religious chapel; a large hall in prison used mainly for prisoners' public recantation

jash: literally 'donkey's foal'; a type of collaborator, usually a military unit composed of people of Kurdish descent that cooperates with enemy combatants against the Kurdish army,

Kurdish rebels, or the Kurdish civilian population. The term is considered derogatory in a cultural sense in much the same way as quisling is.

Jebhe Melli, National Front: a coalition of Iranian nationalist individuals and groups.

kaniz: female slave

Komala: Organization of the Revolutionary Toilers of the Iranian Kurdistan is a local Kurdish group that demanded the right of the Kurdish people to self determination. The *Peshmerga* of *Komala* were heavily attacked by the *pasdars* and military men sent from outside of Kurdistan in 80s.

Komitehs: Islamic Revolutionary Committees located in each neighbourhood in the city of Tehran, as well as in other cities.

Koran: the holy book of Islam.

kuffar: infidels.

La'nat Abad: literally land of the cursed or the damned place; The portion of the cemetery in which the political prisoners are buried.

mahr, mehriyeh: marriage portion payable to the wife at any time after the marriage; a sum of money or any valuable that a man gives or pledge to give the wife at the time of marriage.

mahram: permissible to one another

malik: slave owner.

mojahed pl. *mojahedin:* literally, a warrior, a fighter; a crusader; refers to those affiliated with the *Mojahedin-e Khalq* Organisation.

Mojahedin-e Khalq Organisation (People's *Mojahedin* of Iran): an Islamist political organization that enjoyed a strong popular base in the early 1980's. The *Mojahedin* also became the subject of the Islamic Republic's anger. After the events of June 20, the *Mojahedin* officially announced their entry into the armed phase which led to armed struggle with the regime. In the later years until now, this organization has mainly been active outside of Iran and mostly out of their base in Iraq.

Mojahedin of the Islamic Revolution Organization: an Islamist organisation combined from seven armed Islamist groups which opposed Shah's regime.

muharib: enemy of God.

muharibih: waging war against God, war against God and the state; enmity against God.

munafiq pl. munafiqin: hypocrite; a derogatory term used by the regime to refer to Mojahedin, those affiliated with the *Mojahedin-e Khalq* Organisation.

murtad :apostate.

namous: sexual honour; a man's honour derived from the conduct of his women folk.

Nehzat Azadi: Iran Liberation Movement; committed to the ideas of Iranian nationalism, Western liberalism, and Shii Islam funded in 1961 by Mehdi Bazargan. Ayatollah Khomeini appointed Bazargan as the head of the transitional government.

nifaq: hypocrisy.

pasdar: Revolutionary Guard.

peshmerga: literally, those who face death; armed Kurdish fighter.

Peykar: Peykar Organisation for the Liberation of the Working Class was another Marxist and leftist organisation that opposed the regime. The supporters of this organisation sustained heavy blows form the Islamic Republic.

qisas: retribution covering bodily harm and homicide; defined as matters of private claim.

qusl: total immersion of the body (or the object) into a pool of still water for ritual purity which is duty of a Muslim in some occasions such as after having sex.

Rah-e Kargar: Organisation of the Revolutionary Labourers of Iran (*Rah-e Kargar*): a Marxist organization that stood opposed to the Islamic Republic.

Ranjbaran: Iranian Toilers Party (*Ranjbaran*): a small organisation supported Bani Sadr at a certain period. Their collective policy was to oppose the Islamic Republic.

Razmandegan, Combating Organisation of Iran for Liberation of the Working Class (*Razmandegan):* a leftist opposition group opposed to the Islamic Republic. The Organisation was active in certain parts of Iran and was closely affiliated with *Peykar.*

Sahand, Union of Combating Communists (*Sahand*): a Marxist organisation established by a group of leftist students outside of Iran. Later, *Sahand* became affiliated with *Komala* and established the Communist Party of Iran, which itself went through a series of splitting.

Sar-beh-daran, Communist Union of Iran (*Sar-beh-daran*): a Marxist-Leninist-Maoist organization that believed in armed struggle. The organisation supported Bani Sadr during a certain period and after that started armed operations which lead to their heavy loss.

sar-e moze: refers to prisoners who maintained their stand and refused to repent.

SAVAK: *Sazeman-e Ettela'at va Amniyat-e Keshvar.* Organisation of Intelligence and National Security; the secret police; domestic security and intelligence service established by Iran's Mohammad Reza Shah.

Sepah: Sepah-e Pasdaran-e Enghelab-e Islami: Islamic Revolutionary Guards Corps (IRGC).

shari'a: Islamic law; rules and regulations that are derived in principle from the *Koran* and traditions relating to the words and deeds of the Prophet; these rules govern the lives of Muslims.

siqih: temporary marriage; a renewable contract of marriage for a defined duration from a few hours to ninety-nine years; a wife in such a marriage.

ta'zir. discipline; punishment at the discretion of a judge; discretionary punishment; lashing.

taquti: Idol worshipper; demonic; Westernised person; Individuals referred to as *'taquti'* were a diverse group comprised of people such as Shah government officials to venture capitalists, factory owners, farming land owners, private and commercial property owners and upper class women.

tavvabs : prisoners who recanted their political opposition, expressed their support for the regime and collaborated with the *pasdars.*

team house: a place that the supporters and members of a political organisation secretly live and work together.

Tudeh Party of Iran: one of the oldest parties of Iran that after the 1979 revolution supported Soviet Russia as well as the Islamic Republic. In spite of the party's total support of the regime, in 1983, it was violently suppressed and many of its supporters and leaders were arrested, imprisoned and executed.

Toufan. a Marxist-Leninist Organization which was active in certain parts of Iran.

Velayat-e faqih. the rule of guardianship of the Islamic jurisprudence. It refers to Ayatollah Khomeini's thesis about the guardianship of the *faqih* as the head of state, which constitutes the basis of the Constitution of the Islamic Republic.

zina: sexual intercourse between parties not married to one another. In the Islamic Republic *zina* is a crime punishable by flogging or stoning to death.

zina bih anf: rape; literally '*zina* by force.'

zir-e hasht: a small entrance hall in front of each ward that separated the main ward from the guard's office, often used for punishment; food was also divided and distributed there.

References

Books:

1. Abrahamian Ervand. Radical Islam: the Iranian Mojahedin. I. B. Taurus & Co.: 1989
2. Ardavan Soudabeh. Prison Memoirs: 2004, Sweden
3. Dehghani Ashraf. The Epic of Resistance, Siahkal Publication
   http://www.siahkal.com/publication/Hemaseh/contents.pdf
4. Ismailpour Jahangir. "Adel Abad, A Lasting Grief," Baran Publication, Sweden
5. Jaberi Homa. Islands of Torment. Amir Khiz Publication: August 2007
6. Khomeini Ruhollah. Tahrir al-Wasilah, Vol 4: 1997, Darolelm, Qom
   http://www.hodablog.net/files/obook/tahrir4.htm
7. Mirdar, Morteza. Memoirs of Hojjatolislam Nategh-Nouri. Islamic Republic Documentation Centre: 2005
8. Montazeri Hossein-ali. Memoir of Ayatollah Montazeri. Ketab publication, Winter 2000. Page 350-352 and Volume 2
   http://amontazeri.com/farsi/khaterat/html/1097.htm
9. Mousavi Ahmad. Goodnight Comrade. Baran Publication, Sweden: 2005
10. Razi Abolfotouh. Rozoljanan o Rouholjenan fi Tafsire Alquran, The 10th volume. Moasses Tahghighat va Nashr Maaref Ahlebeit

Papers, Articles & Periodicals

1. Ayandegan Newspaper: 2nd August 1979.Page 3
2. Amnesty International Document. MDE 13/09/87-mde130081987
3. Ettelaat Newspaper, 18th October 1981. No. 16553
4. Ettelaat Newspaper. Mehdi Bahadoran's report re Gharna: 17th September 1979
5. Ettelaat Newspaper. No. 16475: 21st Tir 1358 [12th July 1979]. Page 2
6. Ettelaat Newspaper: 19th April 1981. No. 16406, page 15, and: 19th May 1981. No. 16431. Page 3 and 13.
7. Ettelaat Newspaper: 22nd December 1981. No. 16607
8. Guardian Newspaper. Interview with Ayatollah Khomeini: 6th November 1978
9. KAR magazine, the official publication of the Fadaian-e Khalq – Minority. No. 112: 3rd June 1981
10. Khabar Jonoub. Press Conference of Hojjatolislam Mir Emadi, General and Revolutionary Prosecutor of Shiraz: Rumors of the Unsanitary Prison Conditions and Situation of Prisoners, Execution of 300 Prisoners and Marrying of Girls to Boys Prior to their Execution is an Absolute Farce. No. 889: 10th August 1983. Page 1
11. Khorasan Newspaper. "Mr. Prosecutor, Boldly, Boldly,": 25th August 1981. No. 9294. Page 1
12. Khorasan Newspaper. Response of the Revolutionary Prosecutor of Mashhad to the article "Mr. Prosecutor, Boldly, Boldly,": 31st August 1981. No. 9298. Page 1-2
13. Khorasan Newspaper: 2nd August 1981. No. 9294. Page 1
14. *Mojahed* Publication: 23rd June 1981. No. 127
15. Talebi Shahla, Who is Behind the Name?. A Story of Violence, Loss, and Melancholic Survival in Post Revolutionary Iran. Journal of Middle East Women's Studies. Vol. 7, No. 1: Winter 2011. Page 51

Online Articles, News & Papers

1. Aftab News: 28th June 2011
    http://www.aftabnews.ir/vdcjyhevvuqe8hz.fsfu.html.

2. Aftab News: 2nd October 2009
    http://www.aftabnews.ir/vdcewp8o.jh8wpi9bbj.html

3. Amin Shadi. One Hundred Years of Pleasure, Sexuality and Power
    http://www.shabakeh.de/archives/individual/001199.html#more.

4. Amnesty International. "Iran Election Contested Repression Compounded":
    2009
    http://www.amnesty.org.uk/uploads/documents/doc_19994.pdf

5. Amnesty International. For instance, please see the report: "Iran, Election
    Contested, Repression Compounded": December 2009
    http://www.amnesty.org/en/library/asset/MDE13/123/2009/en/1e69
    a8fb-dcf1-4165-a7fc-a94369e364bf/mde131232009en.pdf

6. Amnesty International. IRAN: BRIEFING PAPER. MDE 13/008/1987:30th
    April 1987
    http://www.amnesty.org/en/library/info/MDE13/008/1987/en

7. Amnesty International. Law and Human Rights in the Islamic Republic of
    Iran. MDE 13/003/1980:1st February 1980
    http://www.amnesty.org/en/library/info/MDE13/003/1980/en

8. Amnesty International. Rape and sexual violence: Human rights law and stan-
    dards in the International Criminal Court. Index No. IOR 53/001/2011:1st
    March 2011
    http://www.amnesty.org/en/library/info/IOR53/001/2011/en.

9. Amnesty International. Rare and Sexual Violence: Human Rights and Stan-
    dards in the International Criminal Court:1st March 2011
    http://www.amnesty.org/en/library/info/IOR53/001/2011/en.

10. Amnesty International. Seeks to Send Mission to Iran in Effort to Stop Execu-
    tions. AI INDEX MDE 13/13/81:12th October 1981
    http://www.iranrights.org/english/document-174.php.

11. Arash Publication. Second war of Turkmen Sahra, interview with Abbas
    Hashemi (Hashem), Fereidoun
    http://www.arashmag.com/content/view/476/47.

12. "Biography of a Classmate": 18th September 2009
    http://shivaf.blogspot.co.uk/2009/09/blog-post.html

13. For more information about Landlord-Tenant plan
    http://www.psri.ir/mojahedin/18-3.pdf.

14. Ghahari Nouriman. Arash Magazine, Cognitive Dissonance
    www.arashmag.com/content/view/676/47

15. Hashemi Seyyed Mahmoud. "Who is a *muharib* and what is *muharibih*?. Part 2.
    Fiqh-i Ahl-i Bayt, No. 13
    http://www.hawzah.net/fa/articleview.html?ArticleID=85967

16. Human Rights Documentation Centre. Haunted Memories: The Islamic Re-
    public's Executions of Kurds in1979,Iran
    http://www.iranhrdc.org/english/publications/reports/3508-haunted-
    memories-the-islamic-republics-executions-of-kurds-in-1979.html

17. Iran Human Rights Documentation Centre. "Violent Aftermath - The 2009
    Election and Suppression of Dissent in Iran": February 2010
    http://www.iranhrdc.org/english/publications/reports/3161-violent-
    aftermath-the-2009-election-and-suppression-of-dissent-in-iran.html

18. Islamic Republic Documentation Centre. Formation of the Revolutionary
    Council,

http://www.irdc.ir/fa/calendar/77/default.aspx

19. Makhmalbaf Mohsen, Fariba Valiat, Behnam Bavandpour .Deutche Welle. Sexual raping in Iranian prisons is a certain matter… : 16th August 2009
http://www.dw-world.de/dw/article/0,,4575831,00.html

20. Mir Hosseini Ziba. Broken Taboos in Post-Election Iran. Middle East Research and Information Project:17th December 2009
http://www.merip.org/mero/mero121709

21. Plan of Bani Sadr's Lack of Competence in Majlis June 20, 1981
http://www.ical.ir/index.php?option=com_mashrooh&view=session&id=187&page=3051&Itemid=38

22. Prosecutor v. Germain Katanga and Mathieu Ngudjolo Chui, "Decision on the Confirmation of Charges": 30th September 2008. International Criminal Court, Decision No. ICC-01/04-01/07. Page 397
http://www.legal-tools.org/doc/67a9ec/
and
http://www.icc-cpi.int/menus/icc/situations%20and%20cases/situations/situation%20icc%200104/related%20cases/icc%200104%200107/court%20records/chambers/appeals%20chamber/

23. Raja News . "A report of the players of the Cultural Revolution + Image: Occupying the strong hold of the Marxists and closure of universities".
http://rajanews.com/detail.asp?id=85511.

24. Saham News. "Karroubi's Letter to Hashemi Rafsanjani Was Published after Ten Days: Young Boys and Girls Were Raped in Prisons; Please Follow Up!": 10th August 2009
http://news.gooya.eu/politics/archives/2009/08/091965.php

25. Shahrvand Emrooz. Interview with Mohammad Atrianfar re interrogation of members of *Forqan* Group
http://www.fardanews.com/fa/pages/?cid=50960.

26. Tabnak. Reactions of the then Head of Judiciary, as well as then Head of the Majlis in Response of Hashemi Shahroudi to Karroubi's letter: 14th August 2009
http://www.tabnak.ir/fa/pages/?cid=59567

Websites:

1. Abdorrahman Boroumand Foundation Website
http://www.iranrights.org/farsi/memorial-about.php.

2. Bidaran
http://www.bidaran.net.spip.php?article152.

3. Elmiyeh Seminary of Qom's website
http://www.hawzah.net/fa/questionview.html?QuestionID=9894&ListQuestionSubject=True&List KeywordAl-pha=True&SearchText=%DA%A9%D9%86%DB%8C%D8%B2;
http://www.hawzah.net/fa/questionview.html?QuestionID=10932&ListQuestionSubject=True&ListKeywordAlpha=True&SearchText=%DA%A9%D9%86%DB%8C%D8%B2;
http://www.hawzah.net/fa/questionview.html?QuestionID=63593&ListQuestionSubject=True& ListKeywordAl-pha=True&SearchText=%DA%A9%D9%86%DB%8C%D8%B2;
http://www.hawzah.net/fa/ question-view.html?QuestionID=63593&ListQuestionSubject=True&ListKeywordAlpha=True&SearchText=%DA%A9%D9%86%DB%8C%D8%B2.

4. http://amontazeri.com/farsi/frame4.asp.
5. http://justiceforiran.org/human-rights-violators-individuals-
    databank/hajdavud/?lang=en
6. http://peiknet.net/09-juli/news.asp?id=39528&sort=Iran
7. http://www.iranrights.org/farsi/memorial-case--3439.php
8. http://www.mojahedin.org
9. http://www.redress.org/downloads/country-reports/Iran.pdf
10. http://www.wired.com/science/discoveries/multimedia/2008/02/gallery_abu
    _ghraib,
11. http://middleeast.about.com/od/iraq/tp/abu-ghraib-complete-guide.htm.
12. http://www2.ohchr.org/english/law/ccpr.htm
13. http://untreaty.un.org/cod/icc/statute/romefra.htm

Witness Testimonies and interviews:

1. Justice For Iran Witness Testimony of Banoo Saberi
2. Justice For Iran Witness Testimony of Hayedeh Ravesh
3. Justice For Iran Witness Testimony of Homa Sadegh
4. Justice For Iran Witness Testimony of Mehri Elghaspour,.
5. Justice For Iran Witness Testimony of Mona Roshan
6. Justice For Iran Witness Testimony of Niloufar Shirazi
7. Justice For Iran Witness Testimony of Ruhangiz
8. Justice For Iran Witness Testimony of Sara L.
9. Justice For Iran Witness Testimony of Shahin Chitsaz
10. Justice For Iran Witness Testimony of Siba Nobari
11. Justice For Iran Witness Testimony of Soheila Bahadori
12. Justice For Iran Witness Testimony of Soraya Zangbari
13. Justice For Iran Witness Testimony of Tahmineh Pegah
14. Justice For Iran Witness Testimony of Tuba Kamangar
15. Justice For Iran. Witness testimonies of Sa'ideh Siabi
16. Justice For Iran. Witness Testimony o Kianoosh Etemadi
17. Justice For Iran. Witness Testimony of Amir Mirza'ian
18. Justice For Iran. Witness Testimony of Ashraf Adelzadeh
19. Justice For Iran. Witness Testimony of Azar al-e-Kanaan
20. Justice For Iran. Witness Testimony of Fariba Sabet
21. Justice For Iran. Witness Testimony of Farkhondeh Ashna
22. Justice For Iran. Witness Testimony of Farzaneh Zolfi
23. Justice For Iran. Witness Testimony of Golrokh Jahangiri
24. Justice For Iran. Witness Testimony of Iraj Mesdaghi
25. Justice For Iran. Witness Testimony of Kobra Bane'i
26. Justice For Iran. Witness Testimony of Leyli Shokati
27. Justice For Iran. Witness Testimony of Mahshid Mojaverian
28. Justice For Iran. Witness Testimony of Manijeh
29. Justice For Iran. Witness Testimony of Manzar Bokhara'ee
30. Justice For Iran. Witness Testimony of Marina Nemat
31. Justice For Iran. Witness Testimony of Mersedeh Gha'edi
32. Justice For Iran. Witness Testimony of Mina Farzi
33. Justice For Iran. Witness Testimony of Mitra Haghighat Lager
34. Justice For Iran. Witness Testimony of Mitra Tahami
35. Justice For Iran. Witness Testimony of Mojdeh Arasi
36. Justice For Iran. Witness Testimony of Monireh Baradaran
37. Justice For Iran. Witness Testimony of Nasrin Nekubakht
38. Justice For Iran. Witness Testimony of Nasrin Parvaz

39. Justice For Iran. Witness Testimony of Nazli Partovi
40. Justice For Iran. Witness Testimony of Niloufar Shirzadi
41. Justice For Iran. Witness Testimony of Parvaneh Alizadeh
42. Justice For Iran. Witness testimony of Parvaneh Aref
43. Justice For Iran. Witness Testimony of Rasoul Shokati
44. Justice For Iran. Witness Testimony of Sanam Ahmadi
45. Justice For Iran. Witness Testimony of Sara Raha'ee
46. Justice for Iran. Witness Testimony of Sepideh Farsi
47. Justice For Iran. Witness Testimony of Shayesteh Vatandoust
48. Justice For Iran. Witness Testimony of Shokat Mohammadi
49. Justice for Iran. Witness Testimony of Simin Behrouzi
50. Justice For Iran. Witness Testimony of Soudabeh Ardavan
51. Justice for Iran. Witness Testimony of Taraneh
52. Justice For Iran. Witness Testimony of Violet

Index

Manufactured by Amazon.ca
Acheson, AB